Praise for *Splendours and Miseries of the Brain*

'The guards who patrol the boundary between the two cultures will not like this book. They are sure that neuroscience has nothing to say about art, let alone the ideal love portrayed in art. They are hopelessly wrong of course. First, Semir Zeki is perfectly at home in both cultures and I am confident that there is no other book where you can learn about the cytoarchitecture of the cerebral cortex and the sufi poet Rumi. Furthermore, he can annoy scientists with as much skill as he can annoy artists. Second, this book is not about what neuroscience reveals about love and about art, but it is about what love and art reveal about the brain. Although the border guards may not realise this, all human experience, including love, is mediated through the brain. The more important the experience, the more it can reveal about the fundamental properties of the brain. This is not a bland book. It will challenge your preconceptions. This book reveals the intimate relationship between the fundamental function of the brain and the highest of human experiences.'

Chris Frith FRS, University College London,
and author of Making up the Mind

'The Brain Sciences hold out the great promise of being a natural bridge between the sciences, concerned with the nature of life and the universe, and the humanities, concerned with the nature of human existence. No one is in a better position to bridge this divide than Semir Zeki, and he has succeeded in illustrating how it must be done in this remarkable book, *Splendours and Miseries of the Brain.*

Zeki has earlier pioneered the modern study of visual perception. He then developed a new and brilliant career – explaining the biology of the visual brain to the general reader. Most recently he has opened up a new field – neuroaesthetics – concerned with the biology of the human response to art. In this new book Zeki broadens his highly original approach and explores the neurobiological principles that underlie creativity in art and in literature, in love, and in human happiness, thereby laying down the gauntlet and outlining the challenges that face intellectuals in the 21st century.'

Eric Kandel, University Professor and Kavli Professor,
Director of Kavli Institute for Brain Sciences, Columbia University,
and Senior Investigator, Howard Hughes Medical Institute

Dante, perché Virgilio se ne vada,
non pianger anco, non piangere ancora,
ché pianger ti conven per altra spada

Dante, because Virgil has left you,
Don't weep, don't weep yet
Save your tears for a more bitter sword.

Purgatorio, Canto XXX
La Divina Commedia

Splendours and Miseries of the Brain

Love, Creativity and the Quest for Human Happiness

Semir Zeki

A John Wiley & Sons, Ltd., Publication

This edition first published 2009

Blackwell Publishing was acquired by John Wiley & Sons in February 2007. Blackwell's publishing program has been merged with Wiley's global Scientific, Technical, and Medical business to form Wiley-Blackwell.

Registered Office
John Wiley & Sons Ltd, The Atrium, Southern Gate, Chichester, West Sussex, PO19 8SQ, United Kingdom

Editorial Offices
350 Main Street, Malden, MA 02148-5020, USA
9600 Garsington Road, Oxford, OX4 2DQ, UK
The Atrium, Southern Gate, Chichester, West Sussex, PO19 8SQ, UK

For details of our global editorial offices, for customer services, and for information about how to apply for permission to reuse the copyright material in this book please see our website at www.wiley.com/wiley-blackwell.

Wiley also publishes its books in a variety of electronic formats. Some content that appears in print may not be available in electronic books.

Designations used by companies to distinguish their products are often claimed as trademarks. All brand names and product names used in this book are trade names, service marks, trademarks or registered trademarks of their respective owners. The publisher is not associated with any product or vendor mentioned in this book. This publication is designed to provide accurate and authoritative information in regard to the subject matter covered. It is sold on the understanding that the publisher is not engaged in rendering professional services. If professional advice or other expert assistance is required, the services of a competent professional should be sought.

Library of Congress Cataloging-in-Publication Data

Zeki, Semir.
  Splendours and miseries of the brain : love, creativity and the quest for human happiness / Semir Zeki.
     p. ; cm.
  Includes bibliographical references and index.
  ISBN 978-1-4051-8558-5 (hardcover : alk. paper) — ISBN 978-1-4051-8557-8 (pbk. : alk. paper) 1. Brain—Physiology. 2. Concept—Physiological aspects. 3. Creative ability—Physiological aspects. 4. Love—Physiological aspects. I. Title.
  [DNLM: 1. Brain—physiology. 2. Art. 3. Concept Formation—physiology.
4. Creativeness. 5. Love. WL 300 Z49s 2009]
  QP376.Z39 2009
  612.8'2—dc22
                                                                                    2008029045

A catalogue record for this book is available from the British Library.

Set in 10.5/13pt Galliard by Graphicraft Limited, Hong Kong
Printed in the United Kingdom by TJ International Ltd, Padstow, Cornwall

1   2009

Contents

List of Figures

Note to the Reader

For a book that is intended for the general reader as much as for the biologist, I have tried to keep references to a minimum. With research work, I have kept to the significant papers or to review articles. In the age of the internet, it should not be at all difficult for a reader interested in one aspect or another to follow the thread through electronic libraries. If a disproportionate number of references belong to me and my group, it is because I am better acquainted with them and because I see the problems I address here through the prism of my work.

Regarding the translations, all those from French and most of those from Italian are mine, unless indicated otherwise. For the latter, I consulted extensively with the previous translations.

Acknowledgments

I have an unusual indebtedness to Anton Burdakov who has been through every page of the manuscript, often providing valuable insights and suggesting improvements in phraseology. I am also indebted to him for the marvelous drawings he made for the book. It was a wonderful collaboration.

I have several colleagues to thank for comments made on various parts of the manuscript: Andreas Bartels, Ray Dolan, Chris and Uta Frith and Riccardo Manzotti.

I have had the good fortune to have been in settings where many of the ideas in this book could be discussed critically. It is a pleasure to thank the many who, through their awkward questions, spurred me to think more.

All have, together, contributed enormously to this book. Only the faults remain mine.

Semir Zeki
London, December 2007

Introduction

Surprising though it may seem, given its coverage, this is not a book about art, music or literature. It is a book about the brain. Its principal thesis is that a central and primordial function of the brain is the seeking of knowledge and that it does so through the formation of concepts. Nor is this concept formation limited to abstract knowledge; it is instead a ubiquitous operation that the brain performs continuously throughout post-natal life, on almost everything that it encounters. It applies it to simple perceptual experiences such as that obtained by viewing, for example, a house or a car, as well as to more abstract entities such as love and beauty. This seemingly effortless capacity, which is supported by a neurological machinery of immense complexity, is a splendid evolutionary triumph of neural engineering, allowing the brain not only to obtain but also to generalize its knowledge. But there is often a heavy price to be paid in return for this exquisite capacity, which is that of misery. Even that price can be turned to advantage, as we shall see, since it is intimately linked to creativity. Hence the title of the book, which is derived from Balzac's great novel, *Splendeurs et misères des courtisanes*[1].

The Repetitive Application of Successful Solutions in Evolution

It is my belief that evolution does not proceed by solving problems. This would be too expensive and dangerous a procedure, which might even entail the extinction of a species. Rather, evolution proceeds in such a way that problems are minimized or do not arise in the first place. One way of securing such an outcome is to use a solution that evolution has devised and that has proved to be successful in other domains, with such modifications as may be needed to apply it to a new domain. Concept formation is obviously a solution that evolution has devised to solve the problem of acquiring all sensory knowledge. Indeed, it would have been surprising if the fundamental approach were not the same for all sensory systems, despite their differences. An analysis of the physiological and anatomical literature shows this to be so. But of course the brain is much more than its sensory systems. It is involved in higher cognitive functions, which also serve to give it knowledge. It is engaged in mathematics, art, music and literature, among other things. Is it conceivable that the brain also forms concepts in these domains, just as it does in the sensory world, that it repeats with variations a solution that has served it so well? Or is it more likely that it brings radically different solutions to solving problems in these disparate fields? That, in a sense, is the question that this book addresses. But it also addresses the consequences of the solution that the brain has adopted to acquire knowledge.

In trying to understand things, scientists use any evidence that is available to them; they evaluate it, accept it if it is rigorous and reject it if it is not. In formulating his theory of evolution Charles Darwin did not find a definitive proof; rather, he scoured the world for any kind of evidence that he might find in favor of his hypothesis. When formulating psychological theories, scientists study behavior patterns and reach conclusions about the organization of behavior. Through the development of brain imaging techniques, we can now go a step further and study the organization of behavior in neural terms, by looking directly into the brain and studying how it reacts in different behavioral conditions. Rapid technical advances in imaging brain activity will allow neurobiologists to profane the secrets of the brain and how they affect and determine mental and emotional states; through the use of these techniques, neurobiologists will be able to explore, as never before, the neurological bases of those subjective mental states that only a few decades ago seemed impervious to a scientific onslaught. By piecing together the evidence, we hope to be able to gain insights into the neural bases of emotional states. In the service of these states mankind has reached the heights of joy and the depths of despair and in the process has created works of art, literature and music which have become an invaluable asset not only to our enjoyment but also to the enrichment of our understanding of ourselves.

Yet this direct evidence, obtained from observing brain activity, is not enough in shaping our understanding of how the brain functions. We cannot proceed in this direction without using the products of the brain in our explorations of its functioning. We need to assess the output of the brain in many domains of life. Considered in this light, it becomes obvious that there is one vast area of evidence that neurobiology has not yet tapped, or has done so to only a trivial extent. That evidence does not depend upon the development of new techniques. It is already there; it comes from art in the broadest sense and has been with us for millennia. It includes not only sculpture and painting but also literature, music, dance and much else besides. It would be surprising if the serious scientific study of achievements in these fields did not give us some insights into how the brain is organized. In this book, I use evidence from visual art and from the literature of love to explore whether they provide us with any evidence that in these areas, too, the brain forms concepts. It may seem strange to raid fields that are traditionally thought of as remote from the province of science. But are not art and literature products of the brain, and can they not therefore provide some insight, however small, into how it works? And is the brain not engaged in the feeling of love and the appreciation of beauty? Might not, therefore, a study of these capacities also tell us something significant about the brain?

Art, love, and beauty are generally considered to be abstract notions even though there is increasing evidence that the experience we have in these areas can be correlated directly with activity in specialized areas of the brain. Of course, much divides the experience of love and beauty from simple sensation, even if there is a link between the two. In seeking for universal principles dictating the organization and functioning of the brain, it seemed important to opt to study systems that are as remote from each other as possible, to learn whether, in spite of the big gulf between them, there is a common thread in terms of brain organization. Can it be that fundamentally the same approach, that of concept formation, is used in simple perception and also in mathematics, art, music and literature? Evidence from these fields suggests that it is. Indeed it is because of this link that there is so close a relationship between ordinary perception on the one hand and art, beauty, love, and creativity on the other, as I will try to show.

If I have concentrated more on the visual system than on other sensory systems it is not because I know more about it but because I know less about the other systems. And this is quite simply because we actually have a great deal more information on the visual system. We also obtain a great deal more information through it, which is why both Plato and Dante, among so many others, considered it to be the king of the senses, and why it has engaged the attention of philosophers much more than the other senses.

In raiding these artistic fields in the service of understanding the brain, I have inevitably had to limit myself to a few examples. And the examples I have chosen are iconic ones. The reputation of the works that I cite, from both Western and Eastern culture, has not dimmed through time but grown by the year. Finding seats for performances of *Tristan und Isolde* is an impossible task, even when performed away from the great metropolises of this world, such as London, New York or Paris. More than a thousand articles and books have been written about the progression of the Tristan chord alone. Dante scholarship has been with us for centuries and admiration for him has continued to increase as he has become more accessible through translation. The legends of Majnun and Leila and of Krishna-Radha continue to inspire and move millions in the Eastern world. It would be hard for any nation but the very wealthiest to raise enough money to purchase one of the great sculptures of Michelangelo, even the "unfinished" ones. Why should this be so? At one level, the answer is simple: one may say that the poetry of Dante is beautiful, as is the love of Radha and Krishna, the music of Wagner and the sculpture of Michelangelo. Thomas Mann may not fit into such a classification, his *Death in Venice*, which I make use of here, being on the whole more disturbing than beautiful. But in this same story Mann gives what I believe to be the correct answer to this question. He writes: "For an intellectual product of any value to exert an immediate influence which shall also be deep and lasting, it must rest on an inner harmony, yes, an affinity, between the personal destiny of its author and that of his contemporaries in general. Men do not know why they award fame to one work of art rather than another. Without being in the faintest connoisseurs, they think to justify the warmth of their commendations by discovering in it a hundred virtues, whereas the real ground of their applause is inexplicable – it is sympathy." Perhaps one should add empathy as well. But why should this be so? It is, I believe, because those who produce art are projecting in their work – be it a novel, a symphony or a painting – certain modes of thought and feeling that are common to many because our brains, at a certain fundamental level, are organized along very similar and common lines. These works deserve to be studied therefore for the light that they may shed on common brain processes and in particular for the capacity of the brain to form concepts.

Variability and Commonality in the Organization and Functioning of the Brain

In his *ABC of Reading*, Ezra Pound stressed the importance of using the scientific, comparative, approach in assessing literary works by studying different "specimens" and comparing them with one another. What I am doing here is in a sense similar, though with a somewhat different purpose in mind. I am comparing the different specimens I have chosen and trying to learn what they have in common, in the hope of deducing something about brain organization that is common to all. Such an approach may outrage some, given that we value art as much for the variety of ways in which it exhilarates, arouses, moves and disturbs different individuals and even the same individual at different times. Medicine in general and neurobiology in particular have not yet progressed sufficiently to be able to address the sources of variability. Their success so far has been based largely on the fact that we are all organized along a common plan, as indeed are our brains. That we can make general statements about the kidney, heart, or stomach, and their functions, reflects the fact that the organization and functioning of these organs in different individuals is almost identical. That we can make general statements about how different parts of our brains are organized at a gross anatomical level or about how the cells in the visual or auditory areas of the brain respond reflects the fact that at this somewhat gross level, and even at the more microscopic level, one brain is fundamentally identical to another in this regard. Once we perfect techniques of studying variability in the human brain, neurobiology will attack this problem unrelentingly, just as medicine is now beginning to attack the source of variability in, for example, the course of cancers in different individuals. Indeed

variability is of cardinal importance in biology. It is the bread and butter of evolution, providing the basis for selection. Perhaps the greatest manifestation of variability is to be found in behavior, which itself reflects the variability of the nervous system. Individuals vary much more in their behavior than in the structure and functioning of their kidneys, lungs, or heart. With time, we shall be able to specify the determinants of this variability. It is not, as some assume, that neurobiologists are indifferent to variability and its importance. It is simply that we have no reliable scientific means of addressing the question at present.

This variability, whatever its determinants, acts on a common plan, which is what I am exploring in this book. Unless one learns about that common plan in detail, one will never be able to address the question of variability, for by definition the latter would look for variations in the common plan. It is nevertheless exhilarating to reflect that, from a common plan of organization and action, so many variations that serve to enrich our experience of life emerge.

In this book, therefore, I have indulged my curiosity about the brain by trying to learn about it, not only through its structure and functioning, as I have in the past, but also by considering its products. Some, perhaps even many, might be tempted to dismiss this as "soft" science. I ask them merely to defer this judgment until they have considered the arguments I present here.

Part I

Abstraction and the Brain

Chapter 1

Abstraction

There are many functions that we can assign to the brain, and more specifically to the cerebral cortex, that thin sheet containing billions of cells that envelopes the cerebral hemispheres. Among these one can enumerate seeing, hearing, sensing, the production of movement and of articulate language and much else besides. But do these diverse functions have anything in common? Is there some overall function of which these particular functions are specific instances? The question is not only interesting but also imposes itself, strangely, because of a simple anatomical fact, namely the general uniform anatomical architecture of the cerebral cortex.

A section taken through the cerebral cortex and stained by some anatomical method that shows how its cells are distributed will reveal two interesting features. One is that its billions of cells can be classified into relatively few types, perhaps even into only two basic ones. One of these is pyramidal in shape and the other is star shaped (Figure 1.1). An expert anatomist may well disagree with such a simplistic classification. He may point out with justice that pyramidal cells come in different sizes, that they can be sub-classified into small, medium, and large, or even "gigantic." He may want to sub-classify the star-shaped cells into those whose processes contain little spines and those that do not. More enthusiastic anatomists will find further subdivisions, indicative of important functional differences and requiring different anatomical techniques to show them. In general, however, examining the brain with a technique designed to reveal the anatomy of the cells in the cerebral cortex will reveal a remarkably uniform picture, one in which cells can be, and have been, classified most easily into these two types.

The other striking feature of the cerebral cortex is the uniformity with which these cells are distributed within it (Figure 1.2).

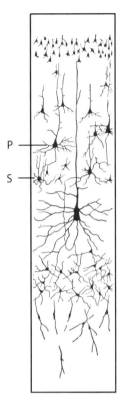

Figure 1.1. Distribution of the two main types of cells – pyramidal (P) and stellate (S) – in the layers of the cerebral cortex. (From Ranson SW, Clark SL (1959). *The Anatomy of the Nervous System*, 10th edn, first published 1920. W.B Saunders Company, Philadelphia and London.)

Throughout, they are stacked upon one another in layers. It is traditional to subdivide the cortex into six layers, with layer 4 containing the star-shaped cells and the layers above and below containing the pyramidal cells. So uniform and ubiquitous is this arrangement that it takes an expert with many years' experience to tell differences in anatomical architecture between one cortical region and another. Even if he can, other experts are certain to dispute it. There are, to be sure, some cortical zones that have an obvious difference, visible at a glance. The primary visual cortex, area V1, has an especially rich layering pattern that makes it easily differentiable from adjoining

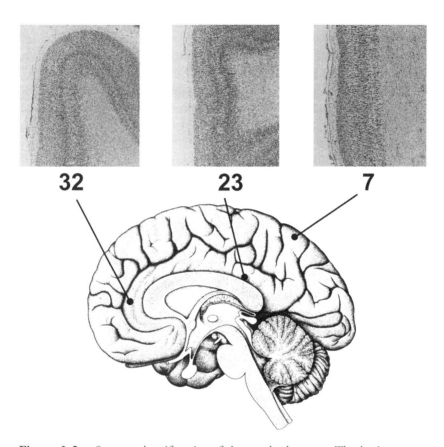

Figure 1.2. Structural uniformity of the cerebral cortex. The basic architecture of the cortex is very similar in different parts of the brain. Three sections through different parts of the cortex are shown, from areas 7, 23, and 32 according to the classification given by the German anatomist Korbinian Brodmann. The sections are stained by an anatomical method to show how the cells are distributed. (Sections taken from Paxinos G (ed.) (1990). *The Human Nervous System*, Academic Press, New York, with permission.)

cortex. The primary motor cortex also has a distinctive architecture, in that it lacks the star-shaped cells. Even these do not constitute radical departures from the common plan but are more in the nature of variations on a theme. Much more impressive is the general architectural uniformity of the cortex. This is surprising, given that different cortical fields and areas, which share the same anatomical architecture, differ so profoundly in function. Apart from the fact that they are both senses, there is a huge difference between hearing and general sensibility (touch, pressure, etc.) and, not surprisingly, these two faculties are assigned different cortical areas. Yet it would be hard to tell the differences in anatomical architecture between the two cortical areas subserving these different functions, except perhaps for the specialist. We now know that there are many different visual areas in the cortex surrounding the primary visual cortex, and that these different visual areas share the same architecture although they have different functions, some being specialized for color, others for visual motion, others for the perception of faces, and so on. This diversity of functions exhibited by cortical areas that have a common architectural plan is surprising. It runs counter to an anatomical law, that organs with different functions have different structures and architectures. If one were to study in a similar way (i.e. by staining the cells in anatomical sections) other organs of the body that are known to have different functions, such as the heart, kidney and liver, one would find huge differences that are visible at a glance even to a lay person, and thus do not require an expert for their detection.

This is an interesting fact that not only requires an explanation but may also give us some useful hints in thinking about what the cortex does. In general, it may be said that cells in different cortical areas derive their differences largely from the fact that they have different anatomical connections, that is, different inputs and outputs, although other factors also influence their specializations. The auditory cortex connects with the cochlea of the ear and the visual cortex with the retina of the eye. Different visual areas outside the primary visual cortex have specific connections reflecting their functional specialization. Yet these different anatomical inputs act upon areas that share the same anatomical architecture. This essential uniformity has sometimes tempted students of the brain to ask whether there is any function, perhaps even a single fundamental function, that the cerebral cortex performs repetitively everywhere, regardless of the specialization of the area, a sort of supra-modal operation. To date, no satisfactory answer has been obtained to that question. Even so, the value of the uniform anatomical picture of the cerebral cortex lies not so much in providing an explanation but in initiating an enquiry into what, if any, uniform function can be ascribed to every part of the cerebral cortex. It is a spur to thinking about the general function of the cerebral cortex.

Abstraction in the Cerebral Cortex

A useful way to begin this enquiry is to study the responses of single cells in different cortical areas and learn what common property they have. Such an approach may seem odd, given that physiologists have tended to emphasize how specific in their responses cells in different cortical areas are and therefore how much the responses of cells in one cortical area differ from those in another: cells in the auditory cortex will respond to auditory stimuli, those in visual cortex to visual stimuli, and so on. Indeed, the description of how cells in different areas of the cerebral cortex differ in their responses is one of the great triumphs of physiology. But in thus emphasizing the specificity in the responses of cells within different cortical areas, physiologists have overlooked another critical feature, namely the capacity of these specific cells – whether auditory, visual, somato-sensory or otherwise – to abstract. In fact, the capacity to abstract seems to accompany, and to be a corollary of, every specificity. It may therefore be said to be a common property shared by a very great majority of cells and therefore areas of the cerebral cortex, of which these cells are the constituents.

What I mean by abstraction is the emphasis on the general property at the expense of the particular. Its meaning in terms of single cell responses in the cortex becomes clearer when one considers actual examples. Let us take orientation selectivity[1], a property of many cells in the primary visual cortex and some other areas of the visual brain (Figure 1.3).[2] These are visual cells that respond to lines of certain orientation, and respond less well to other orientations and not at all to lines oriented orthogonally to their preferred orientation. To that extent, these cells are highly specific for the kind of visual stimulus to which they will respond, a feature that has been often enough emphasized in the physiological literature. What has received far less emphasis, if any at all, is that these cells also abstract the property of orientation selectivity in that they are not concerned with what it is that is of the right orientation for them. An orientation-selective cell that responds to vertically oriented lines only will respond to a pencil

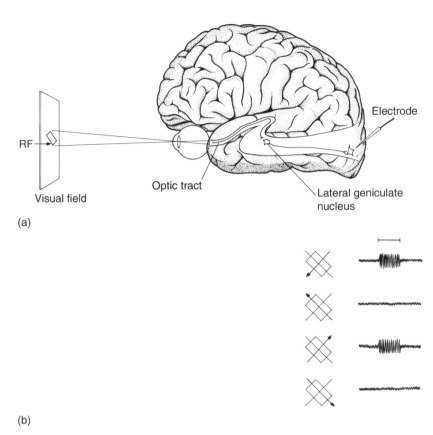

(a)

(b)

Figure 1.3. Response of an orientation selective cell, studied by inserting an electrode into the visual cortex (a) and by flashing light bars of different orientation into its receptive field (RF), that is the part of the field of view which, when stimulated, results in an electrical discharge (response). (b) shows that the cell is orientation selective, responding to an obliquely oriented line flashed into its receptive field and moved in two opposite directions, while being unresponsive to the orthogonal orientation. (From Zeki, S. (1993), *A Vision of the Brain*, Blackwell Science, Oxford.)

if held vertically, or to a ruler, or to a white/black boundary. It will respond as well to a vertically oriented green line against a red background, or vice versa. In other words, its only concern is that the visual stimulus should be vertically oriented, without being concerned with

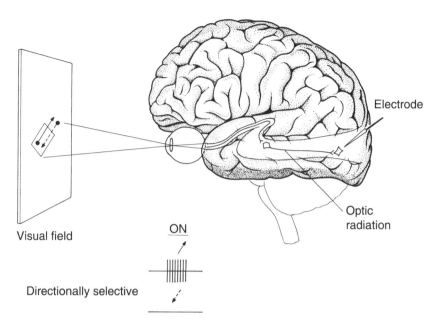

Figure 1.4. The responses of a directionally selective cell in area V5. The cell responds to motion in one direction but not in the opposite, null, direction. Such cells commonly prefer small spots to oriented bars of light. (From Zeki S (1993). *A Vision of the Brain*, Blackwell Science, Oxford.)

what is vertically oriented. The cell has quite simply abstracted the property of verticality, without being concerned about the particulars.

Another example is provided by the cells of another visual area, area V5, which is specialized for visual motion (Figure 1.4).[3] The great majority of cells in this area are directionally selective, in that they respond to motion of a visual stimulus in one direction and not in the opposite, null, direction. But they will respond to a black spot against a white background, or vice versa; they will also respond to a green spot against a red background, or vice versa; and so on. Although these cells usually respond best to spots that are moving in a specific direction, they are capable of responding to almost any form, provided it moves in their preferred direction. In other words, they abstract for the direction of motion without being especially concerned with what is moving in their preferred direction.

These examples of abstraction, observed at the physiological level, are not restricted to areas of the visual brain. A cell in the somato-sensory cortex that is specific for detecting pressure will respond to any stimulus as long as it exerts pressure in the appropriate place on the body surface. A cell that responds to high temperatures is not concerned with what it is that produces the high temperature, but only that there is a high temperature. Similar examples may be given for the auditory cortex.

Nor are the examples limited to sensory areas of the brain. Other examples can be given concerning cognitive properties, but the evidence here is derived from a somewhat different experimental approach. Rather than detecting changes in the responses of individual cells to stimulation, such experiments measure changes in the activity of an entire brain area when humans undertake a specific task such as looking at paintings of a particular type, say portrait paintings, or judging which one of two stimuli has a greater magnitude. The areas of the cerebral cortex that are specifically activated can be inferred from detecting the change in blood flow through them, using modern techniques such as functional magnetic resonance imaging (fMRI). When cells in a given area of the brain are particularly active, their metabolic requirement increases and hence more blood is channeled to the area. These changes in blood flow are thus a good guide to increases in the responses of cells in these areas. In such experiments, if subjects are asked to detect which of two stimuli has the greater value – for example which is brighter, which is larger, which contains the higher number, which is the higher note – the result is always the same and involves the activation of a specific brain area located in the parietal cortex.[4] This suggests that the same brain area is specifically engaged in evaluating magnitude, irrespective of the modality in which the magnitude is presented. Equally, another area but this time located in the frontal lobe detects patterns that change irregularly and unpredictably with time, without being concerned with the precise stimulus that so varies, that is, whether the irregular pattern is that of letters, numbers, or colors.[5] Although the identity and general physiology of these areas has not been worked out with anything like the precision that the visual areas have, the general direction in which they point is the same – that areas of the brain are capable of abstracting. In these instances, the relevant brain areas are not especially concerned with a higher value of some specific modality or a particular temporal irregularity but only with higher values or irregular patterns in general.

Another example concerns works of art. When subjects view paintings of a particular category, for example portraits, the increase

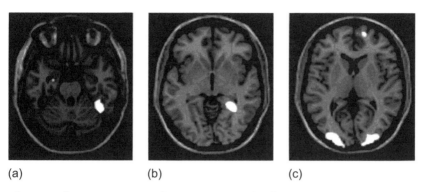

(a) (b) (c)

Figure 1.5. Brain activity during viewing of different categories of paintings. Areas in white show regions of maximum activity when subjects view (a) portraits, (b) landscapes and (c) still lifes. (Figure adapted from Kawabata H, Zeki S (2004). Neural correlates of beauty. *J Neurophysiol* **91**: 1699–1705.)

in activity within the visual brain is specific to those visual areas that have been shown to be specifically engaged when humans view faces in general (Figure 1.5).[6] But activity is also elicited with any portrait, not a specific portrait. A different (and adjacent) visual area of the brain becomes active when they view another category of painting, for example landscapes, an area apparently specialized for registering places.[7] Once again, the viewing of any landscape activates the area. At this level of observation, it may be said that these areas abstract in the sense that they are not specific for any given example of the visual world that they are specialized in but for all examples of that category.

This capacity to abstract seems to operate even at the judgmental level. It has, for example, been shown that judgment of a painting as beautiful correlates with heightened activity in the orbito-frontal cortex, which is part of the brain's reward system (Figure 1.6).[8] But the heightened activity is not observed with only one category of painting. Landscape paintings that are judged to be beautiful are as potent in heightening the activity there as portrait paintings, still lifes, or abstract works that are judged to be beautiful. The common factor is that the painting is judged to be beautiful.

So common is this abstractive capacity that one looks instead for departures from it, for indications that a given brain cell or a given brain area will only respond to a particular example of a particular

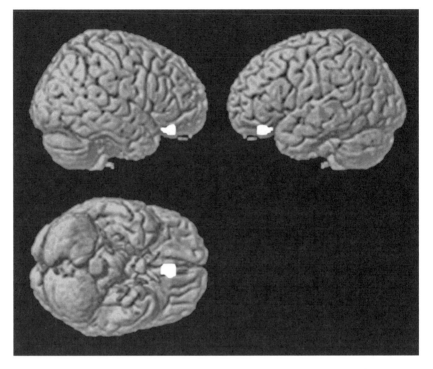

Figure 1.6. Brain activity related to viewing beautiful paintings. Areas in white show regions of maximum cortical activity when humans rate paintings as being beautiful. (Figure adapted from Kawabata H, Zeki S (2004). Neural correlates of beauty. *J Neurophysiol* **91**: 1699–1705.)

category of stimulus. One exception is to be found in the brain areas that are activated when we view the picture of someone we love. Here, any face will not do. It has to be a specific person, one with whom we are romantically involved.[9] But even in this instance, there probably is an abstractive capacity. It is very likely that the areas will become active regardless of the view of the loved person, that is, whether it is a frontal or a side view. I say likely, because the actual experiment has not been done and, in science, there are surprises aplenty. Yet, from all we know about the cortex, the surprise would be if only a particular view would activate these areas.

Once again, we have in the past drawn only some of the conclusions from these experiments, namely that specific visual areas process specific kinds of visual stimuli or that activity in them correlates with specific mental states. In our enthusiasm for these discoveries, we have failed to emphasize the fact that these areas also abstract, in that they are not concerned with specific portraits or landscapes and nor are they concerned with the beauty of a specific painting. This naturally raises the question, so far unanswered, of how it is that one can recognize a specific face or a specific portrait. That we have not obtained an answer to that question, even though we have succeeded in showing that faces in general engage specific cortical areas, is itself eloquent evidence in favor of the view presented here, that these are cortical areas that abstract. Even if future studies show that some of the cells in these areas are selective in their responses to, say, particular faces, the conclusion about their abstractive power will remain hard to argue against, since even the recognition of specific faces involves an abstraction, in that the specific face must be recognized regardless of the distance, the point of view, or the expression worn.

We may thus say that, hand in hand with every specification in the functions of a cortical area goes an abstraction; indeed abstraction is the inevitable by-product of specification. That the capacity to abstract is ubiquitous in the cerebral cortex is just as important when it comes to considering the brain as a knowledge-acquiring system, as we shall see below. Perhaps paradoxically, specification and abstraction are two sides of the coinage of acquiring knowledge. Knowledge cannot be acquired, at least not efficiently, if either property is missing.

Abstraction and Perceptual Constancy

The kind of abstraction that I have explained above is not the only one that the brain undertakes. There is another kind of abstraction, somewhat different though still intimately linked to the first kind, in that it also involves emphasizing the general at the expense of the particular. This latter kind of abstraction is the basis of what is known as perceptual constancy. What is meant by this term can be illustrated by the following example. A house or a face maintains its identity regardless of whether one views them from the front or the side, at dawn or at dusk, from near or from far. We may refer to this as object constancy. Constancy is a very fundamental property of the perceptive systems. Without it, recognition of an object, a surface, or a situation would depend upon a host of highly specific conditions, making it a hostage to every change in these conditions and therefore an almost impossible task. A simple and excellent example of perceptual constancy is provided by what is usually called color constancy. This refers to the fact that the color of a surface changes little, if at all, when the surface is viewed in different illuminants. A green surface, for example, remains green whether viewed at dawn, at dusk, or at noon on a cloudy or sunny day. If one were to measure the amount of red, green and blue light reflected from the leaf in these different conditions, one would find considerable variations. Yet the brain is somehow able to discount these variations and assign a constant color to a surface. Indeed, to speak of constant colors is, in a sense, an anomaly for it implies that there are inconstant colors, while the truth is that there are no colors but constant colors.

Together, these two forms of abstraction emphasize the fact that a ubiquitous function of the cerebral cortex, one in which many if not all of its areas are involved, is that of abstraction. Perhaps this gives a clue to the essential uniformity of the cerebral cortex in terms of how its cells are arranged in layers, and perhaps not. The fact remains that architectural uniformity raises the question and the answer that I have given, even if it turns out not to be the right one and not directly related to the question, is nevertheless an interesting one. And it takes us a step further, to asking why abstraction should be such an important function of the cerebral cortex at large. The answer to that question is best addressed by asking: what is the overall function of the brain in general, and the cerebral cortex in particular?

Chapter 2

The Brain and its Concepts

Acquisition of knowledge is a principal function of the brain, and the brain does so in a seemingly highly efficient way. The efficiency is due in no small measure to the use of concepts, of which there are two kinds, inherited and acquired. These two kinds are intimately linked and indeed one could not exist without the other. The inherited concepts organize the signals coming into the brain so as to instil meaning into them and thus make sense of them. The acquired concepts are generated throughout life by the brain, and make it significantly independent of the continual change in the information reaching the brain; they make it easier for us to perceive and recognize and thus obtain knowledge of things and situations. There is a subtlety in this argument, well recognized by Arthur Schopenhauer. It is not as if perceptions lead to abstractions and concepts, but the other way round: we form our percepts from abstractions and concepts. As Schopenhauer put it: "Concepts and abstractions that do not ultimately lead to perceptions are like paths in a wood that end without any way out".[1]

If it is through these two kinds of concept that the brain acquires knowledge about the world, then it follows quite naturally that there are limitations to that knowledge, emphasized by Immanuel Kant: namely that we can never know the thing in itself (*das Ding an sich*), since our knowledge of it can only be through the operations of the mind (brain). All knowledge is brain knowledge. Although Kant thought about the mind when he wrote, "The Mind does not derive its laws (a priory) from nature, but prescribes them to her",[2] he might as well have been writing about the brain.

Inherited Concepts

A good example of an inherited concept is that regulating the generation of color by the brain, discussed at greater length in the following chapter. This system works within certain constraints. Some of these
are due to the structure and physiological capacities of the receptors
for color vision. In general, human retinal receptors are sensitive to
light in the 400–700 nm waveband. The receptors for color are usually divided into three broad categories, those responding optimally
to red, green or blue light. This leaves many wavebands that our eyes
are not equipped to register. We have no receptors that respond to
ultraviolet light. We can therefore have no direct visual experience of
ultraviolet light. Bees, on the other hand, can sense ultraviolet light
and can experience what we cannot. This restriction thus limits our
knowledge of the external world. Next comes the inherited brain
concept that organizes the incoming signals. With color, the brain has
to organize signals in such a way that a green surface, for example, is
perceived as green even when it is viewed in conditions in which it
reflects more red than green light. This is not such an unusual event.
Leaves often reflect more red than green light at dawn or at dusk,
when there is a lot more of the long (red) wavebands in the light that
is reflected from a leaf. Yet if our perception of that leaf as green were
to change with every change in the wavelength composition of light
reflected from it, then the leaf would no longer be recognizable and
identifiable by its color but by some other attribute. Color would then
lose its significance as a reliable biological signalling mechanism. The
brain has solved this problem by applying a ratio-taking concept to
the signals coming from the green surface and from its surrounds, in
such a way that the ratio of light of any given waveband, say long-
wave (red) light, reflected from the green surface and from its surrounds does not change, as is explained later (see Chapter 3). In this
way, the brain is able to assign a constant color to a surface and make
itself largely independent of the amount of light of any waveband
reflected from that surface alone.

One may wonder why I call such an organizing principle a brain
concept, even though Kant had already done so when he wrote of
the mind as applying a concept to perceptions, by which he meant
that some kind of principle is applied to incoming signals to make

sense of them. Why not call it a brain program or a brain computational process instead, as so many would? I do not do so for two reasons. First, when we consider a sensation like color, we begin to realize that it is generated by the brain and in the brain according to a certain program, which has certain rules because there is a certain concept that is applied to the incoming signals, as described in the next chapter. But we could think of other concepts to apply to the incoming signals that could also result in color vision. Indeed a different concept or principle for organizing signals into the color system of the brain could plausibly even result in a much more efficient color system. We can speculate endlessly about this, but the brain uses the one that it has evolved – a ratio-taking system. Another reason for referring to these inherited systems that organize signals in particular ways as concepts emerges when we look at other systems, such as the one regulating romantic love. As we shall see, romantic love is also regulated by an inherited concept, though a much more complex and even abstract one. This concept, as I shall argue later, is that of "unity-in-love"; it impels partners in a passionate and romantic relationship to seek union with one another, far beyond that provided by sexual intimacy, which, however, comes closest to achieving that biologically ingrained concept. The evidence for this inherited concept of "unity-in-love" comes not from examining the scientific literature, but from examining the world literature of love. It appears to be a concept that is prevalent in all cultures. To speak of it in terms of a computational process, of which it certainly has elements, would be to forget that the concept of unity is a more abstract one, even if it regulates relations in romantic love. This inherited concept has its limitations too. Judging by the literature of love, these limitations are often very severe. The result is that when lovers seek to be united to one another, they are confronted with an almost impossible task. The near impossibility of achieving what that inherited concept dictates has therefore interesting consequences, which I will examine later.

Acquired Concepts

The most critical problem for a knowledge-acquiring system is how to acquire knowledge about the permanent, essential and non-changing properties of objects, surfaces, and situations when the information reaching the brain from them changes continually. We view objects such as cars or houses from different angles and distances, in different lighting conditions and in different settings. Also, a sad expression can be the attribute of many different faces that otherwise differ in their identities. But a single particular face can be happy or sad. The list of examples can be multiplied endlessly. If my ability to identify a house as a house depended upon a particular house only, then I would soon be in trouble when confronted with another house. One way of overcoming this difficulty is to generate a concept of a house. When the brain acquires a concept of a house, the point of view, the precise shape, the distance, the setting, the size and all else cease to matter for the purpose of identification of the house as a house. The brain thus disengages itself significantly from all these changes. Moreover, the brain does not know in advance what kind of experience it will have, but merely modifies its concepts in the light of new experience, which is why the acquired concept has to be modifiable throughout life.

Of course, the use of concepts by the brain to acquire knowledge about the world also has its limitations. Indeed concept formation is perhaps not the only solution that one can conceive of to acquire knowledge in an unstable world. One could conceive of a brain that is organized along different lines. Its organization could, for example, be based on a prodigious memory rather than on concept formation, thus enabling it to remember every single detail that it has ever encountered. This could conceivably also make it independent of the point of view or setting in identifying a house as a house. I have no means of knowing, and nor does anyone else, how efficient such a brain would be, assuming it to be devised by evolution rather than in computational laboratories. Nor can anyone guess what it would look like structurally or how it would function. But this is not the solution that evolution has adopted and so there is little point speculating.

What is clear, and what I hope to explain, is that formation of acquired concepts, though a marvel of neural engineering, also has strict limitations. The concepts formed are synthetic ones, dependent upon the continual acquisition of experience throughout post-natal life. But the momentary experience is of particular examples only, which commonly fail to satisfy the synthetic concept in the brain, as I shall repeatedly emphasize throughout.

It is my conviction that, without understanding something about the knowledge acquiring system of the brain and its limitations, it is difficult to understand not only how the brain functions, but much about what it produces as well. It would, for example, be difficult to understand both art and creativity, since both are ultimately related to the acquisition of knowledge, as I have argued elsewhere,[3] and therefore to the neurological machinery underlying this capacity. Indeed, I would go beyond and say that without understanding something about the concept-forming capacities of the brain, one will fail to comprehend what is at the root of much of human misery (see Chapter 22).

Chapter 3

Inherited Brain Concepts

Characteristics of Inherited Brain Concepts

Color and the concept of "unity-in-love" are but two, though extreme, examples of inherited brain concepts. There are many other inherited concepts that organize inputs into the brain to generate experiences; within the visual brain there are concepts that are related to the recognition of forms and of visual motion and depth; within the auditory brain there are inherited concepts that organize sounds into rhythms and tunes; and so on. In spite of the diversity of inherited concepts, there is an interesting feature that they all share. First of all, we are not at liberty to discard, ignore or disobey them. A normally sighted person with a normal brain cannot dictate that the brain operations that generate color should not come into play and is not at liberty to choose not to see colors when he opens his eyes or to see a surface in any other color besides the one that the brain dictates that it should have, through the comparisons that it undertakes. When we open our eyes at dawn or at dusk and look at leaves, we will see them as green, even though under these conditions they might reflect more long-wave (red) light. We cannot over-ride the brain-organizing principle, which creates constant colors in spite of large variations in the wavelength-energy composition of the light reflected from surfaces. We cannot, in brief, choose to see a green leaf that we know, through objective measurement, to be reflecting more red light as red. There is no free will here! This is not to say that we are not at liberty to choose the color of our tie or of our dress. Equally, a normal person is not always at liberty to choose not to fall in love, or to fall in and out of love at will. Nor, in moments of passionate love, is such a person at liberty to decide that a unity with their lover is not what is desired, even if they do not articulate this desire explicitly and consciously, any more than they would articulate the desire to see a certain color. This is not to say, again, that a person is not at liberty to choose the kind of person they want to love, though it can be argued that even here the choice is not quite as wide as one might imagine or want. Free will is restricted, even in love.

A second feature of inherited brain concepts is that they do not change with time; they are immutable. The brain concept (or program) for generating color does not change with time and experience, nor does the brain system for perceiving faces. Also, the brain has a highly developed system to categorize objects, enabling it to recognize an object regardless of the viewing distance, the angle of view or the lighting condition. This is a stable system and does not change with time or the acquisition of experience. This is quite unlike the acquired concept, which changes both with time and with the acquisition of experience.

A third feature is that of relative autonomy. By this I mean that there are many systems distributed in the brain, each one specialized for organizing the sensory input for a particular attribute, and that these systems are more or less autonomous of one another and even apparently autonomous of the higher cognitive systems of the brain. The generation of color, for example, is dependent upon a specialized cortical system that is independent of the systems for generating other kinds of visual or other sensory experiences (Figure 3.1). As we shall see, the system for color also acts relatively autonomously of the higher cognitive systems of the brain.

These characteristics can be well illustrated by reference to the color system of the brain.

Color as an Example of Inherited Concepts

Color, as Arthur Schopenhauer recognized, constitutes a very interesting introduction to the general problem of knowledge – a theme in this book – namely that the brain creates, according to its own rules, the knowledge that we have. In his book *On Vision and Colors: An Essay*, he wrote that, ". . . a more precise knowledge and firmer conviction of the wholly subjective nature of color contributes to a more profound comprehension of the Kantian doctrine of the likewise

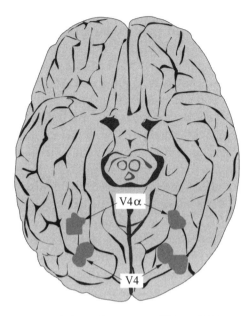

Figure 3.1. Location of the color center (V4 and V4α, comprising the V4 complex) in the human brain as seen from below.

subjective, intellectual forms of all knowledge and hence serves as a very useful introductory course to philosophy,"[1] the problem of knowledge being one of the major problems of philosophy. Kant had aptly written that, "Perceptions without concepts are blind,"[2] meaning that if incoming signals are not organized according to some kind of concept, some organizing principle, we would not be able to make any sense of these signals, and therefore would see nothing.

Color is the supreme example of how the brain constructs a visual attribute, the most powerful way of showing that our experience of the world is determined as much by the inherited operations of the brain as by the physical reality. The color of a surface remains the same regardless of the lighting conditions in which it is viewed, although the shade of the color may change. The most important feature of the color system is therefore the capacity to ascribe a constant color to a surface in spite of wide-ranging fluctuations in the wavelength-energy composition of the light reflected from that surface. Indeed, were it not so and were the color of a surface to change with every change in the lighting environment in which it is viewed, color would not have much biological meaning and, rather than help us to acquire knowledge about a property of objects and surfaces, would actually confuse us. How the brain achieves this remarkable feat, of assigning a constant color to a surface, is known in outline only. For a long time, scientists tried to account for it by invoking higher cognitive factors. The great German psychophysicist Hermann von Helmholtz[3] thought that it involved judgment and learning. He believed that we know that a leaf looks green and therefore we discount the illuminant (i.e. the wavelength composition of the light reflected from the green leaf in different lighting conditions) by a process vaguely defined as the "unconscious inference." Another eminent German psychophysicist, Ewald Hering,[4] believed that another higher cognitive function – memory – played a critical role, a formulation not vastly different from that of Helmholtz. It was left to the American inventor Edwin Land[5] to champion another view, and one with which I am in agreement. Land supposed that the capacity to assign a constant color to a surface is the result of a simple brain program, a computational process. In our terms or in Kantian terms, we would say that color constancy is due to the application of an innate brain concept or organizing principle to the incoming visual signals.

The outlines of the concept that the brain applies to incoming visual signals to generate color are easy to determine even if we are far from knowing exactly how the brain implements it. It is rooted in a golden rule of perception, namely comparison. Color may be accurately described as the result of a comparison, undertaken by the brain, of the amount of light of different wavebands reflected from a surface and from its surrounds. This comparison leads to a ratio, and that ratio never changes. The concept that the brain applies to generating colors is thus the concept of ratio-taking. In a simple example, imagine a green surface surrounded by red, yellow and blue surfaces. If, when viewed in a given illuminant – for example daylight on a cloudy day when there is a good deal more of the shorter (bluish) wavelengths – the green surface is reflecting 60 units (measured in milliwatts) of green light, the surrounds will be reflecting much less because they have a lower efficiency for reflecting green light, and there will be a certain ratio of the amount of green light reflected by the green surface and by its surrounds (Plate 1). Let us call this ratio X. If the same scene is viewed in a different illuminant – for example tungsten light, when there is a lot more of the longer (reddish) wavelengths – and the green surface is now reflecting only 30 units of green light, the surrounds will still be reflecting a lot less because of their lower efficiency for reflecting green light. There will now also be a ratio for the amount of green light reflected from the green surface and from its surrounds, and that ratio is identical to the previous ones (i.e. X), in spite of the significant change in the amount of green light reflected from the green surface in these two conditions. A similar reasoning applies to light of other wavebands. In this way the brain can impose a constancy – it is no longer at the mercy of each and every change in ambient wavelength composition. It can thus acquire knowledge about a surface, namely about its reflectance for lights of different wavebands, and use a visual language – color – to characterize that property. Light itself, even though composed of many different wavelengths, is nothing more than electromagnetic radiation and has no color, as recognized by Isaac Newton[6] when he wrote that "For the Rays to speak properly have no Color. In them there is nothing else than a certain power and disposition to stir up a sensation of this Color or that." That sensation is "stirred up" in the brain, and more specifically within the color centre of the visual brain, by the kind of comparison described briefly above.[7]

The importance of understanding that color is a construction of the brain, that it is a visual language used by the brain and that it is not a property of the physical world cannot be overemphasized. The knowledge that the brain acquires is really about the reflectance of objects and surfaces for lights of different wavelength. A red surface will always reflect red light more efficiently than green or blue light, *compared to its surrounds*. Whenever, therefore, a surface is determined by the brain to reflect more red light than its surrounds, it will invest it with the visual language of red. A white surface, compared to its surrounds, has the highest efficiency for reflecting light of any waveband. Any surface that is determined by the brain to reflect light of all wavebands more efficiently than the surrounds will be labeled, visually, white by the brain. The examples can be multiplied, and it is not surprising perhaps to find that the brain has a special center, located close to the color center in the left fusiform gyrus, that is critical in naming colors.[8] Damage to this centre results in an inability to name colors, though their perception remains intact, a syndrome known as color anomia.

Color is, then, the result of an inherited program or concept that the brain has developed through evolution, which it applies to give sense to the incoming signals and thus gain knowledge about a certain attribute of the world. If the color centre in the brain, V4, is destroyed, the concept of taking ratios as described above can no longer be applied and the subject becomes color blind. This is one reason why I have referred to this part of the cortex as the color center. In a patient with a damaged V4, visual signals still enter the eye and are transmitted to the cerebral cortex normally. But they go to those parts of the cortex that lack the organizing program to take ratios, with the consequence that the patient becomes color blind. This gives substance to the view of Kant, that perceptions without concepts are blind.

Cézanne had said that "Color has a logic and the artist must always obey that logic, never the logic of the brain." The French author and statesman André Malraux was right when, in his book *Les Voix du silence*[9] (*The Voices of Silence*), he described Cézanne's reflections on color as "*cette phrase maladroite*" [this clumsy phrase]. There is, in fact, no logic to color except the logic of the brain. The point is important in this context. The logic of the brain is determined by an inherited brain concept. The artist is at liberty to juxtapose colors as he wants; he may have determined through experience that certain colors, when juxtaposed, have the most desirable effect; he may develop a concept of what colors to invest objects in. He is not at liberty to interfere with the impeccable logic of the brain in constructing colors.

The Autonomy of the Color System

As always, scientists have tended to emphasize the positive evidence without looking into the negative evidence. Human imaging experiments, while implicating the V4 complex strongly in color computations,[10] have not shown any activity related to color computations in the frontal cortex or in other brain areas that are either known or traditionally thought to be implicated in higher cognitive processes or in memory. Nor does damage to the higher centers located in the frontal and parietal areas of the brain lead to color imperception. Hence, one can say with such assurance as the current experiments give that the brain concept that is related to organizing the incoming visual signals to generate colors is not distributed throughout the brain, and is not even distributed throughout the visual brain. It is instead localized to the V4 complex. Abstraction is of course a part of this concept. The ratio-taking machinery within the V4 complex is not concerned with a particular green or red surface, but will apply its computation to any surface indiscriminately. It is simply concerned with relating, through ratio-taking, the amount of light of different wavebands reflected from any given surface to that coming from surrounding surfaces, a comparison that is the essence of perception.

When I speak of relative autonomy, I really mean to say that the application of the brain programs to the incoming signals does not depend upon the healthy functioning of the rest of the brain or even the rest of the visual brain. A patient with damage to other visual centers in the brain, for example those specialized for visual motion or visual form, is not impaired in color vision unless the color center itself is also damaged.[11] There are of course limits to this autonomy. The pathways feeding the color centre, the V4 complex, from other visual areas such as the primary visual receiving centre, V1, and the visual area surrounding it, V2, must be intact and interact with V4 through reciprocal connections (see Chapter 9). The receptors in the retina must be intact. The general system for enabling and regulating conscious experience, almost certainly located in the brainstem, must be intact. But, provided that these systems are functioning normally, the color system appears to be widely independent of what is occurring in the rest of the brain.

Love and beauty provide other examples of inherited brain concepts. Although the sense of beauty has not been studied in any detail from a neurobiological point of view, it is not difficult to surmise that a similar kind of organizing principle is in operation. For each individual, certain signals are qualified by the brain as beautiful according to an inherited brain concept that dictates that certain signals should be so organized, although what is so qualified differs from one individual to the next. The brain is therefore not at liberty not to organize signals in such a way that they affect the relevant reward system of the brain, probably centered in this instance on the orbito-frontal cortex[12] (a region lying at the base of the frontal lobes), although what it qualifies as beautiful will be determined as much by biology as by cultural influences. Much the same applies to desire and to love. The brain must have the capacity to arouse the desire system for a certain kind of visual experience and not for others. Again, the brain does not have the option of not allowing this to happen, although cultural and environmental influences play a critical role in determining when the biological system will swing into action. With desire, although the normal brain's capacity to find individuals as desirable is not negotiable, the kind of person that an individual finds desirable is subject to many post-natal influences and hence varies between individuals. Because of upbringing, family, and cultural influences, many may have a preference for a particular type of person, of a particular stature or hair color, and so on. This is because their brains have formed a concept of the kind of person that is most desirable for them, given their experience. This falls into another category of concept, the acquired concept.

Critical Periods in Nourishing the Inherited Brain Concepts

As stated earlier, an inherited brain concept, or program, is not modifiable with the acquisition of further experience throughout life. A possible exception to this rule is a very general one, namely that the genetically wired brain, which is ready to acquire experience at birth, must nevertheless be nourished post-natally, especially during a critical period right after birth. We have no definitive evidence about what would happen perceptually if an organism with good color vision were to be deprived selectively of all color signals for varying periods after birth. Such an experiment would indeed be very difficult to undertake. But we have evidence from another source, namely the visual form system. The striking characteristic of this system is the presence of orientation-selective cells, which respond to lines of a given orientation and not to other orientations (see previous chapter). These cells are regarded by many physiologists as constituting the physiological building blocks of form perception, even though no one has yet succeeded to show convincingly how they lead to the emergence of cells in the brain that are capable of coding for complex forms. They are present at birth, at least in the monkey.[13] They therefore can be said to be the result of an inherited organizing concept that determines how signals related to form are grouped in the cortex, at least in the initial stages of the form processing system of the brain. What is remarkable is that, if the newborn infant monkey is deprived of vision during a critical period immediately after birth, the organizing principle itself seemingly atrophies. The cells in the brain become very poorly responsive to visual stimuli and lose their specificities for lines of the appropriate orientation.[13] The loss is seemingly permanent and irreparable. Even if full vision is restored to the monkey once the initial critical period is over, it will never recover its full capacity for form vision. It becomes forever blighted. Hence the organizing principle requires to be nourished, at least during the critical period. Deprivation for a similar period in adulthood does not have effects that are as serious, if indeed it has any. Much the same is true of humans who are born blind (due, for example, to congenital cataract) and to whom vision is "restored" later in life. They, too, remain forever blighted.[14]

In the instance of romantic love, the inherited concept is that of unity-in-love, as we shall see in later chapters. There are insufficient examples to determine whether deprivation from all human contact blights that concept. Indeed, the study of the neurobiology of love is in its first infancy. But in pioneering psychological experiments on the maternal love system in the monkey, the American psychologist Harry Harlow showed that depriving the infant of contact with its mother – a requirement for a balanced emotional development – leaves it permanently blighted emotionally. The monkey shuns contact, is withdrawn, does not indulge in playful behavior and behaves generally abnormally compared to normal monkeys.

Inherited brain concepts are critically linked to, indeed are the precursors of, acquired brain concepts. But before examining the latter, we should look into the distribution of the inherited concepts, which constitute the organizing principle for generating experience in the brain.

Chapter 4

The Distributed Knowledge-Acquiring System of the Brain

I have tried to make the point above that the acquisition of knowledge is a principal function of the brain, and that it does so, first, by using an organizing principle so that the input into the brain generates an experience and, next, by using the experience so generated to form concepts. To the extent that many different brain areas are involved in organizing the incoming signals, each according to its specialization, the knowledge-acquiring system of the brain must be widely distributed throughout the cerebral cortex. Each one of these systems has the capacity not only to organize the incoming signals according to its inherited concept, but also to abstract, the latter being a critical step in obtaining knowledge. This distribution of the knowledge-acquiring system in the brain is true not only of signals that are acknowledged to differ widely, such as visual and auditory, but characterizes even the subdivisions within a single modality, such as vision. Indeed, it can be illustrated by reference to two relatively simple visual faculties only, those of visual motion and color.

The Functional Specialization of the Visual Brain

The visual brain constitutes a significant part of the brain, occupying perhaps as much as one quarter of it, which is why we are often described as visual creatures. Vision just happens to be one of the most efficient ways of acquiring knowledge. The visual brain can be subdivided into a number of areas that surround the primary visual cortex, or area V1, a cortical area that receives the predominant visual input from the retina. Different visual areas are specialized for different visual attributes, thus leading to a functional specialization in the visual brain.[1] This can be well illustrated through the color and motion systems. When human subjects view an abstract colored scene with no recognizable objects, the activity is concentrated in the primary visual receiving area of the brain, area V1, and an area that surrounds it, area V2, as well as in the color center, the V4 complex (Plate 2) Both V1 and V2 feed V4 with its (color) signals and are reciprocally connected with it. When, by contrast, subjects view a pattern of black and white dots in motion, with the motion changing direction every few seconds, the activity is now limited to another, geographically distinct area, V5, in addition to the two areas that feed it with its specialized motion signals, namely V1 and V2. The latter two visual areas may be thought of somewhat simplistically as distributing centers, parceling out different visual signals that they receive from the retina to specialized visual areas like V4 and V5.

We have considerable information on how the cells of V5 that respond to motion in one direction and not in the opposite direction, and are hence capable of integrating information from at least two points successively in time, are wired. All indications are that this wiring, which leads to the organizing principle for perceiving visual motion, is genetically determined. It is also very likely that a particular, genetically determined neural wiring endows the cells of V4 with the properties that they have and enables them to generate constant colors, that is, to respond to colors independently of the precise wavelength-energy composition reflected from them. The cells of both areas are capable of abstracting, as explained earlier, in the sense that a color cell in V4 that responds selectively to red is not concerned with the precise nature of the stimulus that is red, but only that it should be red. Equally, a directionally selective cell in V5 is not concerned with the precise configuration of the stimulus that moves in its preferred direction, but only that there should be motion in that direction. Moreover, unlike the consequence of damage to V4, which leads to the syndrome of cerebral achromatopsia (color imperception),[2] damage to V5 results in the syndrome of akinetopsia,[3] when the subject becomes simply unable to perceive motion.

Hence these two different attributes have distinct centers in the visual brain, and this difference is enough to establish the principle of functional specialization, although of course there are many other specializations, among them those for facial recognition, the recognition of facial expression, the identification of forms, and body language.

The difference between color and motion is significant and may constitute part of the reason, though not the only one, why different attributes are processed in separate areas of the visual brain. Kant believed that the inherited concept organizing all experience had two characteristics, space and time. He supposed that these two characteristics are given a priori and are present at birth, before any knowledge is acquired. Yet it is obvious that color and motion have different temporal requirements. With color, signals coming from many different parts of the field of view have to be compared simultaneously, as explained in the previous chapter. With motion, signals coming from different points successively in time must be compared. Hence, if time is indeed a given a priori, inherited, brain concept, it cannot be uniformly applied to all the different visual areas that process different visual attributes, because it has to be applied in different ways for processing different attributes. It is perhaps not surprising to find, therefore, that color and motion are processed in two different areas of the cerebral cortex, the former in area V4 and the latter in V5. It is almost certain that the two areas have different internal physiological machineries for undertaking the necessary computations, given the difference in temporal requirements for color and motion and thus for generating the two distinct percepts.

This difference in the location of the areas in which the two attributes are processed is projected onto the temporal domain. Experiments have determined that color is perceived before motion by about 80–100 ms.[4] In one sense this is a trivial difference, since there are 1000 ms in a second. But in terms of neural time it is a huge difference. There is currently no agreement as to what the standard of time in the nervous system is; the question itself has indeed not been addressed. But one good metric might be the time taken for the nervous impulse to cross from one nerve cell to the next across the synapse, which lies between 0.5 and 1 ms. By this metric, then, the difference in time required to perceive color and motion is enormous. This is not the only difference in perceptual times. It has been shown that color is also perceived before orientation and that expressions on faces are perceived before their identity. But the difference in perceptual times between color and motion is sufficient to make the statement that there is a temporal hierarchy, and therefore a perceptual asynchrony, in visual perception.

The perceptual asynchrony in terms of color and motion has been attributed to the difference in time that the nervous system takes to process these two attributes and the results of elegant psychophysical experiments leave no doubt that this is so.[5] The consequences of this perceptual asynchrony are interesting for the light that they shed on brain operations. Since the demonstration of functional specialization in the visual brain, one question that has much preoccupied physiologists and psychologists is how the brain combines what it has processed in different visual areas to give us our apparently unitary view of the world, where different attributes of an object – its color, its form, its direction of motion – are seen in perfect spatial and temporal registration. The experiments described briefly above show that over small time frames this is not so, that we do not see all the attributes of vision in perfect temporal registration, although of course we do so over longer periods of time, in excess of 250 ms. But these experiments show something else: when asked to pair a color with a direction of motion over these small time frames, subjects invariably pair the color that occurs at time t with the motion that occurred at time $t - \delta t$. In terms of veridical reality, they consequently misbind the color that occurs at time t to a motion that occurred 80–100 ms earlier. What this tells us is that we perceive what the brain has finished processing. It also tells us that there is not an area in the brain that waits for all the processing systems to terminate their tasks. Rather, at any given moment t, it binds what has been already processed and therefore rendered into a percept. It also gives us another reason for believing in the relative autonomy of the systems. The color system of the brain does not apparently have to wait for the motion system to terminate its task.

Collectively, these experiments as well as the clinical observations give us an important insight not only into the organization of the visual brain, but into visual consciousness as well. There has been much talk recently of the "unity of consciousness." But the above experiments do not support such a notion, unless strictly qualified. The argument is a logical one: when we say that we have perceived something, we mean that we have become conscious of it. Color is perceived because of activity in area V4 and motion because of activity in area V5; hence activity in these areas has a conscious correlate. We therefore become conscious of the two attributes because of activity in two geographically distinct locations. Visual consciousness is therefore distributed in space. Also, we become conscious of color before we become conscious of motion. Visual consciousness is therefore also distributed in time. Consequently, there is no such thing as a "unitary" visual consciousness. There are instead many visual consciousnesses that are distributed in time and space. We may refer to these individual consciousnesses as micro-consciousnesses.

It is always dangerous to credit past statements in light of insights gained from recent experiments, but I believe that Kant held very similar views about consciousness, although he of course did not talk about distribution in space, since functional specialization had not been demonstrated in his day and even the location of the visual brain in the cortex was not known. Moreover, he did not discuss the distribution of visual consciousness in time, since the result described above, that different visual attributes are seen at different times, is only a relatively very recent one. But since knowledge cannot be acquired save in the conscious state, consciousness was very central to Kant's thinking. This is what he wrote in an extensive footnote in his book *The Critique of Pure Reason* (first edition):

> All presentations have a necessary reference to a possible empirical consciousness. For if they did not have this reference, and becoming conscious of them were entirely impossible, then this would be tantamount to saying that they do not exist at all. But all empirical consciousness has a necessary reference to a transcendental consciousness (a consciousness that precedes all particular experience), viz., the consciousness of myself as original apperception. It is therefore absolutely necessary that in my cognition all consciousness belongs to one consciousness (that of myself).[6]

The implication here is obvious: that the unified consciousness is a synthesis of many empirical consciousnesses. Since the synthetic, unified, consciousness is that of myself as the source of all perceptions, it follows that the latter, as opposed to the empirical (or micro-) consciousness, is only accessible through language and communication. In other words, animals are conscious but only man is conscious of being conscious.

That color and motion have different temporal requirements is not the only reason why they are processed in separate areas of the visual brain. Different attributes of the visual world occur sporadically and unpredictably, implied in the principle of functional independence.[7] If a visual stimulus moving to the right were always red, then either of the two attributes – its color or its direction of motion – could define the stimulus, and processing one attribute alone would be sufficient for identification and categorization of the object. In fact, a moving stimulus can be of any color. Equally, if a bus always moved in one direction, then either attribute could define it uniquely. But a bus can be of any color and move in any direction. The same principle applies to faces and facial expression. A sad expression is not the privilege of a given face only. A given face in turn can be happy or sad. There are many different visual attributes – faces, facial expressions, body language, movement, color, form, distance, depth – that can occur independently and unpredictably. One solution that the brain has developed for dealing with the independent occurrence of visual attributes is the principle of functional specialization in the visual brain.[7] This principle is really an extension of an overall strategy, that of functional localization in the brain. This refers to the fact that different faculties are anatomically localizable in different and geographically distinct parts of the cerebral cortex, even though the brain shows a unity in thought and action. It should therefore not be surprising that, in spite of the perceived unified visual image, the visual apparatus itself is highly fractionated and specialized. In fact, since the first descriptions of the principle of multiplicity of areas in the visual brain and their functional specialization, many more visual areas have been discovered and each new visual area emphasizes the importance of functional specialization as a brain strategy for acquiring knowledge about the world.

The fact that there are many visual areas in the brain and that motion and color, among other attributes, are processed in separate visual areas and require different inherited concepts to organize the incoming visual signals takes us a step further. It allows us to generalize, by saying that there are many inherited concepts that the brain applies in acquiring knowledge, and that each concept is tailored to processing a specific attribute. It is not hard to see that another brain concept, another organizing principle, must be applied to form, where the relations of one part to another are critical, whereas the precise relationships are not so, or far less so, for color. Another brain concept, again involving comparisons, must be applied to categorize a face as a sad one. The list may be multiplied, and points to one end, that different organizing principles or concepts, both visual and non-visual, are genetically tied to different, specialized, visual areas.

The knowledge-acquiring system of the brain is thus very widely distributed in the cerebral cortex. This means essentially that many cortical areas, both visual and non-visual, are also involved in the formation of synthetic brain concepts (see following chapters). But herein lies an important difference between inherited and acquired brain concepts. Whereas inherited brain concepts are intimately linked to specific areas, with the internal machinery of each area being necessary to organize the incoming signals in a particular way, depending upon its specialization, there is every reason to suppose that acquired brain concepts are strongly dependent upon influences from other, often "higher," areas. This is because judgment, past experience, and memory all play critical roles in updating the synthetic brain concept and modifying it with time.

Chapter 5

The Acquired Synthetic Brain Concepts

To obtain knowledge of this world, the brain must categorize objects and situations and form a concept of them. It is obvious that as we acquire experience post-natally, we begin to form a concept of, let us say, a car. This allows us to categorize an object as a car, regardless of what angle, distance, or lighting conditions we view it from. Equally, we categorize a certain collection of stimuli as a face, and can recognize it as such in very different viewing conditions. Nor is such concept formation restricted only to objects or indeed purely sensory events. Any number of different paintings have celebrated Jesus Christ's last moments on the Cross. The brain is instantly able to categorize such a painting as belonging to a special occasion, at least in Christian cultures, even in spite of the many variations in its depiction. Note that the formation of acquired concepts also involves abstraction. My concept of a car does not depend upon a particular car but on all the cars that I have seen. Abstraction is the critical characteristic that is common to both inherited and acquired concepts.

Acquired brain concepts are distinct from inherited ones in that they are developed by the brain throughout its post-natal life and are therefore capable of being continually modified. The brain may come to develop a concept of what color best suits, for example, a sports car. Henry Ford certainly had a concept of colors for cars when he famously said, "I don't care what color it is as long as it is black." We also develop with time a concept of the kind of person we would like to love, and this concept is no doubt subject to many experiences, including that of social milieu, upbringing and exposure to different individuals. The brain must, almost by definition, be able to develop acquired concepts throughout post-natal life because it cannot know in advance what kind of experience it is likely to encounter in the future.

To develop the acquired concept throughout post-natal life depends upon the acquisition of new experience and incorporating it into earlier experiences. Memory and judgment, which allow for the capacity to compare the new experience with previous ones, are obviously critical factors here. Hence we find that, unlike the inherited brain concepts, the acquired ones are open to wide influences from other brain areas and are critically dependent upon the brain's memory and judgmental systems. They are therefore also critically dependent upon influences from the so-called "higher" brain centers as are to be found in the frontal lobes. A good illustration of this can also be found in color vision. The perception of color depends upon the comparisons that take place largely within the color center of the brain, as described before. It does not depend upon the higher centers located in the frontal lobes. But when we view fauvist paintings in which objects are dressed in "un-natural" colors, by which I mean colors that, through experience, we are not accustomed to seeing them in, then the frontal lobes become activated, as if in trying to solve a puzzle.[1] The frontal lobes become also active when color is perceived not in abstract but as a property of surfaces, that is, when colors are attached to a particular, recognizable, object, since here again memory and experience are involved.

How the brain forms concepts is a matter that neurobiology has hardly touched upon. To date, perhaps the most exciting experiments have been those that have shown that when an adult monkey is shown nonsense objects created using a computer and displayed on a TV monitor, it soon learns to recognize those objects regardless of the point of view from which they are presented. Recordings from cells in the inferior temporal cortex, a cortical zone critical for form perception, shows that most of the cells there are responsive to one of the seen views of the nonsense object only. But a small minority, amounting to about 1% of the total sampled, will respond to the object no matter what view is presented.[2] Though relatively small, 1% still amounts to a very substantial number of cells. Clearly, there is a concept formation system that is at work, even if we are still ignorant about the precise neural implementation. It may occur entirely within the inferior temporal cortex or it may recruit other areas as well. Even so, we can draw one important conclusion about this result: it constitutes a neurological demonstration, if only in outline, of the formation of a synthetic concept in the brain.

Acquired Concepts are Synthetic Concepts
in the Brain

What I mean by a synthetic concept is that, in the example given above, it is a synthesis of all the views that the monkey has been exposed to. In providing such a synthesis, a comparison must have taken place somewhere along the pathway leading to the emergence of such cells in the inferior temporal cortex. It is therefore a concept that is generated by two sets of comparisons: one inherent in the inherited organizing principle that dictates that such comparisons should occur; and another that is the result of comparing the input at any given moment with past inputs belonging to the same category, and stored in memory, and adding to the stored memory and thus modifying it. What distinguishes the synthetic, acquired, concept from the inherited one is that the former is capable of modification throughout life, with the acquisition of experience. Take the example of an aeroplane. Our concept of planes has changed radically since the time that the first plane was launched by the Wright brothers. No one at that time, with the possible exception of some visionaries, would have included a jumbo jet in their concept of planes. Most of us in turn (unless we are aeroplane engineers) have little concept of what planes will look like a century from now. This continual modification of a synthetic concept through the accretion of experience is not limited to visual or auditory or other sensory conditions. Our concept of what is beautiful changes as we view more and more objects or situations, or as we find ourselves in different cultural environments. The synthetic concept of a beautiful dress is not the same today as it was in the 1930s or in Renaissance times. The continual modification of synthetic concepts through cultural influences as well as through the experiences that an individual accumulates is applicable to even more abstract concepts such as love. The inherited concept of unity-in-love does not seem to have changed much through the ages, if one is to believe the literature of love. But the kind of person that one loves varies very much from one culture to another and from one age to another. Indeed an individual's concept of the kind of person that he or she may love can change during a lifetime. The way that one pursues a loved person also seems to vary very much from one age to another. The troubadours and the Sufi mystics commonly exalted chaste love at a distance, a practice that many would not, I suppose, wish to pursue today.

Another feature of the acquired, synthetic, concept is that it may change internally, through thought processes in the brain. A supreme example of this in world literature is Dante's concept of Beatrice and of love, which I will examine later. Here again, we must qualify what we mean by internally. Dante saw Beatrice only during his childhood years, yet she remained with him for the rest of his life, and was the primary inspiration for his great work. His love for her was gradually metamorphosed into love of wisdom and beauty. Such a transmutation occurred in the physical absence of Beatrice and thus in the brain of Dante alone. This does not mean to say that external influences – his experience of other women, his experience of life in general, his reading – did not play a role, perhaps even a critical role, in this transmutation.

The Relationship between Inherited and Acquired Concepts

If inherited brain concepts constitute the organizing principle, thus generating perceptions and therefore experiences, while categories are generated from these experiences through the synthetic, acquired, concepts, it is obvious that the two must be very intimately linked. Indeed, one can say that the former is the basis of the latter, without which the latter cannot exist.

Returning again to a simple example, that of a car, the brain is able to generate a concept of car through its many experiences, a concept that becomes independent of the point of view, the color, the viewing conditions and much else besides. The very process of generating such a concept depends upon an inherited brain program, the capacity to abstract and to generalize. But whereas the capacity to generate both the experience and the concept is the province of inherited brain concepts, and is thus not hostage to the acquisition of new experiences, the generated concept of a car itself is capable of many modifications throughout post-natal life. Indeed, it could be said that the rule for acquired concepts – a synthesis of many experiences – is to be continually modified. Just as the inherited brain concept is indispensable for generating the experience, so the experience is indispensable for generating the acquired concept.

Chapter 6

The Synthetic Brain Concept and the Platonic Ideal

The synthetic brain concept is one that I would like to equate with the brain ideal. It therefore is interesting to compare this view with Plato's Ideal Theory.

Plato believed in a system of universal Ideas that have an existence independent of man. He believed that true knowledge can only be knowledge of these Ideas and that the only way of obtaining such knowledge was through a thought process since Ideas were, to him, supra-sensible. Plato's Ideal Theory went through several hesitations, modifications and enlargements.[1] These can be traced from the early Socratic discourses and especially *Theaetetus* to the later Platonic dialogues. It is arguable whether Plato was ever convinced that he should make Ideas of things such as houses, or trees or horses, and he acknowledged his hesitation in this regard.[2] What is certain is that his main preoccupation was with the idealization of abstract concepts such as justice, honor, beauty and love. He believed that these Ideals exist permanently outside the individual and are not subject to changing conditions to which the sensible world is hostage. In Book X of *The Republic* he used the example of couches to illustrate his point and also question whether art could really ever give true knowledge of objects, since a painting could only depict a particular couch from a particular point of view. This restriction led Plato to express his disapproval of art. Painting, he believed, could only represent one particular facet of a particular object and not the universal, Ideal, object that alone could give knowledge of all objects of that category. He would therefore have banished all painters from his millennial Republic.

I, as a neurobiologist, would not share the same hesitation. I consider instead that the brain does form concepts of particular things as well as concepts for more abstract notions such as love, beauty, honor and justice that preoccupied Plato. I consider, too, that these concepts, which constitute the ideals formed in the brain, have no existence outside the individual although they may be influenced by external events.

In a sense, therefore, Plato believed that knowledge is derived from abstractions; the Ideal is an abstract entity that represents a universal value; knowledge of it can only be obtained through a thought process. My view, and I suppose the general view of neurobiologists, would be the opposite: that sensory data are submitted to abstractive processes in the brain from which a synthetic concept (the Ideal) is built up. We can, therefore, summarize a fundamental difference between the Platonic system and the one that I am proposing here. There is, in the neurobiological system, no universal Ideal of beauty, or of the form of an object, or of a landscape. Each one of these is tailored according to individual experience, and varies from one individual to the next. Another fundamental difference between Ideal as the synthetic concept of the brain and Plato's Theory of Ideals is that while Plato's Ideals are immutable, the synthetic concept changes with time and with the accretion of experience. If one is searching for universals and for immutability, then one must look to the inherited concepts that organize the input into the brain and generate experiences, not the synthetic concepts. Whether we look at color or love, we find that there is a universal element dictating these experiences that varies little, if at all, from one culture to the next or with time. The system for generating colors is immutable, so is the one for generating love. According to the evidence that we obtain from reading the literature of love, the fundamental concept behind the emotion of love – that of "unity-in-love" – is also immutable.

Concept formation is one of the great triumphs of the brain but it also exacts a very heavy toll. The acquired concept in the brain, being a synthetic one, is the result of all the experiences that an individual encounters during life. But an individual's moment-to-moment experience is of only one example of the category that has been conceptualized. And that particular example may not satisfy the synthetic concept in the brain. Through my viewing of many houses, I am likely to have not only the concept of a house, but also of an ideal house. But the particular house that I may visit to purchase may not satisfy the ideal concept of a house formed in my brain through its concept forming machinery. Artists have concepts that they want to translate onto canvas. But the end result may not, and commonly does not,

satisfy them; it constitutes but one example that may not quite correspond to the synthetic concept in their brains. The same is true of a performance. My concept of how *Tristan und Isolde* should be performed is almost certainly dictated by the performances I have attended or heard and by what I have read about the opera. Any given performance may not actually satisfy that synthetic concept constituted in my brain, and that comes to mean the ideal performance. The same is true of even more abstract concepts such as love and justice.

The difference between the system that I am advocating and the Platonic one, though critical, does not exclude substantial similarities. The first of these relates to that golden rule, comparison. Plato supposed that there must be some power in the mind (brain) that can compare the information received and that notions such as "larger" or "more beautiful" that enable comparisons to be made must be innate, in order to supply the power for reasoning. One might therefore consider this inherited (brain) capacity to be an example of a universal, inherited, concept. Comparisons are as critical in Plato's thinking as they are in the system advocated here. Also, the thought process that Plato advocated as the critical element in acquiring knowledge becomes a thread linking the views of Plato, Kant, and more modern neurobiological thought. Like Plato and Kant, I suppose that the construction of a synthetic concept or ideal, leading to knowledge of a particular category, is due to a thought process, but the thought process can equally be a "silent," unconscious process. The example that I have given above, of monkeys forming concepts of nonsense objects, is due to such a "silent" thought process. As Plato and Kant believed, it involves a comparison, in this instance of all the "nonsense" objects that the monkey has viewed to determine what they have in common. Finally, as in Plato's Theory of Ideals, the synthetic concept is also rarely achievable in life.

Splendors and Miseries of the Brain

The splendor of the brain is that it is capable, seemingly effortlessly, of generating so many concepts and thus acting as a very efficient knowledge-acquiring or, if one prefers, knowledge-generating system. The misery that this splendid machinery entails is in fact the result of its very efficiency. The incapacity of our daily experience to live up to and satisfy the synthetic concepts that the brain generates commonly results in a state of permanent dissatisfaction. This does not much matter in many cases. It may be relatively unimportant whether a bottle of wine fits my concept of the perfect wine or whether a house or a symphonic rendering corresponds to my brain-constructed ideals of them. It is quite another matter when the concept of love or a work of art is left unsatisfied.

But is there any evidence that the brain has not only a concept of love but of the kind of person that is to be loved? And is there any evidence that the brains of artists, no less than that of viewers, form a concept of a particular scene or object to be represented? As it stands today, it is difficult to find hard scientific evidence in favor of such a view. If one needs such evidence, one must look for it elsewhere. In fact, examination of the literature of love and of artistic works provides compelling evidence, which the scientist should use, that there are such concepts, that they are universal, and that they are more often than not left unsatisfied. The latter constitutes one of the main motive forces for artistic achievement, as well as for the constant endeavor in the face of numerous dissatisfactions to find in a work of art, or in life, a true reflection of the synthetic concept in the brain. It is for this reason that I have included such a relatively large discussion of concepts of art and love in this book.

Chapter 7

Creativity and the Sources of Perfection in the Brain

Perfection in different domains is something we all seek to varying degrees. In some domains, and for some individuals, it is critical. It would be foolish to think that, except in certain rare cases, most people do not seek the perfect partner. It would be hard to imagine that the artist does not seek to create a perfect work of art, be it a symphony or a novel or a painting. We in turn would all like to read a perfect novel or hear a perfect symphony or gaze at a perfect sculpture. But what is perfection? And what do we mean when we say we seek it? How can we define perfection in terms that are applicable to all that we seek perfection in? Can we do so without reference to the brain?

It is my belief that synthetic brain concepts are central to understanding perfection. Perhaps not all would agree with this view. The Platonic system supposes that perfection is embodied in some immutable ideal that exists in the world outside. This implies that perfection resides outside the brain. But that is only part of the Platonic answer. The more difficult and neurobiologically interesting part is that only through a thought process, and not through the senses, can one get to *know* the ideal and thus acquire knowledge. Hence, unwittingly and probably without realizing it, Plato introduces the brain into his system, for the brain alone is involved in the thought process. That this is so was actually acknowledged by Plato in words spoken by Socrates in *Phaedo*. In a passage remarkable for its time, Socrates asks: "Is it through the blood that we acquire knowledge or through the air that is in us? Or is it none of these but that through the brain we form an opinion and from opinion acquire knowledge?"[1]

That perfection for one individual is not necessarily perfection for another is a clear indication that there is no universal standard of perfection, and hence that there is not some kind of ideal in the world outside. If there were, we would surely all have the same notion of perfection. It is also a sure guide to the fact that perfection resides in the brain rather than in the world outside, though it has to be accessed through a thought process. Some may disagree with this view. They might want to say that there is a perfect ideal in the world outside and the fact that different individuals have a different notion of what constitutes perfection is merely an indication that they have different thought processes. Even accepting such dissent, their argument still revolves around the question of the thought process, and hence the brain.

What then is that thought process? I would like to begin by looking at its end result, which is the creation of a synthetic concept in the brain, because it is through a thought process that we achieve such a concept in the brain, as discussed in the previous chapter. For the artist, it is the translation of that synthetic thought process into a work of art that constitutes the process of seeking perfection, even if the artist may never attain it. For the viewer, if the work of art satisfies the synthetic concept in his brain, then the work of art is perfect, or comes close to it. It is possible that a particular painting or work of art, or the sight of an individual, may satisfy completely the synthetic concept in the brain of the creator or the viewer, though this is, on the whole, a somewhat rare event. It is more likely that even if a work is judged to satisfy the synthetic concept at any given moment, it may not do so at a subsequent time, a fact that we are all familiar with. This may be traced to the argument given above, that the synthetic concept is not immutable. Rather, it is continually modified as the brain acquires new experience. There are, we all know, events, views, and situations that are so perfect that we want to "freeze" them, in the sense that we do not want to revisit a place or re-create a situation because it was so perfect in terms of satisfying us and therefore our synthetic concepts at that moment. In many of his poems Konstantinos Kavafis, considered by many to be the greatest Greek poet of the last century, has recreated such frozen moments, moments that have not developed either through experience or even in his mind, and which have returned in their original form to inspire him later in life and elevate his art (see Chapter 21). In daily life, such frozen moments – of satisfying experiences revisited – are rare, or rather are the exception and not the rule. With new experience, we (or our brain) "unfreeze" what was previously frozen and come to develop a new, or extended, synthetic concept.

Hence the transience of all perfection and of all beauty depends not only on the change in the object that is contemplated but also in the transformation of the synthetic concept of the brain itself, for what is beautiful and therefore corresponds to the brain concept at a given moment may cease to do so at another, because the brain concept itself has changed through the accretion of new experience. The "*I* consider" in Shakespeare's sonnet, which starts with the lines

> When I consider that every thing that grows
> Holds in perfection but a little moment

is of paramount importance.

This analysis also has a bearing on the question of choice. In the modern world, we often believe that the choices made available to us have increased significantly compared to older days. There is no denying the truth of this. But it is also worth considering that the choice available to us is also determined, and sometimes severely restricted, by the synthetic concept in the brain. This effectively means that there is not a straightforward relationship between the variety in the external world and the exigencies of the brain, except in the sense that the variety could modify the synthetic concept in the brain through exposure. It is important to understand that choice is not only a question of what is available in the world outside but of what is available in the brain as well. And a restriction in choice is determined as much, and probably significantly more, by the synthetic concepts of the brain.

By a thought process I do not mean to imply only the conscious effort made in solving a mathematical or technical problem, or in executing a painting or thinking about an event. Nor do I mean the process that we are aware of while listening to a symphony or reading a book. Thought processes are involved in all these activities, but thought processes also involve brain activities of which we are not even aware. The formation of synthetic concepts in the brain is itself also a silent and continuous thought process of which we are unaware. Indeed we are even unaware of the synthetic concept itself but only of its external manifestation, the fact that there are many occasions in which it remains unsatisfied, although of course only very few would trace this dissatisfaction to an actual concept in the brain. By this I mean only that every time we find something imperfect we are doing so with reference to the synthetic concept in the brain, which becomes the standard against which all else is judged.

Neurobiology has not yet managed to unravel the details of the thought process. There is progress in this direction at present but it is still at the macroscopic level, by which I mean that we do not know much about the cellular events involved (see Chapter 6). There is little doubt that the thought process involves quite complex neural operations but we still have not figured out how to study the contribution that individual cells make to this process. More complex thought processes are unique to man and therefore even more difficult to study at the level of brain cells; we just do not have the adequate technology at present. In approaching the problem, we therefore have to limit ourselves to generalities and to hints derived from such neurophysiological studies as we possess.

Perfection is thus achieving or finding in the outer world a reflection of the synthetic concept constructed by the brain. This may be nothing more than the ideal landscape painting, one that is representative of all the landscapes that the brain has experienced and hence can be used to represent each and every one of them. Or it may be the perfect individual, perfect in terms of the seeker's brain. Or it may be even more exalted than that and consist of the perfect union – a brain concept – with the perfect individual. In each case, the perfection is not easy to achieve. In each case it is the attempt to translate into reality what is derived from reality but is no longer real, in the sense that it is synthetic and therefore cannot fit any single particular real example. There are various solutions that artists and writers have used to achieve what is barely achievable and, odd though it may at first seem, these solutions are not qualitatively different between, say, visual art and love as expressed in its literature.

This of course raises the fundamental question of how a synthetic concept in the brain is satisfied. There must be some kind of mechanism to indicate that a certain landscape, for example, comes close to satisfying the synthetic concept of the perfect landscape. The answer probably lies in the reward and pleasure centers of the brain (Figure 7.1). Imaging experiments have shown that when subjects rate a painting as beautiful there is heightened activity in part of the reward system of the brain, the orbito-frontal cortex, which itself is only one part of an extensive reward system that involves other cortical and sub-cortical structures. Although the details of the cellular events that

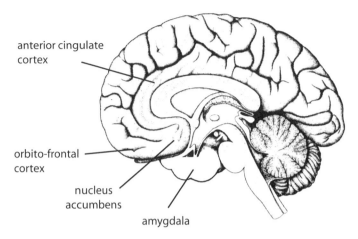

anterior cingulate
cortex

orbito-frontal
cortex

nucleus
accumbens

amygdala

Figure 7.1. The reward circuitry of the brain is complex and includes several stations, both cortical and sub-cortical. Only the forebrain stations are shown, while sub-cortical nuclei, which include the striatum and the insula, are not.

lead to such heightened activity are not known, and nor are the connections between the various cortical sensory areas and the extensive reward centers charted with any precision, it seems highly likely that it is some heightened activity in the reward centers of the brain that signals satisfaction, and conversely that the absence of such activity, or a much reduced activity, signifies the reverse. This is not to imply that the concept itself resides in the reward system but rather, through some as yet unknown mechanism, that the reward system is capable of signaling that the viewed landscape matches as closely as possible the synthetic concept in the brain. Where the concept itself resides is problematic. It is very likely that specialized visual areas are involved. It is possible that other areas are also involved but the problem has not been sufficiently studied to date (see Chapter 5). It is important to point out what must by now be obvious, that the part of the reward system I am referring to, the orbito-frontal cortex, is not activated by a given painting that artists or critics rate as very beautiful, but by what the perceiving individual rates as beautiful. Hence a painting that one individual rates as beautiful will result in heightened activity in this reward center but the same painting rated as not beautiful by another individual will not do so.

Perhaps the most common approach to realizing a real counterpart to the synthetic concept in the brain, and thus satisfying its reward system, lies in trying, and trying again, to come closer and closer to that concept. The difficulty here lies in the fact that the concept itself changes with the experience. Cézanne's series drawings of the *Montagne Sainte Victoire* represent an attempt to come nearer to giving a perfect representation of form, as constituted and as it developed with every new depiction in Cézanne's brain. Artists and writers have often worked and re-worked the same piece over and over again, to try and perfect it. Many remain dissatisfied with the final product and start afresh, either on a new work or on trying to develop the work at hand. Georges Braque had very much the brain concept in mind when he referred to finishing off his paintings, although he did not refer to the brain. He once said that when he painted he tried to put the concept in his mind onto canvas. He often found that when he left a painting untouched for periods of months, and came back to it, the unfinished painting was finished because he had forgotten the original concept. The painting had therefore become divorced from his mind and had acquired an existence of its own!

Another solution is not to undertake a work at all. It is obvious that we cannot give many examples here, for there must be many who do not undertake a piece of work because they find it impossible, but how are we to know? There are, however, examples from artists such as Michelangelo and Sandro Botticelli that attest to this approach and I discuss them later. Another approach is to leave the work unfinished. This approach characterized much of Michelangelo's sculptural work, three-fifths of which were left *non finito*. I shall discuss this in relation to the confessional statements found in his *Rime* or sonnets. It was, after all, Michelangelo who once reputedly said that tragedy does not lie in setting high aims and not achieving them but rather in setting low aims and achieving them. Another example is to be found in the work of Cézanne, much of which is left in an unfinished state, a state of which, interestingly from a neurobiological viewpoint, many and indeed perhaps most viewers are unaware, though artists and art critics once criticized these works severely for their unfinished status. There are substantial advantages to this approach, of leaving things unfinished, in terms of the difficulty of realizing in the real world the synthetic concepts of the brain. Translated to the literature of love, this characteristic becomes the glorification of the unfinished in love, the unconsummated love affair – a characteristic of much of the great literature of love, from troubadour poetry, to the myth of Majnun and Leila, to Tristan and Isolde.

The crushing disappointment of realizing how much things can depart from the synthetic brain concept is described in a light-hearted way by Virginia Woolf in *Orlando*, a description that conforms very much to the neurobiological view I am presenting here. She describes how the illusion of wit in a salon depends upon there being no wit uttered: ". . . as it is notorious that illusions are shattered by conflict with reality, so no real happiness, no real wit, no real profundity are tolerated where the illusion prevails. This serves to explain why Madame du Deffand said no more than three witty things during the course of fifty years. Had she said more, her circle would have been destroyed . . . When she made her famous 'mot de Saint Denis' the very grass was singed. Not a word was uttered. 'Spare us another such, for Heaven's sake, Madame!' her friends cried with one accord. And she obeyed. For almost seventeen years she said nothing memorable and all went well."[2] Better leave the synthetic concept undisappointed. "Is nothingness not a sort of perfection?" asks Gustave von Aschenbach in more sober tones in *Death in Venice*.

Implicit in what I am saying is that creativity itself must depend in a major way not only on the synthetic brain concept but, even more importantly, on the difficulty of realizing it in real life. Not for nothing did Thomas Mann write that art is "the sole and painful way of getting a particular experience."[31] In similar vein, Wagner wrote to Liszt, "Since never in my whole life have I been able to experience the real happiness of romantic love, I mean to raise the greatest of all monuments to this most beautiful of dreams,"[4] implying that he could not realize in life the perfect romantic happiness which his brain conceived of, which he therefore hoped to realize in his work. Here, indeed, lack of actual experience which may conflict with the synthetic concept may enrich the artistic output. The rich imagination that the incapacity to have direct experience generates was alluded to by the novelist John Irving.[5] Irving was puzzled about his father whom he had never met and whom no adult in his family ever talked about, even though the father had asked, in letters to Irving's mother, for some limited contact with his son. In the interview, Irving said: "My mother's greatest gift to my imagination was by denying me any access to my father or any information about who he was. I began imagining him at a very early age and I think that you could say that easily 8 out of 11 of my novels are about a missing father or a missing parent." The concept that he formed of his father was now sovereign and uncontaminated by reality.

The sources of perfection thus lie in the brain, and more specifically in the synthetic concepts formed by the brain. Synthetic concepts are commonly difficult to experience, particularly since they often depart significantly from the individual experience. One way of getting closer to a brain concept lies in creating a work, be it of art or music or literature. Even here there is commonly a mismatch between the brain concept and the artistic product. These are of course all creative efforts, and creativity depends upon a host of factors, among them a brain capacity – for drawing or writing music or playing tennis – and a host of other factors such as drive that must ultimately depend upon neural organizations about which we know little. There is little doubt in my mind that one of the factors determining creativity is the attempt to satisfy the dis-satisfied brain concept. Hence, a permanent dissatisfaction is one of the most powerful ingredients driving creativity. Once one satisfies the brain concept, creativity diminishes rapidly, because one need no longer create what one already has. As Lucian Freud once wrote:

> A moment of complete happiness never occurs in the creation of a work of art. The promise of it is felt in the act of creation and disappears towards the completion of the work. For it is then that the painter realises that it is only a picture he is painting. Until then he has almost dared to hope that the picture might spring to life. Were it not for this, the perfect painting might be painted, on the completion of which the painter could retire. It is this great insufficiency that drives him on. That process of creation becomes necessary to the painter perhaps more than the picture itself. The process in fact is habit-forming.[6]

Part II

Brain Concepts and Ambiguity

Chapter 8

Ambiguity in the Brain and in Art[1]

I have so far emphasized the fact that the brain is interested in obtaining knowledge about essential and non-changing characteristics in a world that is in perpetual flux, a problem that has much preoccupied philosophers, who are concerned with the problem of knowledge, of how we acquire it and how sure we are of what we know. To do so, the brain has inherited concepts or programs that organize experience and make it as independent as possible from external change, the generation of constant colors being among the best examples. There are many other examples that one could give and they all share two features in common. One is their stability, since it is not easy to fool the brain into thinking that a house, for example, is anything but a house regardless of viewing conditions. The other is their relative autonomy, by which I mean that the stimulus is perceived by the brain to be a given color or a given form through the activity of the specialized visual areas and without the mandatory intervention of the higher cognitive centers such as the frontal lobes. Another way of putting this is to say that the operation of the inherited concepts that regulate the activities within the specialized areas to generate percepts does not necessarily depend upon higher cognitive centers.

Figure 10.2 in Chapter 10 illustrates what is *apparently* a radically different situation, one in which the stimulus is stable but the percept varies. This cube, known as the Kanizsa cube after the Italian psychologist Gaetano Kanizsa who made a detailed study of such figures and their perception, can be in one of two recessional planes. What appears to be the front (i.e. towards the observer) can spontaneously change position and occupy a rear position away from the observer, and vice versa. Here, then, is an example of a lability or instability in the brain's response to a physically unchanging stimulus. This is apparently the exact opposite of its response to a perpetually changing stimulus to which it gives stability, as in the example of color. Here, the brain is instead projecting its own apparently unstable operation onto the stable physical stimulus. Why the brain should have developed such a system is not immediately clear but is very likely to be due to the fact that some, indeed many, stimuli in the world can be deceptive in the sense that they can be given more than one interpretation. If the brain did not have the capacity to project more than one interpretation onto the stimulus, it may find itself in a dangerous situation. A good example is that of a smile on the face of someone one may fancy. If one were to give only one interpretation to that smile – a desire for greater intimacy – one may soon end up in trouble. Better for the brain to entertain several possibilities and thus protect itself.

There are several interesting features about stimuli that are capable of being interpreted by the brain in more than one way, and chief among these is that they always seem to engage higher cortical areas in the frontal and parietal lobes of the brain, quite unlike the perception of color or form, although the precise role that these cortical areas play in the interpretation is not straightforward. We commonly refer to these stimuli as illusory or ambiguous, although in fact there is nothing either illusory or ambiguous about them, as I shall try to show. Nor is there such a radical difference between them and apparently stable stimuli, such as that found in color vision. For both types of stimuli, the brain projects its own operations onto the incoming visual signals and organizes them according to its own inherited and acquired concepts. The difference between the two is that in the so-called ambiguous examples that we shall consider the brain can project more than one acquired concept onto the incoming signals. What we have here is a stable brain system with a huge range for acquiring knowledge about the world, extending from those stimuli to which the brain gives only one interpretation to those that are amenable to many interpretations. This capacity of determining that there is more than possible solution is itself due to an inherited brain concept, which dictates that more than one group of cells or more than one area is engaged when viewing a scene that cannot be definitively resolved into one stable and unchanging entity, regardless of viewing conditions. It is, as we shall see, a stable inherited concept that is very difficult to disrupt, as all inherited brain concepts are. To understand the neural basis of "ambiguity" requires us first to reiterate an important point and understand that the brain is not a mere passive chronicler of external events. Perceiving is not therefore something that the brain does passively.[2] Rather, the brain is an active participant in constructing what we see. Through its participation, it instils meaning into the many signals that it receives and thus gains knowledge about the world. The percepts that the brain creates are the result of an interaction between the signals that it receives and what it does to them.

There is another interesting feature about multiple interpretations, which is in line with what I have said before, that once evolution hits upon a successful solution it uses it repetitively with such modifications as may be necessary for every new departure. We shall thus see that the implied instability in the brain's response to the Kanizsa cube is merely an example at one end of the scale, where the number of interpretations is limited to two. At the other end, the brain uses this same strategy to give multiple interpretations to, for example, works of art.

The *Oxford English Dictionary* defines ambiguity in the sense in which most people understand it: "uncertain, open to more than one interpretation, of doubtful position." Ambiguity is a protective characteristic that the brain has developed but which has been put to good use in enriching many works of art. But ambiguity should not be thought of as a characteristic of some great works of art. Rather, it is a characteristic of the brain in its knowledge-seeking role, a characteristic that the artist exploits and uses to sublime effect and thus enriches his work. Equally, the viewer uses this same potential in providing different interpretations and thus enhances his or her experience of the work. To understand this better, we must (as we have done in earlier chapters) look at the brain, its function and its capacity to form concepts. Such an undertaking leads us to another, and neurobiological, definition of ambiguity that is the symmetrical opposite of the dictionary definition. My aim in this section is to show that there are different levels of "ambiguity" dictated by neurological necessity and built into the physiology of the brain. They all involve the application of brain concepts, whether inherited or acquired, onto the image. These different levels may involve a single cortical area or set of areas; they may involve different cortical areas with different perceptual specialization or they may involve, in addition, higher cognitive factors such as learning, judgment, memory, and experience. Whether the result of activity in a single area or in different areas, these different levels are tied together by a metaphoric thread whose purpose is the acquisition of knowledge about the world and of making sense of the many signals that the brain receives. They are united no less by a single operation, which nevertheless differs from one condition to another. That operation is the application of brain concepts onto incoming signals.

Chapter 9

Processing and Perceptual Sites
in the Brain

Before we consider the neurobiological foundations of ambiguity, it is instructive to give a more general view of the organization of the visual brain, particularly in relation to the processing and perception of the visual input. In more precise terms, it is instructive to enquire into the perceptual capacities of the visual processing centers in the brain. The question is not trivial. Many have supposed, either implicitly or explicitly, that processing sites are separate from perceptual sites, that visual signals are processed in some cortical area and that what has been processed is then relayed to another cortical area, through which we perceive and thus become conscious. Alternatively, once signals are processed, other signals from higher centers of the brain dictate the interpretation of what has been processed, in "top-down" fashion. Both suppositions raise difficult problems, in particular of what dictates that the processing is terminated and thus to be relayed to another area, or what dictates that there should be an intervention from a higher area. The resolution of these problems has interesting consequences for understanding the more general problem of ambiguity and how it is handled by the brain.

As outlined earlier, the visual brain consists of many different visual areas, specialized to process different attributes such as form, motion, color, faces and so on. We think of these areas as being specialized to process these different attributes, without being very specific about what processing means since we do not really know much about the detailed neural mechanisms that are involved. But it is worth considering a further proposition, that these processing sites are also perceptual sites, that is, sites at which what is processed becomes perceptually explicit without the mandatory involvement of further or "higher" areas, leading us to perceive the attribute that they have processed.

Processing Sites in the Visual Brain are also Perceptual Sites

Strong evidence that processing sites are also perceptual sites comes from experiments designed in such a way that the same stimulus is delivered to the two eyes separately and is sometimes perceived by the subject and sometimes not, depending upon the configuration used, even though in both instances the appropriate signals reach the eye and are relayed to the visual brain. These experiments utilize what is known as dichoptic viewing conditions, in which the two eyes are stimulated separately in rapid succession, say at 100 ms intervals. When an identical stimulus, such as a green outline house or face against a red background, is presented separately to each eye, the two images are fused into a single image and the subject can report consciously and correctly what the stimulus was (i.e. the subject can tell whether the stimulus was a face or a house). But if the same stimulus is presented to each eye in the same way though with opposite color contrasts, the two colors cancel each other in the fusion and the subject is no longer able to tell whether the stimulus was a face or a house. For example, if a green outline house against a red background is presented to one eye and a red outline house against a green background is presented to the other, the subject perceives only yellow, since the two (opponent) colors cancel each other out (Figure 9.1). The stimulus cannot therefore be recognized by the subject, even though the visual input to the eyes is the same as in the condition when the stimulus was correctly perceived.

Houses and faces are processed in distinct areas of the visual brain[1] and constitute therefore good systems for testing the proposition that processing sites are also perceptual sites, using the experiment outlined above. If they are, then one would expect areas that are specialized for the perception of faces to be active whether the faces are (consciously) perceived or not, as long as there is the appropriate visual input to them from the eyes. If they are not, then one would expect that the area would not be active when the stimuli are being processed but not perceived, that is, when the subject cannot recognize the stimulus even though the adequate signals are entering each eye and are being relayed to the appropriate cortical area. One might, in addition, expect that the entire pattern of activity in the brain would be

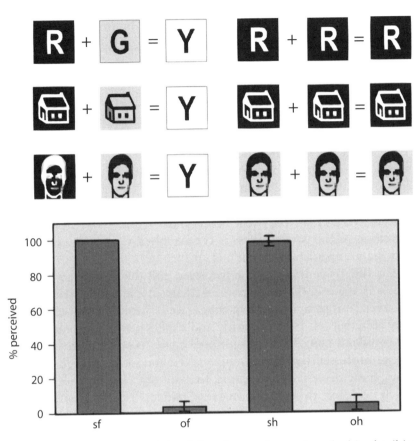

Figure 9.1. Illustration of the dichoptic experiment described in detail in the text. When identical stimuli (representing, for example, a face and a house) are delivered to the two eyes, subjects can recognize the identity of the stimulus (as shown in the right three columns and the underlying histogram). When the two stimuli are of opposite color contrast, the two cancel each other out and subjects cannot recognize the stimulus; instead, they see yellow (see histograms, which show the percentage of stimuli correctly recognized). R = red; G = green; Y = yellow; sf = same face stimulus delivered to each eye; sh = same house stimulus delivered to each eye; of = opposite color contrast face delivered to each eye; oh = opposite color contrast house delivered to each eye.

substantially different during the processing stage (with the presentation of faces in opposite color contrast when the subject cannot identify a face) and during the perceptual stage (when the two stimuli are presented in identical color contrast and the subject can easily identify a face). The same logic applies to the perception of houses, for which a contiguous brain area is specialized. But the brain imaging experiment described above showed that the same stimulus-specific areas are activated regardless of whether the stimulus is perceived or not.[2] Thus when the stimulus is that of a face, the area in the brain specifically implicated in the perception of faces is specifically activated, regardless of whether the stimulus is perceived or not. A similar result is obtained with stimuli depicting houses, which activate a different, specialized, part of the visual brain. Indeed, the pattern of cortical activation in the cortical areas is remarkably similar in the perceived and the non-perceived conditions (Figure 9.2).[3]

The difference between the perceived and the non-perceived condition is that, in the former, the activity in the specialized areas is stronger. Surprisingly, one big difference is in the frontal lobes, the very area that has been implicitly and explicitly thought of as critical for conscious perception.[4] The frontal cortex is active when the stimuli are processed but remain unperceived and inactive when they are consciously perceived, for reasons that are not clear. In fact, there is much evidence, though of a negative nature, that the frontal cortex

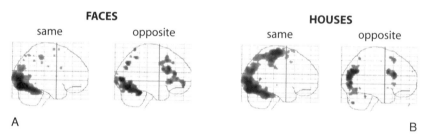

A   B

Figure 9.2. A reconstruction of the distribution of brain activity when subjects viewed the stimuli in the dichoptic experiment shown in Figure 9.1. Note that the same part of the occipital lobe of the brain (A) is activated with the two different stimuli but that the activity is stronger when subjects perceive the stimuli correctly than when they do not (the strength of activity is not shown in this figure). Note also that when the subjects are not able to perceive a face or a house, there is activity in the frontal cortex (B).

is not necessarily involved in all perceptual states, the example of color perception given earlier being among the best.

This demonstration shows that the cortical perceptual sites are not separate from the cortical processing sites. Processing sites instead are also perceptual sites. This is not to imply that other cortical areas are never involved in the perception of houses and faces. There is little doubt that the frontal and parietal lobes of the cortex are involved during the perception of visual stimuli to which more than one inter-pretation can be given and that the memory system is involved when the identification is that of a particular house or a particular face. The importance of the demonstration lies in showing that there is not a separate site specialized for perceiving, as opposed to processing; this is an important point to bear in mind in what follows. In general, all the evidence suggests that a processing site becomes a perceptual site when the neural activity in it passes a certain threshold, though no one knows if this heightened activity is due to the recruitment of new cells in the relevant area or to the increased activity of cells that are already engaged in processing.

Nodes and Essential Nodes in the Visual Brain

It is useful to introduce here the concept of nodes and essential nodes, by giving a very rough sketch of the organization of the visual brain (Figure 9.3). In essence, a very prominent part of the input from the retina reaches the primary visual cortex, known as area V1. Signals belonging to different attributes are distributed to specialized com-partments within V1. V1 is surrounded by another visual area, V2, which also has specialized compartments that receive input from their counterparts in V1. V2 itself is surrounded by further visual areas, promin-ent among them being V3, V3A, V4, and V5, all of them special-ized visual areas that receive distinct inputs from the specialized compartments of V1 and V2. These specialized areas have diffuse return anatomical connections with areas V1 and V2 and also reciprocal con-nections with further visual areas, but the details do not concern us here. There are therefore many visual areas in the brain and each receives input, directly or indirectly, from area V1, and is reciprocally connected with it.

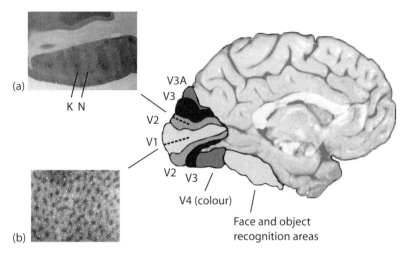

Figure 9.3. Organization of the visual brain. A medial view of the brain to show the distribution of some of the visual areas. (a) Section taken through V2 and stained as for section in (b). Now the cytochrome oxidase rich zones appear as stripes, which are alternately thick (K) or thin (N). The wavelength selective cells in V2 are concentrated in the thin stripes. (b) Section taken through V1 and stained for the metabolic enzyme cytochrome oxidase to show the distribution of islands (blobs) of high cytochrome oxidase content which also contain cells that are specific for different wavelengths of light.

By a *node* I mean a stage in the visual pathway, for example area V4 or area V5, or a specialized sub-compartment within the pathway, for example the compartments of V1 and V2 that feed V4 or V5 (Figure 9.3). An example of the latter would be the blobs of V1 and the thin stripes of V2, compartments that are rich in the metabolic enzyme cytochrome oxidase that can therefore be easily visualized when brain sections passing through the two areas are stained for that enzyme. These cytochrome oxidase compartments (blobs of V1 and thin stripes of V2) contain cells that respond selectively to some wavelengths of light and not to others, and project to area V4 where color is generated by the brain. An *essential node* is one at which activity becomes perceptually explicit without the need for further processing.[5] In other words, when activity at a node acquires a conscious correlate, it becomes an essential node. Each node can potentially become an essential node. I refer to the conscious correlate that is the result of activity at an essential node as a *micro-consciousness*;[5] activity at different essential nodes leads to a micro-conscious correlate for different attributes. Activity of a certain strength at V4, for example, leads to a conscious correlate, that of color, while activity of a certain strength in V5 leads to another conscious correlate, that of visual motion. Visual consciousness consists therefore of many micro-consciousnesses that are distributed in space, since they are the correlates of activity in spatially distinct locations that reach perceptual endpoints at different times (see Chapter 4).

Area V4 provides a good example of an essential node. Activity in it leads to the generation and conscious perception of color without the need for further processing by other visual areas. We therefore say that a micro-consciousness for color is generated as a correlate of activity within the V4 complex. In the intact brain, the nodes that feed V4 (the blobs of V1 and the thin stripes of V2) are not necessarily essential nodes as far as color vision is concerned, in that activity in them is processed further, at the level of V4 (although they are of course intimately linked to the generation of color since they pass wavelength signals to V4 and are reciprocally connected with it). They become essential nodes in two conditions: one occurs when activity in them leads to conscious awareness of the fact that the dominant wavelength has changed, as happens when a scene is viewed under two different illuminants with different wavelength compositions, for example successively in tungsten light and in daylight. This is a consequence of the fact that most of the wavelength selective cells in areas V1[6] and V2[7] are concerned with the wavelength composition of the light and seem to lack the machinery for generating colors. The other condition is when V4 is damaged, leading to a perceptual state produced by activity in the blobs of V1 and the thin stripes of V2 and characterized by an inability to construct constant colors. In patients rendered achromatopsic (cortically color blind) by damage to V4, the intensity of lights of different wavebands can be detected, but no colors can be ascribed to them[8] or, if the damage is sub-total, the attributed color is heavily dependent upon the dominant wavelength in the light reflected from a surface.[9] In this instance, a green leaf would appear red at dawn and at dusk (when a good deal more of the long (red) wavelength is reflected from the leaf). This is of course quite unlike what happens in a normal person with an intact V4. In the latter, the leaf would remain green (though change in shade) because the brain is able to compare the amount of light of different wave-bands (including red) reflected from the green leaf and from its surrounds. Clinical evidence suggests, therefore, that when V1–V2 become the essential node for color vision (in the absence of V4) their physiological capacities are reflected perceptually by an unstable color vision in which color constancy is a primary casualty.

   This brief background description of the organization of the visual brain allows us to consider different levels of ambiguity in the brain, from the totally non-ambiguous to the highly ambiguous state.

Chapter 10

From Unambiguous
to Ambiguous Knowledge

The Unambiguous Nature of Color Vision

Color vision provides perhaps the best example of unambiguous conditions, when the brain has no option but to interpret signals in one way and one way alone. It is important to emphasize here that when I say that the brain has no option, I mean that it has no option given its genetically determined neurological apparatus and wiring and given the physical reality of the visual world. The question that we ask in color vision is: what is the formal contribution that the brain makes in acquiring knowledge about color, what is the "concept" that it applies to the incoming signals, and what are the limitations that it imposes, given its neurological apparatus. As discussed earlier, the color of a surface remains substantially the same even in spite of wide-ranging variations in the wavelength composition of the light reflected from it, a phenomenon generally known as color constancy. I have described in Chapter 3 how, for generating color, the brain is principally interested in acquiring knowledge about the constant and invariant characteristic of a surface, namely its reflectance. This it does by comparing the wavelength composition of the light reflected from it with the wavelength composition of the light reflected from its surrounds. By doing so, the brain is able to discard all the variations in the wavelength-energy composition of the light reflected from a surface and assign a constant color to it.

There is no ambiguity in the knowledge thus gained since surfaces have definite reflectances for lights of different wavebands. The brain merely has to compare the reflectances of these surfaces and their surrounds for the same wavebands and determine which has the higher reflectance for light of one waveband and of another. Given that reflectances are immutable, the brain has no option but to reach the conclusion that it does. It has developed an efficient and unfailing machinery for doing so, and a significant part of that machinery, related to ratio-taking mechanisms, is vested in the color center of the brain, the V4 complex.[1,2]

It is interesting to consider the apparent chaos that is caused when, through partial damage to the color center, the ratio-taking mechanism of the brain becomes imperfect though not completely non-operational. The consequence is to give the brain several options, in that the color of a surface now becomes hostage to the wavelength composition of the light reflected from it and changes its color appearance every time the wavelength composition of the light in which it is viewed changes. These options are strictly dependent upon the physical reality and are not generated internally by the brain itself, in that the perceived color of a surface will change markedly only when the wavelength composition of the illuminating light also changes markedly. These options are therefore useless, for they cannot give a correct interpretation of the reflectance of a surface and hence of its color. The perceived color follows slavishly the physical reality and is related to the dominant wavelength in the light reflected from a surface, without the added comparison with the surrounds. The different options thus do not have equal validity as in the truly ambiguous situations that we shall consider below. In a healthy brain with an intact color center, there is no room for many different interpretations of what the reflectance of a surface and hence its color is, which is not to say that the color that one individual sees is the exact replica of what another sees. Whether two individuals see the same identical quality in color is not known and would be very difficult to verify. But for a given individual, there is no luxury of giving different interpretations to the reflectance of a surface, a luxury that in this case would only lead to confusion and false knowledge.

Doubtful Ambiguity: the Kanizsa Triangle

The same physiological straightjacket, determined strictly by the rules of the brain, is at play in interpreting other patterns of signals, which are nevertheless not as rigid as color vision in allowing no options. Consider Figure 10.1a. The configuration here is interpreted by almost all normal people as a triangle. There are of course other possible

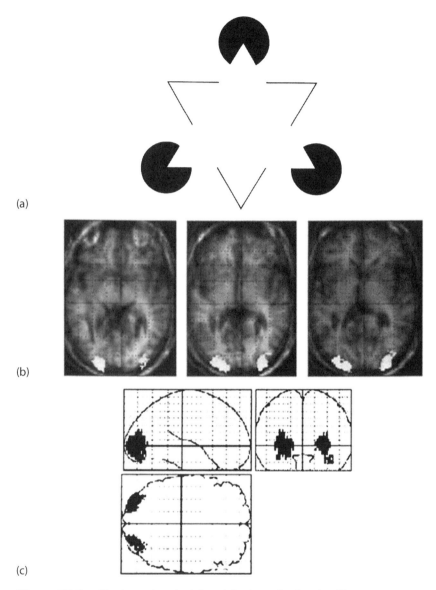

(a)

(b)

(c)

Figure 10.1. Kanizsa triangle (a) and brain activation by illusory contours (b). Activity produced in the brain of subjects when they view the Kanizsa triangle is shown in the glass–brain projections (c) in black. The activity is restricted to the posterior part of the brain, where the visual areas are located. Note the absence of activity in the frontal lobes. For details see text. (From ffytche D, Zeki S (1995) Brain activity related to the perception of illusory contours. *NeuroImage* **3**: 104–108.)

interpretations that one can give, if one should insist perversely to complete the gaps in the figure in bizarre ways. But this would be very unusual and I certainly have never encountered anyone who has done so. In fact, the interpretation conforms very much to the physiology of one category of cells in the visual brain. These are the so-called orientation-selective cells, referred to earlier. They respond to a line of specific orientation, less well to lines of other orientation and not at all to lines that are orthogonal to the preferred orientation. Such cells are found in abundance in specific compartments of areas V1 and V2 and constitute a substantial majority of cells in area V3.

Physiological recording experiments[3] have shown that the orientation-selective cells of the brain are capable of responding to virtual lines such as are constituted in Figure 10.1. Given that these cells, by definition, respond optimally only to their preferred orientation and not at all to the orthogonal orientation, it becomes obvious that they are not free to respond in other ways, thus forcing only one plausible interpretation. There are many variants of this Kanizsa figure and their characteristic is that they are all open to only one plausible interpretation, probably dictated by the physiology of orientation-selective cells in the cortex. But the patterns in the Kanizsa figures, though consisting of lines, nevertheless constitute objects, in this instance a triangle. It is not surprising to find therefore that viewing the Kanizsa illusory figures activates, in addition to areas V2 and V3, an area within what is known as the lateral occipital cortex of the brain, an area that is critical for object recognition in the human brain (see Figure 9.3 for simplified diagram of visual brain areas).[4] In terms of our description, the lateral occipital complex could be referred to as a processing-perceptual center for objects. As with color vision, where V4 collaborates with the areas feeding it with visual signals and with which it is reciprocally connected, the lateral occipital complex presumably works in collaboration with areas V2 and V3, with which it is reciprocally connected.

Essential Nodes and "Top-Down" Influences in Resolving Ambiguities

To interpret the "unfinished" picture of Figure 10.1b as a triangle naturally involves a semantic element, which itself is shaped through experience. This, among other reasons, is probably why many have thought that a "top–down" influence is brought to bear upon the pattern of signals, forcing their interpretation in a certain way. What is meant by "top-down" is vague in neurological terms, but what is implied is that a "higher" thought process influences the way in which we interpret things or that a "higher" area influences neural activity in a "lower" area. Implicit in such thinking is the supposition that processing and perception are always entirely separate, that a processing site in the brain is different from a perceptual site or, more accurately, that an interpretation has to be brought to bear upon the result of processing in an area, the interpretation emanating from a different source than the processing site. Effectively, this means that we can only become conscious of the triangle in the Kanizsa triangles, or of a color, if some "higher" area, located for example in the frontal lobes, forces the interpretation of the ambiguous figure in a certain way. If this were invariably so, one would expect that, when the brain is constructing colors, cortical areas such as those in the frontal lobes that have been implicated in higher thought processes would be engaged and that their activity could be demonstrated with imaging experiments. We have already seen that the mandatory involvement of higher areas is not necessary for what is processed in an area to become perceptually explicit. The V4 complex, for example, consti-tutes an essential node for color, activity at which has a conscious cor-relate and does not need to be processed further. Just as it had been supposed that the involvement of higher cognitive factors is necessary for color constancy, so it has been supposed that the interpretation that the brain gives to the configuration shown in Figure 10.1 is imposed "top–down." [5] If so, then "higher" areas of the brain should become engaged when subjects view such figures. But imaging experiments show that, when human subjects view and interpret such incomplete figures as triangles, activity in the brain does not involve the frontal lobes (Figure 10.1b and c).[6] The reason for the absence of any frontal lobe involvement, and hence the absence of "top–down" influences as traditionally understood, is becoming obvious and it entails a major shift in our thinking about perceptual and processing sites in the brain and about consciousness too. While older theories assume, either explicitly or implicitly, that a processing site is different from a perceptual site, evidence from physiological and imaging experiments, discussed above, shows that this is not necessarily so and that in many instances a processing site is also a perceptual site (see also Chapter 9). This seems not to be so with figures that are genuinely "ambiguous" or more accurately unstable, in the sense that the brain is capable of interpreting them in more than one way.

Ambiguous Bi-stable Images

The situation is rendered more complex when one considers the Kanizsa cube (Figure 10.2). Here the intersecting lines could all be in the same plane, or some could be in a plane that is closer to the viewer than others. The brain has no means of knowing, and thus allows for all three interpretations or rather projects three possible interpretations to this physically unvarying stimulus. At any given time only one interpretation is possible, and that interpretation is as valid as the other interpretations. It is a sort of interpretational flip-flop, one or the other but not the two simultaneously. It is difficult to tell whether this interpretational flip-flop is due to any "top–down" influences, that is, to activity of areas beyond the ones that register and combine the oriented lines into particular groupings. Imaging experiments show that every time the interpretation shifts from one plane to another, activity in area V3 increases. But they also show that there is an activation of the fronto-parietal cortex. The interpretation of the latter result is not straightforward; it might be due to sudden surges and shifts of attention, since the fronto-parietal cortex is known to be

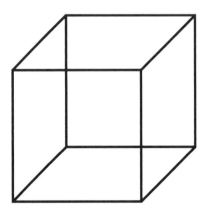

Figure 10.2.   The Kanizsa cube.

Figure 10.3. *Composition* by Nathan Cohen (private collection).

involved in attentional states. Or it might be due to some top-down influence that dictates that a shift in perception should occur. Either way, the result is substantially different from that obtained with viewing colors, when there is no activation of the fronto-parietal cortex. Whichever interpretation is the correct one, the results show that a micro-consciousness that is due to activity at a single essential node can be in several, mutually exclusive, states. One of the reasons that leads me to this conclusion is the obligate nature of the recessional planes seen in other instances, of which a good example is provided by the work shown in Figure 10.3.

Obligate Metastability

The abstract compositions in this figure make original use of a long-known perceptual effect, namely that juxtaposed rectangular forms of different shades can be interpreted by the brain as being in one of two recessional planes, either towards or away from the viewer at the point of juxtaposition, but not in both simultaneously. What this work shows compellingly is that, with the addition of further elements (rectangular shapes) of the same type, there develops an obligate perceptual relationship in the planes occupied by the contiguous rectangular forms. In the composition shown in Figure 10.3, when the plane at the point of convergence of the central rectangles is towards the observer, the two surrounding ones are shifted to a plane away, and vice versa. There is no choice in this obligate relationship, which raises interesting physiological problems that are worthy of study. One would suppose, not unreasonably, that there must be some reciprocal relationship between cells in the same visual area that are capable of signaling recessional planes, in that when cells that signal a plane towards the viewer are active, cells that signal a plane away from the viewer are silent or inhibited, and vice versa. One supposes further that such a reciprocal relationship depends upon the lateral connections between cells in a given area, assuming of course that there are no "top–down" influences. Given the strong topographical relations involved, one would also suppose that the meta-stability is due to activity in an area with a good topographical map (i.e. a map of visual space) in it. Given that many cells in the third visual complex (areas V3 and V3A) are depth selective and capable of signaling what occurs in front of, and behind, the fixation plane,[7] and given the topographic representation of the visual field in the V3 complex,[8] it becomes reasonable to suppose that this perceptual meta-stability is due to the instability of the responses of cells in V3, in the sense that the activity of some cells dominate perceptually at one moment and that of others at another. Such perceptual alterations can be attenuated or even abolished if the (ambiguous) visual stimulus is periodically removed from view, suggesting that uninterrupted viewing is necessary for the unstable physiological mechanisms that lead to multistable vision.[9] While the critical experiments have not been done, it is interesting to note what the consequence of such a demonstration is. It implies that the physiology of a single area, or a limited number of what are called "early" visual areas, allows a multiple perceptual interpretation of incoming signals. That interpretation is nevertheless strictly circumscribed by the basic physiology of the cells in the visual area, without involving factors such as memory and learning, although it may involve attentional signals from the fronto-parietal cortex. Accepting that activity at an essential node can have a micro-conscious correlate, one is naturally led to the conclusion that the micro-consciousness can be in more than one state, though we can only become conscious of one state at any given moment. This raises the question of whether what regulates the change from one state to another of the same micro-consciousness (due to activity in the same essential node) is identical to the mechanism that regulates the change from one micro-conscious state to another when the switch is due to activity at two different essential nodes.

Ambiguous Interpretations of the Same and of Different Visual Categories

In the above examples, I have hypothesized that the same cortical area is engaged during the bi-stability or meta-stability where the meta-stability involves the same object or attribute, with possible intervention from further areas. I may be wrong in this supposition and only further experiments will clarify the picture. My reason for doing so is to be found in the principle of functional specialization in the visual brain, discussed earlier, which tells us that the processing of distinct visual attributes is the privilege of distinct visual areas. A cube is a cube, whether one of its planes is closer to the viewer or further away; hence one supposes that it is differences in processing in the same area that leads to different versions of the cube. The same reasoning holds for other and more complex bi-stable images, such as the "wife–mother-in-law" image (Figure 10.4), though with a difference. Since each one of the two images seen in this bi-stable image is that of a face, I assume (though without much direct evidence to support my assumption) that the bi-stability involves a change in the pattern of activity in the same area. But here the two faces differ substantially in other attributes, principally that of age but also in viewing angle, making it plausible to suppose that other, top-down, influences will be brought into play to dictate how the change in activity is regulated to give one of two different interpretations. The involvement of more than one area when viewing perceptually unstable figures is even more plausible in examples such as the

Figure 10.4. The "wife–mother-in-law" bi-stable figure (left). To the right we show that adding spectacles to the mother-in-law does not abolish the instability, in that the figure can still be interpreted as being the "wife."

Figure 10.5. The Rubin vase.

Rubin vase (Figure 10.5) where the two images, faces and a vase, belong to different categories. One supposes that two different areas (essential nodes) are involved and that as perception shifts from one to the other – from the area concerned with face recognition to the one involved with object recognition – "third" areas may become engaged and may indeed even dictate the change.

Imaging experiments[10] have shown that the switch from one percept to another during the presentation of bi-stable images (when the stimulus remains the same but the percept changes) is indeed accompanied by a shift in the activated areas. For example, a shift from faces to vases entails a shift in the site of activation, from the region of the visual brain that is specialized for the recognition of faces to the one that is specialized for object recognition. However, they have also shown that the fronto-parietal cortex is engaged whenever a percept changes from one condition to another. The shift of activity from one area to another distinguishes this kind of ambiguity from the more straight-forward one that involves activity within a single area alone. The involvement of the fronto-parietal cortex in both examples suggests that third areas are involved in the shift in both cases, though it is possible that their involvement may differ for the two examples. One interpretation might be that the fronto-parietal cortex is the "higher" area dictating the percept and hence that we only become conscious of the interpretation through the intervention of the fronto-parietal cortex. This would be tantamount to saying that the areas in the fusiform gyrus that are activated are not totally sovereign in dictating what is perceived, and hence that a processing site, though also a perceptual site, is not really sovereign in dictating what is perceived, or only partially so. But there is yet another interpretation of the involvement of fronto-parietal cortex. Experiments[11] have shown that where the reversal is that of a single attribute – the change in the direction of motion that is perceived when a configuration such as that of Isia Leviant's *Enigma* (Figure 10.6) is viewed – the activity is restricted mainly to V5 and to V3B, the former an area that is critical for motion perception and the latter an area that is important in extracting contours.[12] But here again the fronto-parietal cortex is engaged. One conclusion that can be drawn from these studies is that the fronto-parietal cortex is involved when there is a perceptual change of which we become aware, without necessarily being involved in or dictating the percept that we become aware of. Such an interpretation, if correct, would lead us to the conclusion that activity in the parieto-frontal cortex is critical for us to become aware of a change, but that these cortical areas do not necessarily dictate what should change, or how. To become aware of what has been processed or what has changed, (heightened) activity at a specialized processing site (essential node) is critical.

Figure 10.6. *Enigma* by Isia Leviant. Many, but not all, viewers perceive rapid motion in the rings that, upon prolonged viewing, reverses direction spontaneously.

The Stability of Perceptual Instability

The extent to which the machinery of the brain is programmed to allow of different interpretations, and the seeming poverty of "top–down" influences, can be demonstrated by showing that it is not easy to disambiguate these ambiguous figures. This may be readily ascertained by examining the so-called staircase illusion (Figure 10.7). Adding features to the illusion that, one might have thought, would oblige the brain to perceive the figures in only one way does not lead to perceptual results that can be interpreted in only one way. The same is true of the "wife–mother-in-law" illusion (Figure 10.4). Adding a number of features to the figure, to force the brain to interpret it in one way only, is never successful. The brain retains the options of

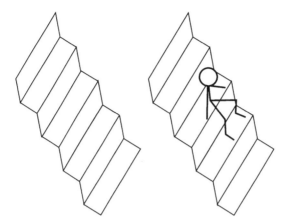

Figure 10.7. The staircase illusion. Trying to force the interpretation in one direction, as on the right, cannot abolish the instability that makes the lines appear in different recessional planes.

interpreting it in two ways. This suggests that the brain does not have much choice in the multi-interpretations that its organization makes possible. *The ambiguity, in other words, is stable.* The stability of multi-interpretations is also, in a sense, an inherited brain concept applied to certain categories of incoming signals. The brain is organized to project its own interpretation to the incoming visual stimulus. And as we have seen, inherited brain concepts are immutable. The stability of multi-interpretations also argues against ubiquitous "top-down" influences, because the addition of further visual features that, top-down wise, would have imposed a single interpretation on the figure fails to do so. The ambiguous or unstable system of the brain is therefore highly stable in its instability. To force the brain to give one interpretation alone, even where extra knowledge is provided, is very difficult.

The overall conclusion that we can draw from these experiments is that, in a totally unambiguous condition, as in color vision, there is no mandatory involvement of higher areas in the frontal or parietal cortex. In ambiguity that involves one attribute only, as in the example of the Kanizsa cube, the change from one perceptual state to another involves a heightened activity within the essential node that is specialized for the processing and perception of that attribute, together with an involvement of the fronto-parietal cortex, which may do so either to dictate the change or to register attentional shifts or to register changes in the state of consciousness. Where ambiguity involves more than one attribute, as in the example of the Rubin vase, the change in the perceptual state involves a shift in activity between specialized areas, together with an engagement of the fronto-parietal cortex, the involvement of the latter being subject to the same interpretations as given above. It cannot be too strongly emphasized that, wherever there is a shift in the perceptual state, we can only be conscious of one state at any given moment.

The fact that other areas, beyond the essential nodes, may become involved in shifts in the perceptual state implies that other influences, including memory, may be brought to bear on what it is that we perceive with the same stimulus. They may crucially involve the imposition of other concepts that could dictate what we perceive. And this leads us to the true ambiguity that is often a characteristic of great art.

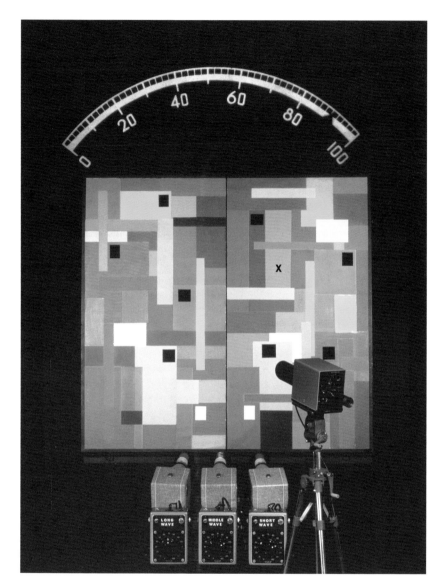

Plate 1. The Land Mondrian Experiment. In this figure the amount of green, blue and red light reflected from the green patch (marked with a cross) can be made to change by varying the intensity of light coming from the corresponding projectors. The intensity of light of each waveband reflected from the patch can be measured by a telephotometer (bottom right). When the amount of the three wavebands reflected from the patch is varied, the color of the patch remains green. For details see text.

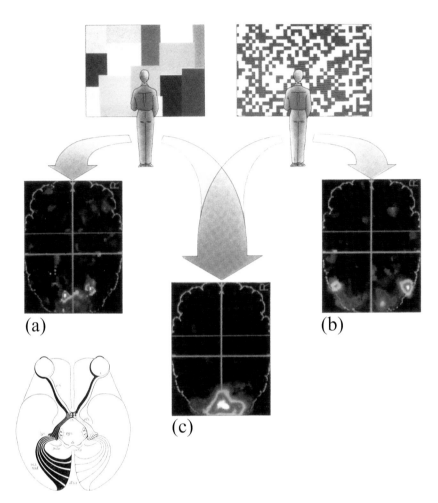

(a)

(b)

(c)

Plate 2.   The results of a an imaging experiment, to show on horizontal sections (a, b, c) of the brain the areas activated when subjects view a multicolored abstract scene (left) and when they view a pattern of black and white dots in motion (right). The activation is shown in white, red and yellow. Note that in both instances the primary visual cortex, area V1 (center panel), is activated but that color activates a different part of the brain than visual motion. a, b and c are horizontal sections through the brain taken at the level indicated in the schematic diagram to the lower left, which shows the termination of the optic nerve fibers in V1.

Chapter 11

Higher Levels of Ambiguity

One of the functions of the brain, as emphasized earlier, is to instill meaning into this world, into the signals that it receives. Instilling meaning amounts to finding a solution. But the brain commonly finds itself in conditions where this is not easy, because it is confronted with several meanings of equal validity. Where one solution is not obviously better than the others, the only option is to allow several interpretations or rather to project several interpretations, all of them valid. Such a higher level of ambiguity is to be found in the multiple narrative interpretations, or concepts, that can be given, for example, to Vermeer's *Girl with Pearl Earring* (Figure 11.1). Note that this is a single stable image, and the only variable is that the brain of the beholder can offer several equally valid interpretations of the expression on her face, depending upon the concepts that it has acquired. Though physically stable, the image is cognitively unstable. The girl in the painting is at once inviting, yet distant, erotically charged but chaste, resentful and yet pleased. These interpretations must all involve memory and experience of what a face that is expressing these sentiments would look like. The genius of Vermeer is that he does not provide an answer but, by a brilliant subtlety, manages to convey all the expressions, although the viewer is only conscious of one interpretation at any given moment. Because there is no correct solution, the work of art itself becomes a problem that engages the mind. "Something, and indeed the ultimate thing, must be left over for the mind to do,"[1] wrote Schopenhauer. There could be no better illustration of this than the work of Vermeer, where nothing is explicit.

Vermeer's *The Music Lesson*[2] provides another example. This revolves around the relationship between the man and the woman. Many interpretations are possible. He could be her teacher, brother, husband,

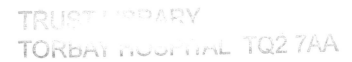

Figure 11.1. Johannes Vermeer, *Girl with Pearl Earring*, Royal Picture Gallery Mauritshuis, The Hague.

or a suitor. They could be discussing something quite banal like the quality of her playing, or something a good deal more serious such as a separation or a reconciliation. All these interpretations have equal force and validity. Each depends upon the concept that the brain has formed. The brain must entertain them all and try to find the correct solution, the right concept, except that in this instance there is no correct solution or concept. It is this that led me to offer a neurological definition of ambiguity that is quite different from common dictionary definitions of it, namely that it is not vagueness or uncertainty, but rather certainty, the certainty of different scenarios, each one of which has equal validity with the others.[3] There is no correct answer, because all answers are correct. Schopenhauer wrote, ". . . through the work of art, everything must not be directly given to the senses, but rather only so much as is demanded to lead the fancy on to the right path . . . for Voltaire has very rightly said, '*Le secret d'être ennuyeux, c'est de tout dire*' [the secret of being boring is to tell everything]. But besides this, in art the best of all is too spiritual to be given directly to the senses; it must be born in the imagination of the beholder, although begotten by the work of art. It depends upon this that the sketches of great masters often effect more than their finished pictures."[4]

When we say that a painting or situation is ambiguous, we invest the painting or the situation with that characteristic. In fact, there is no ambiguity there but the possibility of multiple interpretations projected by the brain onto the painting. Each of these projections is a brain reality and each has a validity and a certainty for a limited time. Much the same is true of the term "illusory," which implies that there is a departure from the physically determined reality. This fails to take into account that, for the brain, the only reality is brain reality. When the Kanizsa cube appears in a certain recessional plane, the reality for the brain is that it is in that recessional plane while the viewer perceives it to be in that recessional plane. There is nothing illusory here.

Ambiguity and the "Unfinished"

It is obvious that there is a relation between works that display such ambiguity and unfinished works. Both are cognitively unstable because in both instances the brain is able to give multiple interpretations that are of equal validity to the same work. In each, it can bring multiple concepts to bear upon the interpretation. I have written elsewhere of the unfinished sculptures of Michelangelo as an example.[5] Even in spite of their unfinished status, they have commonly led to interpretations that are so self-contained that one is left with the conclusion that they must have been "finished off" by the viewer. Charles De Tolnay's[6] lyrical description of the *Rondanini Pietà* (Figure 11.2) as a work that "comes to represent in the personal life of the artist that state of beatitude to which his unsatisfied soul aspired" could be a description of a finished work except that in this instance it refers to an unfinished work. It is thus interesting to compare the "unfinished" triangles of Kanizsa with the unfinished sculptures of

Figure 11.2. Michelangelo Buonarroti, *Rondanini Pietà*, Castello Sforzesco, Milan. (Courtesy Riccardo Manzotti.)

Michelangelo, although many might regard such a comparison as demeaning to the great sculptor. In trying to make sense of the pattern that constitutes a Kanizsa triangle, the brain "finishes it off" in the only way possible; when trying to make sense of the pattern that constitutes the Kanizsa cube, the brain can interpret the intersecting lines as being in one of three planes. In Michelangelo's *Rondanini Pietà*, the capacity to give many interpretations is taken yet a step further. Now the solutions are, by comparison, large in number. Many concepts can be brought to bear upon the interpretation, upon the completion. Hence the capacity to give multiple interpretations is not a separate faculty invented or used by the artist. It is instead tied to a general capacity of the brain to give several interpretations, to instil meaning by applying several concepts, a capacity that is important for it in its role of acquiring knowledge. It is on this physiological basis that the prized quality of ambiguity in art is built.

It is perhaps interesting to note here that these multiple concepts that the brain brings to the interpretation of the single image that constitutes a work of art are, in the instances referred to in this chapter, acquired brain concepts. Such concepts, as I have described earlier, are less stable than inherited brain concepts and are indeed susceptible to continual modification through life. It is not surprising to find therefore that the ambiguity in a single painting is less stable than the ambiguity in, for example, the staircase illusion referred to. In a single painting whose ambiguity depends upon the projection of multiple acquired concepts, the ambiguity can be reduced and stabilized. Marcel Duchamp's re-working of Leonardo's enigmatic *Mona Lisa* testifies to this, as do many similar re-workings by more recent artists such as Salvador Dali.

One can therefore conjecture that there are graded steps, not only from non-ambiguous to ambiguous stimuli, but also in the number of areas or distinct cortical sites that may be involved during the perception of what are called ambiguous figures. At the highest levels, as evidenced by the capacity to give multiple, equally valid, interpretations to a work of art, the ambiguous state may involve several distinct areas that are able to bring their influence. The Vermeer paintings referred to above provide a good example. Here, memory, experience, learning and much else besides can influence what is perceived at any given moment. This almost certainly involves a "top-down" influence from diverse sources, not just the frontal lobes. Thus, opening up the capacity for a given brain area to be influenced by another area is merely one step in opening up the capacity to be influenced by multiple other areas and therefore by multiple concepts. Hence, the artist exploits intuitively this potential of the brain that allows multiple areas to influence what is perceived. In fact, of course, the ambiguity might be greater than is implied here. The visual brain has been developing over a much longer period of time than the linguistic brain and many visual images, though highly evocative, resist a semantic classification. Images may also acquire a richness through ambiguous visual signals that are not easily communicated, or are inaccessible, through language. It is not ambiguity itself, therefore, that is aesthetically pleasing, even though some artists such as Arcimboldo and Salvador Dali deliberately made ambiguity an artistic form. It is rather the capacity to project multiple concepts and experiences onto a work.

Ambiguity and Contradictions

In the examples given above, of Vermeer's work, the possible interpretations are not only many but are also sometimes contradictory. Some will see the girl in Vermeer's masterpiece as being alternately chaste and erotically charged, or approachable and resentful. These of course are interpretations that my brain is giving to this composition, and it is not implausible, though not certain, that others will see similar contradictions or others. In fact, it is ambiguity that allows us to give contradictory or conflicting interpretations. Such is the case with a work that is in a highly incomplete state and that allowed Johann Winckelmann to perceive it as embodying contradictory elements. Winckelmann, often regarded as the father of art history, had a very definite view, one might say a concept, of beauty as reflected in Greek sculpture, which he related to his view of Greek culture in general.[7] For him, Greek art was born out of, and in, a free social and political setting, yet one that was beset by a contradiction or tension that, he thought, was reflected in its art. That tension was between "an 'active' manly freedom realized in the violent struggles of the early phases of Greek culture . . . and a free sensual enjoyment of things." Winckelmann, of whom Goethe interestingly wrote that "his gift was

Figure 11.3. *Torso Belvedere*, the Vatican Museums, Vatican. (Courtesy Riccardo Manzotti.)

to search in the outer world what nature had laid in his inner world,"[8] chose the *Torso Belvedere* (Figure 11.3), an "unfinished" work, as representative of the highest beauty in Greek art and as one depicting most forcefully this apparent tension. In fact, of course, the *Torso*, which occupied a very privileged position in Winckelmann's writings on art,[9] and which is uncertainly attributed to the Greek sculptor Appolonius, is a fragment now and was a fragment when Winckelmann saw it. As exhibited today in the Vatican Museum, it is surrounded by finished sculptures from the Greek and Roman periods, yet it is this fragment that arrests and dazzles. It was found in Rome during the papacy of Julius II. It was seen and greatly admired by Michelangelo, who reputedly wept when he saw it and referred to it as his "teacher." It is its incomplete status that allowed Winckelmann to read so much into it and, what is more, so much that is visually compelling, at least to anyone who may not be acquainted with the history of the *Torso*. He thought of it as "the high ideal of a body raised above nature, a nature of mature manly years, as it would appear when elevated to a state of divine contentment."[7] To him, "The apparent calm and stillness, which recall the blissful self-absorption of ideal youth, are charged by intimations of the naked physical power of a hero laying waste all that came in his way."[9] The *Torso Belvedere* is thus characterized as being actively heroic and passively contended. And these contradictory interpretations, united in a single figure, can compellingly become, or become acceptable, as the interpretations of the spectator, as concepts brought to bear upon the fragmented sculpture, even though we are only conscious of one interpretation at any given moment. For Joshua Reynolds, who thought that all art is an abstraction, the *Torso* kindled a "warmth of enthusiasm as from the highest effects of poetry. From whence does this proceed? What is there in this fragment that produces this effect, but the perfection of the science of abstract form."[10]

That Winckelmann himself attributed a primary role to the imagination (to us, the brain) in this instability becomes evident in his description of the *Torso Belvedere*, which he asked the viewer to admire for its continuous flow of one form into another. As the viewer interprets these ever-changing forms "[the artist] will [also] find that it is not possible to reproduce this accurately by drawing since the curve that the drawer believes himself to be following changes its direction imperceptibly and confuses both eye and hand with its new direction."[11] In Anton Burdakov's drawings inspired by the *Torso Belvedere* (Figures 11.4 and 11.5), this instability becomes apparent in the energetic and yet indeterminate flow of lines, which again empower the brain to give multiple interpretations, the drawings being themselves the products of the brain, produced through multiple concepts.

The point to note here is that it is to some considerable extent, visually at least, the fragmentary status of the *Torso Belvedere* that allowed Winckelmann to make, and allows us to consider, contradictory interpretations that are visually convincing. It is perhaps not entirely

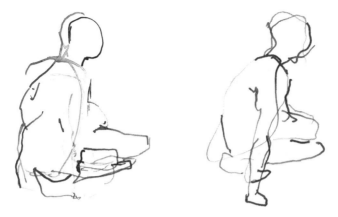

Figure 11.4. Anton Burdakov, *Two Figures A*, 2005. (Private collection, Courtesy Anton Burdakov.)

Figure 11.5. Anton Burdakov, *Two Figures B*, 2005 (Private collection, Courtesy Anton Burdakov.)

fortuitous, then, that Winckelmann chose an incomplete work to represent his highest ideal of Greek beauty.

Perhaps one of the highest points of ambiguity reached by an artist is to be found in Sandro Botticelli's drawings, "*per essere persona sofistica*" (for the sophisticated person), of Dante's *Divine Comedy*, commissioned by one of Botticelli's patrons, Lorenzo di Pierfrancesco de' Medici, the first cousin once removed of Lorenzo the Magnificent and head of the younger Medici line. Several of the drawings, especially those illustrating the *Inferno*, have been lost but enough remain to establish two points, one about abstraction and the other about ambiguity. As the poetry of Dante becomes more abstract, in the sense of dealing with complex concepts that even Dante confessed he could not handle, so the drawings of Botticelli become more abstract and more sparse. This becomes especially evident when one compares the rich illustrations for the *Inferno* with the much sparser ones for the *Paradiso* where many show Dante and Beatrice within an outline circle, considered at that time to be the most perfect form, with little else to surround them. The effect is to leave more to the imagination of the viewer, to allow a greater intrusion of the viewer's concepts in the interpretation of the drawings. The second point concerns specifically the pages illustrating Cantos XXXI and XXXIII of the *Paradiso*. Already in Canto XXX, Dante is confessing the difficulty of transcribing the beauty of Beatrice as constituted in his mind (brain) and therefore his failure (which to him is the failure of every artist) in representing perfection. In Canto XXXI, he confesses to his inability even to conceive of her delights, while in the last Canto (XXXIII) his powers of description fail him, for his concept is much too grand for words. And so, faltering like the geometer who does not understand how to square a circle, he simply yields his will and desire to love – and to the imagination of the reader to interpret his ecstatic vision.

Cantos XXXI and XXXIII are left unillustrated by Dante, while Canto XXXII is very sparsely illustrated. It is perhaps Botticelli's summary way of conveying to the viewer that abstract notions such as love and beauty are conceptually much too grand to be illustrated, just as Dante conveyed this verbally in his poetry. They must instead be left to the imagination. It is therefore just possible that, at one level of analysis, one of the greatest artists of the Early Renaissance did what many others do routinely, which is not even to attempt a work – just one step removed from leaving it unfinished.

The general point that I make here is that there is a continuum in the operations of the brain, the basis of which is to seek knowledge, which it does through the formation of concepts, to instill meaning into the world. In this continuum, we proceed on the one hand from conditions where the brain has no option in its interpretation of the signals that it receives, as in color vision, to those in which there are two equally plausible interpretations and, finally, to those in which there are many interpretations. There would also appear to be a gradation in the degree to which activity in a given cortical area is influenced or modified by activity in another, or other, cortical areas. The generation of color appears to depend upon activity in the color pathways and principally in the color center. The color that is ascribed by the brain to any given object in our field of view is determined by the operations of the color centre and is not easily modifiable by influences from other cortical areas. One supposes, on the other hand, that the cortical area in which faces are registered is susceptible to influences from other cortical areas, which could determine the interpretation given to the expression on the face. If, as I have written elsewhere,[5] the function of art is an extension of the function of the brain, namely the acquisition of knowledge about the world, and if the brain does so by forming concepts of all that it experiences, then it stands to reason to suppose that the mechanisms used to instill meaning into this world are the very ones used to instill meanings into works of art. It is those basic mechanisms that artists have used in creating their works and it is those same mechanisms that we use to interpret their achievements.

Part III

Unachievable Brain Concepts

Introduction

If the realization of a synthetic brain concept, or the brain ideal, is commonly difficult or impossible in real life, or even in art, a solution might be to present it in an incomplete form – since it is the complete form that is unattainable – and leave it to the imagination of the perceiver, the artist no less than the viewer or the reader, to complete the experience according to the synthetic concepts in their brains at any given moment. In the following pages I describe this strategy in art, concentrating on the work of Michelangelo and Cézanne and on literary works by Balzac and Zola directly related to the unachievable in art.

Chapter 12

Michelangelo and the *Non finito*

Michelangelo was convinced that he was the greatest sculptor of his age. He soon managed to convince everyone else of that too. When the Pope once asked for "Michelangelo the sculptor," he replied, "I am Michelangelo Buonarroti. I know of no competitor and admit of no equal." It is perhaps hard to believe that two thirds of the sculptures by this self-declared genius, admired for centuries, should have remained unfinished. Yet we find that running through his art as well as his view of his art are the same cracks and fissures that characterize the work of other artists and these can be traced to the near impossibility of satisfying brain concepts. To the end, it left Michelangelo in a state of permanent dissatisfaction.

Throughout his life, Michelangelo was dominated by the overwhelming desire to represent not only physical but also spiritual beauty and divine love, an almost impossible undertaking to even attempt for all but a very few of his stature. Even he, however, faltered and failed. There is little doubt that in his Neo-Platonic culture both physical and spiritual beauty were entwined and not easily separable, that he formed several amorous relationships, and that he yearned for a physical and spiritual dimension to these relationships. Like Tristan and Isolde, and countless other lovers, he longed for that unity that is a brain concept and a hallmark of passionate love. In a poem dedicated to Tommaso de' Cavalieri, the handsome young Roman nobleman who dominated his emotional life in his later years, a relationship that seemingly left him unsatisfied, he wrote lines that are strikingly similar in sentiment to those of the chaste lovers in Act 2 of *Tristan und Isolde* (see Chapter 20). Indeed, they can be said to mirror perfectly the main theme of that opera.

If a chaste love, if an excelling kindness,
If sharing by two lovers of one fortune,
Hard lot for one the other's concern,
Two hearts led by one spirit and one wish,

And if two bodies have one soul, grown deathless,
That, with like wings, lifts both of them to Heaven,
If love's one stroke and goldendart can burn
And separate the vitals of two breasts,

Neither loving himself, but each the other,
With one delight and taste, such sympathy
That both would wish to have a single end,

If thousand thousands would not be one inch
To love so knotted, such fidelity;
And mere affront can shatter and unbind.[1]

Both his artistic achievements and his *Rime* (sonnets) and madrigals testify to Michelangelo's deep dissatisfaction with his life, no less than with his art. This state of dissatisfaction is characteristic of many, perhaps all, great artists. But it is no less a characteristic of many ordinary women and men, and can be traced directly, I believe, to the failure of reality to match the synthetic brain concept that it has generated. The discrepancy between the two is simply greater in artists of talent and genius. But it is a difference in magnitude, not in kind. One solution that many ordinary people adopt when they realize the magnitude of the task at hand is to abandon all efforts at it. Talented people may have the desire to write a novel or perhaps compose a symphony. Many who have the necessary linguistic or musical skills abandon the attempt once they realize the difficulty of translating their brain concepts into art, or leave the work unfinished. Michelangelo adopted in part the same solution. It is known that, in general, this man who had been "ravished" by beauty, who had spoken in his sonnets of beautiful faces, nevertheless abandoned the attempt to represent them systematically as portraits. He quite simply refused to execute portraits, the two exceptions being those of Tommaso de' Cavalieri and of Andrea Quaratesi, with both of whom he was romantically involved. For it was not the model that he was interested in translating to perfection in his art but the concept in his brain, as he relates in the sonnet below, the "forza d'arte" being what I interpret to be the unhindered concept in the brain.

> When that which is divine in us does try
> to shape a face, both brain and hand unite
> to give, from a mere model frail and slight,
> life to the stone by Art's free energy.[2]

Notice that he speaks of the divine in "us," not in the subject or the model. Notice, too, that it is the brain and the hand of the artist that unite to give form to the divine (concept) in the artist, not the small and frail model. He is saying, quite simply, that he is executing the concept in his brain. The solitary genius who thus strove for perfection ended up in at least one domain, that of portrait painting, producing almost nothing. After all, with nothingness, the brain concept is not translated into an unsatisfactory and pale version.

The concept, or *concetto*, plays a central role in Michelangelo's theory of art. He was firmly of the view that the artist had a concept in his mind and the artist of genius had a concept that was divine, close to God. But for the Neo-Platonic Michelangelo these concepts were somehow tailored to the art that is "out there," in the world outside, for art-forms have an existence in the world outside that is quite independent of the artist. The function of the artist, and above all the sculptor, is to hack away until the concept is revealed in the stone. The Florentine historian Benedetto Varchi, who analysed one of Michelangelo's most celebrated sonnets (*Non ha l'ottimo artista alcun concetto*) before the Florentine Academy in 1546, understood clearly the artistic theory of Michelangelo and recalled the philosophical notion of the Peripatetics, that any creation is translation from the potential (the concept) to the actual. The opening lines of the sonnet are:

> The best of artists have no thought
> to show what the rough stone in its superfluous shell
> does not include. To break the marble spell is all that
> The hand that obeys the brain can do[2]

the *intelletto* having, according to Varchi, a close relationship to the *fantasia, immaginativa* and *cogitiva*. (It is useful to recall here that the *fantasia* during the time of both Dante and Michelangelo meant the concept generated by a sensory input.)

With one significant exception, Michelangelo's view of the translation of the brain concept into a work of art is similar to that of the

Alexandrian Neo-Platonic philosopher Plotinus, with whose writings Michelangelo was acquainted. In his *Enneads*, Plotinus had written that "Statues and hand-wrought things cannot be realized out of their materials until the Intellect-Principle imparts the particular Idea from its own content." But rather than supposing, as Michelangelo did, that the form is in the stone and the function of the artist is merely to bring it out, Plotinus rather more realistically in terms of modern neuro-biology believed instead that the "form is in the artist long before it ever enters the stone." In fact, even in spite of Michelangelo's belief that the artist merely brought out what is in the stone, there is good room in his thinking for the brain concept or the *intelletto* that, in Latin, meant "perception" or "a perceiving."

All women and men have a concept in their brain of what consti-tutes a beautiful thing. Leonardo da Vinci, Lorenzo Ghiberti and Leon Battista Alberti, who like all other artists also had their brain-based concept of beauty, believed that this could be translated into painting, or at least approximated, by some kind of formula. Leonardo sought for perfection by copying nature, advising painters to use mirrors.[3] Alberti and Ghiberti believed that harmony, symmetry and mathematical proportions constituted the foundations of beauty, the former sup-posing that beauty had at its basis a sort of harmony constructed accord-ing to some fixed number that "the highest and most perfect law of nature demands."[4] He in fact used what we would now call morphing by a process of averaging, which would "eliminate the imperfections of natural objects by combining the most typical parts,"[4] a process that Xenophon, the ancient Greek writer and historian, had recom-mended centuries earlier when, in one of his Socratic dialogues, he argued that, in painting a body, the artist must combine the most beau-tiful parts from a number of human bodies so that he could combine the best features of each in his work. Raphael, too, complained that he should combine the beautiful aspects of many women but that he could not find enough of them.[4] Such a process, if one thinks about it, naturally constitutes an attempt to re-create a synthetic brain concept. For what is this process of averaging but a synthesis of many views undertaken by the brain? It amounts to generating a brain concept and then translating it, but by rules that artists thought were important.

The "divine" Michelangelo was impatient with such rules. He came closer to articulating the thought in this book, that the beautiful is a divine concept created and planted in the mind through exposure and that, far from copying nature, the artist should try to give free reign to that divine concept in his brain through "Art's free energy" (*forza d'arte*). In transposing as well as he could the concept in his brain, he departed from the proportions found in nature and "from the work regulated by measure, order and rule which other men did according to a common use and after Vitruvius [and] . . . to which he would not conform."[4] Michelangelo was indifferent to mathematical measurements. To him, there was a higher measurement, achieved by the brain. Such a departure allowed him not to represent the reality outside, but the reality embedded as a synthetic concept in his brain. Giorgio Vasari quotes Michelangelo as saying that "it is necessary to keep one's compass in one's eye and not in the hand, for the hands execute, but the eye judges."[3] He is said to have designed the model for the cupola of St. Peter's in Rome "without rules, without calculations, with only the feelings that guide a great artist."[5] That "feeling" is of course nothing more nor less than the concept in his brain. Michelangelo's artistic creations, in sculpture no less than in painting, may lack these elegant mathematical harmonies and symmetries. They may not be true copies of nature and his proportions may commonly be "wrong", as a brief inspection of one of his most celebrated creations, the ceiling of the Sistine Chapel, will convince. But his art possesses that *terribilità* that has dazzled so many precisely because it comes close to representing the essence of his concept. The Virgin in his St. Peter's *Pietà* is as young and perhaps even younger than the Christ on her lap, a fact much commented upon, and which Michelangelo defended by saying that her virginity and purity kept her young, perhaps recalling the line of Dante, whom he much admired, in the *Paradiso*: "*Virgine madre, figlia del tuo figlio*" (Virgin Mother, daughter of your son). Many of his other works, both statues and paintings, do not resemble real-life images. It is what was in his brain, the ideal, that interested him most.

That Michelangelo remained perpetually dissatisfied with his attempts to give life to his concepts through his works of art, indeed dissatisfied enough to turn against art, is expressed in one of his late sonnets, dedicated to Vasari, his friend and biographer:

> Now I know how fraught with error was that fantasy
> That made art my idol and my king

No brush, no chisel can quieten the soul
Once it turns to the Divine love of Him who from the Cross,
Outstretched his arms to take us unto Himself.[4]

Is it any wonder that, like Dante in *La Vita Nuova*, he recorded in another sonnet his wish to end, in death, this eternal strife:

When will that day dawn, Lord, for which he waits
who trusts in Thee? Lo, this prolonged delay
destroys all hope and robs the soul of life
Why streams the light from these celestial gates,
if death prevent the day of grace, and stay
our souls forever in the toils of strife?[2]

These lines, and many others like them, testify to the difficulty that he experienced in translating his brain concepts into art, just as Tristan and Isolde wish for death to free them from the imprisonment of their unattainable brain concept of love. Another solution to this difficulty, for him as for so many others, was to leave the works *non finito*, or unfinished, just as the love affair between Tristan and Isolde is left unfinished, in the sense of being unconsummated. In both, the imagination reigns supreme.

To most people, leaving things unfinished means leaving them incomplete. Its meaning in art is slightly more complex. For a long time, the ideal in painting was a detailed representation, in which accuracy of depiction was greatly valued and where everything was brought to a complete finish. The Académie in Paris often cited Raphael as the supreme example of what was desirable in a painting. In fact, departures from this apparently ideal state began early on, in the High Rennaisance. The *sfumato* (smoky haze), a technique for blurring sharp edges by gradual blending of tones, was used by Leonardo Da Vinci in, among other paintings, the *Mona Lisa* and *The Last Supper*. Titian's spot or splotchy painting (*pittura di macchia*) characterize some of his greatest paintings, including *The Flaying of Marsyas* (State Museum, Kromeriz) and *The Entombment* (Accadémia, Venice). In these, boundaries are no longer distinct, they merge into each other, the coherence of the picture increasing if it is not viewed too closely, just as Titian intended (this approach was later to be used by Rembrandt). It was especially well suited to Titian who wanted to depict form through color and movement. It is reputed that he often painted with his fingers rather than with a brush. Of course, this approach also represents a departure from nature with its sharp boundaries. It also departs from conformity for accurate representation. It subordinates the external reality to the greater reality, that of the synthetic concept formed in the brain and derived from the experience of many realities. For the viewer, the approach adopted lacks distinct, easily definable, boundaries; he therefore invests the painting with an imaginative, emotional and poetic quality, which is why Titian referred to these paintings as his "*poesie*" and why we often now refer to Titian's "mature *poesie*." The paintings, though "unfinished" in the context of what was expected from a painting then and even much later, were not incomplete in terms of how the brain could handle them.

It is really but one step from this to the *non finito* of Michelangelo, though I of course speak conceptually not chronologically. The *non finito* was adopted by Donatello, who left many of his sculptures unfinished, to the disapproval of Michelangelo. The unfinished status of Donatello's work has been attributed to his frustration with his commissions or to the general lack of time in completing what he had undertaken to do. Michelangelo, in spite of his disapproval of unfinished works, adopted the same approach. He worked for many years on some of his sculptures, like the *Rondanini Pietà* (Castello Sforzesco, Milan), on which he was still working when he died. It and other unfinished sculptures like the *Palestrina Pietà* and *San Matteo* (both at the Galleria dell'Accademia, Florence) evince powerful feelings of pathos and resignation. The unfinished here refers to the fact that part of the marble slab is not worked at all, while others are crudely finished and lacking definition. The unfinished status of Michelangelo's works has often been explained away in a similar way as that of Donatello's, that it can be traced to nothing more exalted than exigencies of money or time, or that he had too many commissions. It is true that he was inundated with commissions, often with persistence, from the rich and the influential. The persistence was sometimes subtle, as with François I and Beyazid II who deposited money in Michelangelo's name in banks before making a commission.[3] It is also true that some patrons were dilatory in paying him and haggled over sums in a way that he found humiliating. But it is also true that others, like Giovan Francesco Aldovrandi (a patron in Bologna) and Pope Clement VII, were generous, the latter paying him three times more than asked for. What is not to be doubted is that Michelangelo died a very rich man. A more convincing explanation for the unfinished status of his work, therefore, is that he left some of them deliberately unfinished because he found it difficult to translate his brain concepts into sculptures that satisfied these concepts. There are two categories of unfinished sculptures. In one category are those whose unfinished status correlated well with his view, expressed in one of his sonnets (see above), that the sculptor struggles to release the form that is buried in the marble (see for example his *San Matteo*, which emerges incompletely from the stone). But if, as Plotinus had observed, the form is in the artist long before it ever enters the stone, if it is true, that is, that the artist is shaping the stone according to his brain concept, then the unfinished status is merely an implicit admission of the difficulty of realizing the brain concept in a sculpture, and hence the struggle to release it from the stone and actualize it. In the other category, of which the *Rondanini Pietà* is a good example, the sculpture itself is detached from the block of stone without any hint of the artist trying to release it. Rather, it is the detached sculpture that is left with rough and unfinished edges, giving more the impression of the inability to translate beauty, divine love and tenderness into stone. Whichever of the two unfinished examples one chooses, it seems therefore that there is a better explanation for why Michelangelo, the perfectionist, sculptor of that great "requiem in marble" at St. Peter's in Rome, should have left three fifths of his sculptures unfinished. It is given by Vasari: "Michelangelo's non finito reflects the sublimity of his ideas, which again and again lay beyond the reach of his hands."[6] In other words, he was not able to translate the concept in his brain into a work of art. It is hard to believe that he continued to work for ten years on the *Rondanini Pietà* for any other reason than that he was left perpetually dissatisfied with it, that he felt unable to translate his grandiose concepts of beauty into stone.

The *non finito* has another aspect too, which is a virtue in a work of art: it stirs the imagination of the viewer, who can finish it off mentally according to his own brain concept(s); the viewer is no longer circumscribed by the concept in the artist's brain. It seems to me much more likely, then, that Michelangelo brought his sculptures to a certain finish, which he judged to be adequate to convey as well as he could the concept in his brain, leaving it to the viewer to complete the unfinished, even if he did not articulate such a thought explicitly. Otherwise he would have destroyed them, as indeed he did with many

of his drawings. He as much says so in one of his sonnets, which is somewhat difficult to render into English and difficult to understand even in the original Italian:

> When my rude hammer to the stubborn stone
> Gives human shape, now that, now this, at will,
> Following his hand who wields and guides it still,
> It moves upon another's feet alone:
>
> But that which dwells in heaven, the world doth fill
> With beauty by pure motions of its own;
> And since tools fashion tools which else were none,
> Its life makes all that lives with living skill.
>
> Now, for that every stroke excels the more
> The higher at the forge it doth ascend,
> Her soul that fashioned mine hath sought the skies:
>
> Wherefore unfinished I must meet my end,
> If God, the great artificer, denies
> That aid which was unique on earth before[2]

In it, I think that Michelangelo, the believer in the divine but also in the divine "in us," is essentially saying that the development of a sculpture is not in his control but in a Divine being in Heaven, and that he will leave his work unfinished unless there is divine intervention, for otherwise it would be impossible to translate his "divine" concept into his work.

It is perhaps because of their unfinished status that sketches for paintings are often more appealing than the finished paintings themselves, as Schopenhauer remarked (see Chapter 11). Vasari wrote that, in their sketches, painters are guided by an inspiration that gives them "a certain measure of boldness; but afterwards, in finishing it, the boldness vanishes." For Kenneth Clark, the quality of a sketch is "smothered by labour."[7] Michelangelo understood this. As we shall see, Frenhofer, in Balzac's *Unknown Masterpiece*, did not, to his cost.

Chapter 13

Paul Cézanne and the Unfinished

Paul Cézanne is generally regarded as one of the most influential painters of modern times. His work has left a deep mark on twentieth century painting and presaged the appearance of Cubism. In surveying his work, one cannot help but notice an evolution towards the unfinished, towards objectively empty patches of canvas that somehow do not give the impression of emptiness. An excellent example is provided by *La Route tournante* (Figure 13.1). In addition, the objects that he painted have themselves a certain unfinished quality, and again become absorbed by the viewer to such an extent that they look finished. The series of drawings of the mountain outside Aix-en-Provence known as the *Montagne Sainte Victoire* (Figures 13.2 and 13.3) begin with natural-istic renderings and become increasingly more abstract, with the fields, houses and trees merely hinted at by brilliant brush-strokes of differ-ent color. Often the entire canvas consists of nothing more than a series of patches, rectangular in shape, some finished, others not, the whole assembled together in such a way as to give the perceiver much flexibility. Cézanne was a meticulous painter, deliberating at length over each detail. He also felt unsatisfied with much, perhaps all, of his work and destroyed many of his canvases. It is perhaps because of this that he was commonly considered to be irresolute and simply incapable of finishing his work. Yet a closer look at Cézanne's work shows that nothing was quite left unfinished in haste, and nothing was left to chance. Though knowing nothing about the visual brain he was nevertheless remarkably insightful into its workings, and had also been influenced by literary works that have a theme central to this book – the difficulty of representing the synthetic brain concept or ideal, and the advantages of leaving much to the mind. It is not surprising there-fore that a large body of his work has, on objective analysis, an unfinished

Figure 13.1. Paul Cézanne, *La Route tournante,* 1902–06, Courtauld Institute of Art, London.

aspect. This engages the viewer imaginatively and gives him different possibilities, although the viewer may not be consciously aware of it. But there is an additional factor at work in Cézanne, as no doubt with many other artists, although Cézanne was explicit about it. As the painting developed, so the concept in his brain changed, since the synthetic concept is capable of forever evolving. I have already referred to moments that seem so perfect to the artist that he chooses to "freeze" them, to re-create later, thus protecting the concept from development. Konstantinos Kavafis is a very good example of this in poetry. But this was not characteristic of Cézanne. Henri Matisse once said of Cézanne that "After a certain time, [he] always painted the same canvas of Bathers. . . . A Cézanne is a moment of the artist, [not] of nature . . . Despite the continual use of the same means, there are different effects; *it's the man, Cézanne, that has changed*"[1] (my emphasis), or rather the concept in his brain as he paints. Matisse himself had a similar approach, and wrote: "I'm driven by an idea that I

Figure 13.2. Paul Cézanne, *Montagne Sainte Victoire*, 1887, Courtauld Institute of Art, London.

really grasp only as it grows with the picture."[1] It has been said of Cézanne that his "work can be understood simply as a series of continued sketches, that each item is merely a link in a chain and thus subordinate to the artist's œuvre as a whole,"[2] Cézanne often describing himself as merely progressing towards his artistic ideal, without ever attaining it,[3] which he decidedly could not, since the ideal itself (the brain concept) was forever changing.

Finished and "unfinished" paintings appeared in Cézanne's first one man show, at the Amboise Vollard Gallery in Paris in 1895. That he should have allowed the finished and the "unfinished" to be displayed together, in a first one-man show, suggests that he himself was not any more dissatisfied with his "unfinished" work than his "finished" ones, even though both Cézanne and his work were stigmatized and ridiculed by critics for their "unfinished" status. Such criticism was nothing new. Earlier, following the first Impressionist exhibition of 1874 in which Cézanne had exhibited three works, among them *A Modern Olympia*, one critic (Jean-Antoine Castagnary) wrote of the

Figure 13.3. Paul Cézanne, *Montagne Sainte Victoire vue des Lauves,* 1904–1908, Kunstmuseum, Basel.

poor example set by the unfinished status of Cézanne's work, fearing that others may pursue the same perilous path, "with that degree of untrammeled imagination, where nature is only a pretext for reveries, where the imagination will be powerless to formulate anything other than personal fantasies."[4] In a sense, in criticizing Cézanne's work, Castagnary was actually showing its power. Many thought that Cézanne's unfinished works were due to some brain disease, personality disorder, or some other physical disability. Cézanne, apparently largely indifferent to worldly success, may himself have unwittingly encouraged such a view, and not only by leaving most of his paintings unsigned. In a letter to Émile Bernard, he complained that his age and failing sight is why ". . . my image or tableau is incomplete."[5]

Bernard himself may not have been the wisest choice to confide in on such matters. His view of Cézanne was extremely ambiguous, often degenerating to outright hostility. Using language that mirrors well that of the stagnant Parisian academic source, the Académie, Bernard castigated Cézanne as anti-classical, and wrote of him contemptuously: "Let us learn only from the finders, not from the eternal seekers, whose search only bogs them down more."[6] Nor did such criticism come only from artists and art critics. Perhaps the unkindest cut of all, as Cézanne saw it, was from his boyhood novelist friend, Émile Zola, who reviewed the third Impressionist exhibition, to which Cézanne had contributed seventeen works. Zola wrote: "The day when Monsieur Paul Cézanne is in full command of himself [*se possédera tout entier*], he will produce completely superior works." Later, Zola was to describe Cézanne as a tragic artist, one who could not complete his works: "Never anything taken all the way to the end with tenacity and magnificent force. In sum, no realization."[7] In a novel entitled *l'Oeuvre* Zola wrote of Claude Lantier, whom Cézanne perceived as a thinly disguised substitute for himself: "There were always superb bits; he was pleased with this one, that one, the other. Then why the abrupt gaps?" (see Chapter 14). Zola's book has been interpreted in different ways. Some think of it as a portrait of Cézanne, others view it as that of an artist, Claude Lantier, with Edouard Manet, Claude Monet and Cézanne all acting to contribute to his personality. Some, amongst whom I include myself, do not consider the book to be hostile or unsympathetic to Cézanne. Indeed, its major point – that the richness of concepts in an artist of genius is such that they are difficult to present in a work of art, that such an artist must be full of doubts and irresolution and that the unfinished is an expression of this inner struggle and an expression of genius – is not dissimilar to one of the main arguments in this book. Whatever these interpretations, Cézanne himself took exception to the book, which led to a rupture in relations between the two.

Others saw things differently and explored the significance of the unfinished. Charles Beaudelaire had written (in defense of the painter Corot), that ". . . a work of genius . . . is always well executed when it is sufficiently executed. Furthermore, there is a great difference between a *completed* work [*un morceau fait*] and a *finished* work [*un morceau fini*]; generally what is *completed* isn't *finished*, and something *highly* finished may not be *complete* at all"[8] [original emphasis]. Writing to his son about the 1895 Exhibition, Camille Pissaro said of Cézanne's work: "There are exquisite things, *still lifes* of irreproachable accomplishment, *others much worked* but left in a suspended state [*laissées en plan*] that are still more beautiful than the others, land-scapes, nudes, heads that are still unfinished yet truly grandiose . . . Why? Sensation is there!" [my ellipsis, original emphases].[9] Perhaps most important of all, there is Cézanne's own statement, in a letter to his mother in 1874 (the year before the first Impressionist exhibition in Paris): "I have to work constantly [but] not in order to strive at *finish*, which attracts the admiration of imbeciles . . . This thing, which is so much admired, is only the feat of an artisan's skill and renders every resulting work inartistic and common. I must strive to *complete* only for the satisfaction of being truer and more artistic"[10] [original emphasis and ellipsis in the quote].

Finished and unfinished do not quite have the same import in the work of Cézanne as in the work of, for example, Michelangelo. Yet they can both be ultimately traced to the same source, the overall brain strategy of concept formation and the difficulty of realizing that concept in a work of art or even in a series of works. To understand the unfinished component in Cézanne's work it is necessary to take a broader look at his art and at what he was trying to achieve. Here, perhaps more than in Michelangelo, the entire output of Cézanne, as well as individual paintings, should be considered. And his attitude towards "unfinished" works is more explicit than that of Michelangelo's.

Cézanne's main preoccupation was with form. He was painting at what one might call a transitional time, when the influence of that autocratic and dictatorial organ of art, the Académie in Paris, was beginning to be challenged and to wane. In the classical tradition of the Académie, what was emphasized above all was a realistic depiction of nature – anatomical accuracy, a correct rendering of relations and proportions, with color added on to express mood, the Italian master Raphael usually being the reference point. There had been some departures, alluded to in the previous chapter, and prominent among these is the patch painting (*pittura di macchia*) in Titian's mature works. In these, Titian had dispensed to a significant degree with exact detail and rendering. This more free painterly approach was perhaps first initiated by the "trembling" brushstroke and the *sfumato* of Giorgione, in whose workshop Titian had worked as an assistant. But, for a long time, the approach did not have many followers.

Cézanne dispensed much more with the precise and realistic representation of form. His main concern was the rendering of nature but he believed that he could represent nature in a more abstract way.

Instead of copying details, he set out to represent the overall form by patches of color. Patches become a dominant feature of his later work. These patches, he believed, would give the entire canvas a harmonious unity; from their interaction on canvas a scene or theme would emerge. But where would such an interaction occur and who would give them that unity? It is of course the brain of the viewer, not the canvas itself. Such a view – which should be easy for us to understand today, with all that we have learned about the brain – did not come naturally to many who viewed the work of Cézanne and to many of his critics, the prevailing view being rather that of an image impressed upon the retina and interpreted rather than constructed by the brain. But Cézanne himself seems to have had a remarkably sophisticated view of the seeing apparatus, the visual brain, one that was neuro-biologically sound, even if he knew nothing about the visual brain. He believed strongly that seeing is an active process, one in which eye and brain collaborate to give a pictorial unity to what is being depicted, summarized in his favorite word "*réalisation*." This view of painting may have been influenced to some extent by the theorizing of Denis Diderot, one of the most original thinkers of revolutionary France. Cézanne's admiration for Balzac's short story, *Le Chef-d'oeuvre inconnu* (*The Unknown Masterpiece*), certainly suggests this, since Balzac is known to have been much influenced by Diderot, whose views he incorporates almost verbatim in his story (see Chapter 14). In an essay published in 1776, entitled *Pensées détachées sur la peinture*, Diderot had emphasized the importance of unity – "Nothing is beautiful without unity." The details were not as important. Objects could be distorted if they served the higher purpose, that of unity. To achieve that unity, the entire canvas had to be painted and to advance at once, advice given to Cézanne by Pissaro and accepted enthusiastically. Cézanne said: "I advance . . . all of my canvas at once, together. In the same movement, the same conviction, I bring into relation every-thing that is scattered." [11] In describing one of his late works, created of patchworks of color extending over the canvas, Cézanne said, "Only from their sum, their relation and interaction, do the objects they define reveal themselves to the viewer." The precise formal content is not specified. Moreover, by leaving so much of it apparently unfinished, he leaves open the possibility that the paintings themselves could have been developed in a number of ways, both for the painter and the viewer. How it is integrated and developed depends on the viewer, or

rather on the brain of the viewer, and may change from one viewing
to the other. The *"réalisation"* of which Cézanne spoke so consist-
ently and so fervently could only be given to the work by the brain,
indeed achieved in the brain. And that "realization" must depend upon
a brain concept. In giving it that unity, the brain also takes account
of the unfinished parts of the canvas. These unfinished parts – sometimes comprising significant extents of the canvas – constituted part
of the unity and the harmony. To fill in all the details was to destroy
that unity. On this Cézanne was quite explicit. He wrote: "I conceive
of it [painting] as a personal apperception. I situate this apperception
in sensation, and I ask that the intelligence organize it into a work."
For Cézanne, to see (*voir*) is always also to conceive (*concevoir*).[3]

The notion that a work of art should not be pushed too far, that
an "unfinished" work can in fact stir the brain imaginatively, was
central to the work of Cézanne and to his thinking. In comments on
Cézanne that Émile Bernard attributed to Julien Tanguy (a dealer in
artists' materials and a friend of Cézanne) about how slowly Cézanne
worked and his inability to finish his paintings, there is one telling
line: "The slightest thing costs [Cézanne] a great deal of effort *and
nothing is accidental in what he does*" [my emphasis].[12] This would imply
that even the gaps and the unfinished parts were pre-meditated. It is
no wonder that Cézanne identified closely with the principal character of Balzac's *Unknown Masterpiece* and with Diderot's opinion
expressed in his *Essais sur la peinture* and reflected in Balzac's novel:
the painter, like the writer, cannot render all that he knows, sees or
feels, or all the concepts in his brain. His work therefore leaves him
unsatisfied and this dissatisfaction "propels him forward and deceives
him on what he can achieve and spoils his creation."

As we shall see, in Balzac's book the artist pushes the work too far
and spoils his creation, admitting failure and defeat at the end. With
Cézanne, it was not a question of admitting failure. The unfinished
forms an integral part of his work. Terence Maloon writes that sensation had a special and, from our viewpoint, very significant meaning for Cézanne and Pissaro.[4] It meant, he says, a sort of primal
vividness. "It never resolved into a precise image – that would have
made it too objective and have changed it into something else. One
can infer that . . . [they] considered sensation to be essentially indeterminate. They believed that the evocation or trace of sensation . . .
was spoilt by attempts to stabilize and confine it . . . Hence, their

concern for 'sensation' translated in their paintings into qualities associated with lack of finish" (my ellipsis). In other words, they left it to the viewer's brain to construct the final image. Cézanne had learnt a lesson from Frenhofer. He did not overwork his canvases. But of course he was never satisfied with them. Like Thomas Mann (see Chapter 21), he was driven by permanent dissatisfaction in trying to translate the concepts in his brain onto canvas.

Chapter 14

Unfinished Art in Literature

The art of the unfinished and the inability to finish have been both celebrated and lamented in literature. Here I want to concentrate on the two novels mentioned in the previous chapter, both of which have had substantial impact. The shorter one is by Honoré de Balzac and the longer one by Émile Zola. Interestingly, both combine art with love. In both there is a central conflict between art and life: the artist is seemingly not only dissatisfied with his output but also with his lover, and the artistic impulse seems to overwhelm and conquer all. The artist tries, unsuccessfully, to create the perfect lover on canvas; the lover on canvas gradually displaces the real lover in the affections of the artist, though neither is able to satisfy the concept in the artist's brain.

Balzac's *The Unknown Masterpiece*[1] has left a deep impression on many artists and thinkers, including Picasso who, it is reputed, was so haunted by it that he rented the apartment in Paris where the story was set. Its central theme is the progressive destruction of a work of art by over-working it through richness of concepts. In a letter to Mme Hanska, who later became his wife, Balzac wrote that the "execution and composition of music, just like the execution of a work of art, can be destroyed by a richness of concept in the creator."[2] In writing his novel, he may well have been influenced by Ernst Hoffmann, the German author who gave his name to *The Tales of Hoffmann* by Jacques Offenbach, and in particular the work entitled *Der Artushof* (*The Court of Arthus*). In it, a young painter encounters an old master whom he persuades to view his paintings. Invited to the old master's atelier, the young painter is told of his timely visit since the master has just put the finishing touches to what he considers to be a great painting, one that he has worked on for more than a year. He (the master) becomes ecstatic and comes to believe that his painting is coming alive. But the young painter can only see a totally empty canvas. The master can in fact only dream and fantasize about his work, which he is incapable of translating onto canvas.

Similarly, in Balzac's story, a young painter interestingly identified as the painter Nicholas Poussin (whom Cézanne much admired and copied frequently at the Louvre) visits an elderly painter, Porbus, by chance in the company of a recognized great painter, Frenhofer. The latter is deeply critical of the work of Porbus: "you content yourself with its first appearance, or the second, or the third; this is not the way of the victorious fighters . . . they persevere until nature is reduced to revealing itself all naked and in its real spirit." Frenhofer is an exigent artist, just like Cézanne after him. He has a predilection for color and impresses upon his interlocutors the extent to which color is so much more important than line in the execution of a painting. Cézanne, too, was very much concerned with rendering form through color. Frenhofer, the artistic creation of Balzac, resembles (superficially at any rate) Cézanne, the real artist. Both persevere even though they are irresolute, and unable to finish a painting. Is it any wonder that Cézanne once said, "*Frenhofer, c'est moi!*"

Frenhofer has, it transpires, been working on a canvas for ten years. It is the portrait of a woman. But this is no ordinary woman. She is "not a creature but a creation." Just like von Aschenbach in *Death in Venice*, who has in his brain the ideal concept of a beautiful youth (see Chapter 21), so Frenhofer has the ideal woman as a concept in his brain. But unlike von Aschenbach, who found his brain ideal in Tadzio, even if only fleetingly, Frenhofer has sought in vain to find the true likeness of his "glorious lady of my mind" (Dante) in nature. He says: "I have yet to meet an irreproachable woman, whose body contours are of a perfect beauty . . . where does she live . . . this lost Venus of the ancients, so often sought for . . . to see for a moment, just once, the divine nature, complete, the ideal, I would give away all my fortune . . . like Orpheus, I would descend to the hell of art to bring her to life" (my ellipsis). The use of the term "hell of art" is itself not uninteresting – it suggests a perpetual struggle. Frenhofer's painting is in fact "not a painting, it is a sentiment, a passion." He jealously guards this painting, his passion, from view. No one is allowed to see it.

The three – Porbus, Poussin and Frenhofer – agree a deal. Poussin's mistress, Gillette, is of incomparable and heavenly beauty, and indeed may be the very woman whom Frenhofer would give away his fortune to meet. Frenhofer is doubtful at first, for he knows that the ideal in the brain (the creature he had tried to paint) cannot find its copy in nature. "What mistress?" Frenhofer asked. "She will betray him sooner or later. Mine will always be faithful." After all, as von Aschenbach had realized in *Death in Venice*, beauty is ephemeral. To create a woman who is forever beautiful and forever faithful, one has to create the "glorious lady of one's mind" untrammeled by reality, as Dante did. Frenhofer nevertheless agrees. In exchange for a glimpse of the divine Gillette, he agrees to show the masterpiece he has been working on for ten years, and which no one has yet set eyes on. Unlike Frenhofer, Poussin "had discovered a model in the woman whom he loved and who loved him." But here Balzac, with his usual insight, introduces a powerful hint into the ideal formed in the brain and its unrealizability in life, which is in fact the theme of his story. Things are not as simple because, while trying to translate that ideal model, his lover Gillette, onto canvas, "the look of the lover [Poussin's] had metamorphosed into the look of the painter. And this metamorphosis has lost him his love . . . because he himself, by making of her a model, had already left her." She is in fact not the real model. The real model is the immaterial concept in his brain. Gillette senses this, and refuses to sit for him any more because "in these moments, your eyes say nothing to me; you no longer think of me, though you are looking at me." The real woman becomes jealous of the conceptual woman being created on canvas.

At the arranged meeting, Poussin and Porbus are astonished when they view the painting that Frenhofer had been toiling at secretly for ten years. They see nothing but "a mass of confused colors contained within a multitude of bizarre lines which formed a wall of painting." The whole canvas is vastly overworked, save for a divinely painted foot, a mere fragment. They remain "petrified in admiration before this fragment that had escaped an unbelievable, slow and progressive destruction." The next day, Frenhofer is found dead and his painting destroyed, perhaps having realized, like von Aschenbach, that beauty – the concept in the brain – cannot be easily experienced. Sometimes it may even be impossible to experience it in a work of art.

The main theme in Balzac's novel – the enormous difficulty of translating a synthetic brain concept into a work of art (especially if the synthetic concept in the creator is rich) and the difficulty of finding a counterpart for that concept in real life – are taken up by Émile Zola in his novel, which forms part of his series of novels depicting a family, the Rougon-Macquart, in nineteenth century France. Although the two French writers, the brothers Goncourt, accused Zola of plagiarism when he published his book (specifically of their *Manette Salomon*, published some fifteen years before Zola's novel appeared), all the evidence suggests that Zola had planned early on a novel that would depict the struggle of the artist. In outlining his projected novels for the Rougon-Macquart series, Zola had at the very beginning reserved a place for a "novel about art" in which he would expose "the sick (*maladives*) concepts of the brain that extend to madness (*qui montent jusqu'á la folie*)."[3] It would be about a painter who has "irresistible and wild intellectual appetites . . . The violence with which he undertakes to satisfy the passions of his brain render him impotent . . . the terrible drama of an intelligence that devours itself."[3] It is more than likely that, in writing his novel, Zola was influenced by Balzac's novel, as Balzac is known to have been influenced by others, and the others by the reality of the synthetic concept in the brain that commonly does not find a counterpart in life or in art.

Although many believe that the character portrayed in Zola's novel is a compound of three artists (see previous chapter), many more believe that Cézanne was the sole model. If Cézanne did indeed see himself as the artist described in an unfavorable light, he gave no hint of it in the letter that he wrote to Zola upon receipt of the book, in which he wrote "I thank the author of Rougon-Macquart . . . and ask him to allow me to shake his hand while thinking of yesteryears." There is indeed much that Cézanne would have been grateful for in Zola. He was the first to believe in and to encourage Cézanne, and to instill in him the importance of the "idea" in painting. In a letter, written while Cézanne had still not embarked upon his artistic career, Zola wrote: "Take courage; seize your brushes, and let your imagination roam. I have faith in you. Courage above all, and think hard, before engaging yourself in this path, of the thorns that you are likely to encounter." [4] Whatever the truth, the book is interesting in the insights that it gives us about artists, especially since it comes from a man who was familiar with artistic circles and indeed was an artist himself, in the sense of being a literary author. More than that, the portrait of the struggling artist, in the form of the writer Sandoz in the novel, is almost certainly modeled on himself. In his own notes, Zola wrote that "With Claude Lantier, . . . I will describe my intimate life of productivity, this perpetual and painful delivery (*accouchment*); but I will enlarge the subject by the drama, with Claude who is forever dissatisfied, who is exasperated . . . and who finally commits suicide before his unfinished work."[5] What is especially interesting about the novel is the language that Zola uses to describe the artistic effort and artistic failure. There are many passages in which he demonstrates that he understands that the difficulty for any creator is to represent the concept in his brain, although Zola does not use such language explicitly. I quote some of these lines below.

L'Oeuvre, translated into English as *The Masterpiece*, is the story of a painter, Claude Lantier, who on a rainy night in Paris finds himself somewhat fortuitously giving shelter to an apparently innocent country girl, Christine, lost in Paris. She soon returns to thank him for his succor and they eventually fall in love. He is working on a canvas, with a reclining woman as its centerpiece. Christine is just the model that he has been seeking, or so he believes. He soon realizes, with fatal consequences, that neither Christine nor the painting he is so desperately trying to execute satisfy the synthetic concept of the ideal woman in his brain. That this is so is implied by the fact that he uses several other models, and indeed changes models weekly. As he works and re-works the painting using Christine as a model, the conflict between the reality of life and art begins to loom large: "his excitement mounted, it was his chaste passion for the flesh of a woman, a delirious love for nudes desired but never possessed, an impossibility to satisfy himself, *to create that flesh of which he dreamt*" (my emphasis). His misfortune is twofold: he does not find in real life the flesh of which he dreams and he cannot transform the flesh of which he dreams onto canvas. The resulting permanent dissatisfaction begins to work its destructive effects. The painting is worked and re-worked, almost finished and then re-started. "And he felt unable to make corrections, a wall, an impregnable obstacle, beyond which he could not go, rising. If he re-worked it twenty times, he aggravated the mistakes twenty times." He is exasperated by "This effort of creation in a work of art, this effort of blood and tears which agonized him, to create the flesh, and blow life into it. *Always this battle with the real, and always beaten, the struggle against the Angel*" (my emphasis), the angel being understood as the perfection that resides only in the brain. As he surveys his canvas, he wants to destroy it. He looks at the painting with "a fixed and ardent gaze, in which was burning the awful torture of his impotence . . . Was it a lesion in his eyes that prevented him from seeing correctly? Had his hands ceased to belong to him, since they refused to obey him?" (my ellipsis). "He is racked by one of these doubts that made him execrate painting, the execration of a betrayed lover."

That the brain concept of what Lantier wants to represent on canvas is a synthetic one, to which all particular views that he has seen have contributed, is evident from the description of his efforts to paint a view of the Cité in Paris. He wants to see the Cité at sunrise, disengaging from the mist; he wants to see it at noon and at dusk. The importance of the first impression in shaping the synthetic concept is acknowledged, because "before these twenty different Cités, regardless of the time, he always returned to the Cité he had first seen, at four o'clock one beautiful September evening." But his incapacity to translate his synthetic brain concept (which has synthesized all these views) into a work of art exasperates him. He makes continual errors, through which he spoils the painting. Sandoz, when told by Christine that the painting is finished, surveys it with embarrassment. He sees that it is rather in the form of a rough outline, "as if the painter had been afraid to spoil the Paris of his dreams by finishing it," for which one could readily substitute his synthetic brain concept of Paris.

His painting is refused by the Salon. His doubts begin to return, "Ravaged by his struggle against nature. Each canvas seemed to him weak and above all incomplete, not achieving the desired effect." It was this impotence that exasperated him, more than the refusal of the jury. He suffers from never having been able to give of himself completely to the masterpiece that could not give birth to his genius. But hope is always there, and always aids the pursuit of the unattainable. Without that hope, art itself would be dead. The disappointment at his inability to execute to perfection on the canvas at hand what is in his brain is forever alleviated by his high hopes for the next one. "By a constant phenomenon, his desire to create worked faster than his fingers, he never confined himself to a single canvas without conceiving of the next one. He was impatient to conclude what he had started and over which he agonised. No doubt it would not be worth much. He would have to make fatal concessions, cheat, do all that an artist had to abandon out of conscience (*'il en etait aux concessions fatales,*

aux tricheries, a tout ce qu'un artiste doit abandonner de conscience');
but what he would do next, he saw as superb and heroic, unassailable, indestructible." There is always the next time, the next one: "The perpetual mirage that whips the courage of the damned of art."

Nor does reality, in the form of Christine, his model and lover, satisfy his brain concept of the perfect woman. As she gets incorporated into the painting, she notices that any resemblance to herself begins to fade in the hands of this dissatisfied artist, who re-works each piece a hundred times. Even though it is the painting that unites them, she nevertheless begins to feel less close to him with every fading trait of herself. "Does he not love [me]," she wonders, "that he should allow [me] to thus fade away from his painting? And who is this new woman, this vague and unknown face that pierced her face?" She is not able to comprehend that it is his synthetic brain concept that is taking over, that no single model could ever satisfy him. The unrealized woman that he is trying to create on canvas is the one he really loves, not Christine who merely comes close to the conceptual woman. It is a repeat of the story of Poussin and Gillette, who suspect him of transferring his attention to the woman on the canvas. But in his vain attempt to give life to his brain concept, Christine becomes his accomplice and willing victim, happy to satisfy him "without understanding what a formidable rival she was giving herself" in the woman on the canvas. She sees that Lantier's painting robs her of her lover more every day. But "she was not able to fight, she ceded, allowed herself to be carried away with him, to be united to him in a single effort. But an infinite sadness accompanied the beginnings of this abandon, a fear of what was awaiting her. She neglects her son. It was the man she adored and desired who become her child, and the other, the poor creature, remained a simple witness of their great past passion." He was, to be sure, with her and close to her. But how she felt his distance, there "in the inaccessible infinity of art." In fact, it is not the art that is inaccessible but rather the brain concept.

The passion between them dies. They understand it, once they disentangle themselves and yet find themselves lying next to each other, "henceforth strangers, with the feeling of an obstacle between them, of another body, whose coldness had brushed against them, on certain days, since the ardent beginnings of their liaison. They would now never again be able to be unified. There was there something irreparable, a crack, a void had been produced. The wife diminished the lover, the formality of marriage seemed to have killed love and the woman on the canvas destroyed the lover."

Christine becomes jealous, agonizingly so, but not of other models. "She had only one rival, this painting, who was stealing Lantier from her. He could no longer look at her body, which he had previously covered by a lover's kisses; now he adored it only as an artist. He loved in her nothing but his art, nature, life." She poses for him endlessly, ready to offer herself while he was burning for that other woman, the one he was painting. As with Gillette in Balzac's novel, "She no longer saw herself in his eyes . . . She feels humiliated and conquered by that other woman." The woman on the canvas had transformed his life. Even "His carnal passion had transferred to the canvas. It was for him the eternal illusion, and he preferred the illusion of his art, this pursuit of a beauty that is never attained, this mad desire that nothing contained. To see them all, to create them all according to his dream." To her, it was on the other side of the canvas that Lantier was now living, with that other woman. And thus beaten, Christine begins to feel "the weight of the sovereignty of art."

As Christine surveys the woman on the canvas disbelievingly, shocked by the thighs in gold and the flowers beneath the belly, she exhorts him to look at his painting, to wake up, to return to existence, to understand that she, Christine, is there in flesh and blood, still alive, still loving. Lantier obeys, looks at the painting and is in turn stupefied by his creation. "Who could have painted this idol of unknown religion?" he thinks, "Who had made her of metal, of marble and of gems, blossoming the mystic rose of her sex, between the precious columns of her thighs, under the sacred vault of her belly? Was it he who, without knowing it, had been the creator of this symbol of insatiable desire, of this extra-human image of flesh, become gold and diamond between his fingers, in his vain effort to give it life?" Christine was the reality, the end that the hand attained, and Claude, the "soldier of the uncreated" (*soldat de l'incrée*), becomes disgusted.

At the end, Christine finds Claude hanging, dead, his head facing the painting, "next to the Woman with the flowering sex of a mystic rose, as if he had breathed out his soul in his last groan" and she is "crushed by the fierce sovereignty of art."

I have quoted almost at random from the book, not necessarily in the order they occur. There are many more passages that illustrate the same point, namely that the struggle of the artist is with translating the synthetic concept in the brain into a work of art. In Zola's novel, no less than in Balzac's, the emphasis is also on the difficulty of finding in a particular example, be it that of a lover, an adequate reflection of the synthetic concept in the brain. Both novels also draw an implicit and close relationship between artistic creativity and libidinal feelings, since both are self-reproductive impulses. The unfinished in art represents a failure to realize the synthetic concept in the brain. The unfinished in love represents the failure to realize the biologically ingrained concept of unity.

Part IV

Brain Concepts of Love

Conte by Arthur Rimbaud

A prince was tormented at never having been employed except in the perfection of generous vulgarities. He foresaw astonishing revolutions of love and suspected his wives could afford him better than this agreeable indulgence in luxury and a mere glimpse of the heavens. He wanted to experience the absolute truth, the moment of desire and the quintessential satisfaction. Whether an aberrant piety or not, he wanted the satisfaction of that essential desire. He possessed at least a sufficient earthly power.

All the women he had known he executed. What an upheaval in the garden of beauty. Under the sabre, they blessed him. He did not order any new ones. – The women reappeared

He murdered all those who followed him, after the hunt or the libations. – They all followed him

He amused himself by slitting the throat of these luxurious beasts. He torched the palaces. He attacked people and annihilated them – The crowds, the golden roofs, the beautiful beasts continued to exist.

Can one find ecstasy in destruction, regain youth through cruelty! The people did not murmur. None offered alternate views.

One evening, while he was galloping proudly, a Genie appeared, of an ineffable, even unavowable, beauty. From his physiognomy and his comportment sprang the promise of a love that was multiple and complex! Of an inexpressible, even unbearable, happiness. The Prince and the Genie were extinguished, probably in essential health. How could they not have died? Together then they died.

But this Prince died, in his palace, at an ordinary age. The prince was the Genie. The Genie was the Prince.

The knowledgeable music escapes our desire.

Source: Arthur Rimbaud, *Illuminations*, quoted in Pierre Brunel (2004), "Éclats de la Violence – Pour une lecture comparatiste des Illuminations d'Arthur Rimbaud". José Corti, Paris, p. 105.

Chapter 15

The Brain's Concepts of Love

It is part of our biological make-up to fall in love and we commonly do so even with the least likely or socially acceptable person. To others, they may seem faulty; to us, they appear faultless. This suspension of judgment in affairs of the heart is so common that it is not unreasonable to suppose that it has a sound neurobiological basis. Though love may sometimes seem vagrant and irrational, there is a good and rational biological basis for that irrationality since it constitutes a device that maximizes the chances of ensuring variability. But, being vagrant and irrational, so are commonly the responses to it. An irrational response to a biologically rational system is bound to fail, collectively and in the long term. Fighting against love is fighting against biology, a battle that no one has ever succeeded in winning in the long term. Resistance to love is futile as so many lovers have discovered. Barriers against it have never succeeded in eradicating the feeling, as religious leaders and orthodox families of all persuasions have discovered when trying to prevent their children from contracting liaisons of which they disapprove. In his opera, *Die Walküre*, Wagner highlighted the power of love against all convention by making the love between a brother and a sister, Siegmund and Siegelinde, the central theme of the opera.

There is a deep contradiction in our thinking about love, one that is evident in the language that we use to describe that state, at least in English and in French. It is nevertheless a contradiction that may illuminate us about the nature of love in the brain. While we all tend to regard falling in love as a desirable state that everyone should experience, we nevertheless speak and write of "falling in love."[1] This is strange. In general, to fall is not a desirable state. No one would possibly want to "fall" in the estimation of others or to "fall" in position. Used in these latter contexts, the verb "to fall" presents no contradiction and no problem. "Fallen" women or men may generate feelings of pathos, pity and sympathy in us, but people who fall in love incite our pleasure, envy, anger, or jealousy. There clearly is some kind of contradiction there; if not a contradiction, it is at least a pointer to the fact that love has its splendors and its miseries as well, and that the two can be of equal power. If not of equal power, the advantage does not always lie with the splendors. The contradiction extends beyond language and invades the use to which language is put to paint the great lovers in literature. While the state that follows the "fall" might be considered to be a desirable one by most, a state that constitutes an equilibrium and balance and an adjustment to oneself and to one's society, to the great lovers in literature it leads instead to an all-consuming experience of estrangement from society, where the question of balance and even happiness ceases to matter.

This contradiction is evident in the world literature of love, which, more often than not, paints a gloomy picture – of dissatisfied lovers, of adulterous partners, of the inevitable and strangely desirable death that either extinguishes the passion or promises its epiphany in another world, beyond earthly human existence.

These strange contradictions demand an explanation, and that explanation is perhaps best found in the brain and its concepts. For the capacity to love, with all the intricate neural machinery that governs its operations, involves an inherited concept of love. We also have an acquired concept of what love should be and of the kind of person we want to love. Acquired brain concepts are synthetic and therefore change with experience. The troubadour concept of love is perhaps a little different from that prevalent in Elizabethan England, and we in turn have a concept of love that is different from both. Equally, the sort of person that one might want to love at one stage in one's life might be different from the sort of person one may desire later. Yet these differences are trivial compared to the more enduring, seemingly inherited, concept of love celebrated by poets and writers. That concept can be summarized in one word, unity. It is the desire of lovers to be unified with one another, to become one. And, projected to love, that one word has ingrained within it both the splendors and miseries of the brain. The "unity-in-love" is a brain concept that invokes splendors of heaven. That heaven can never be permanently attained on earth; it is against reality. And if it is a brain

concept, not one tied to cultural traditions, one should find pancul-
tural evidence for it in the world literature of love, as celebrated in
different ages.

Some of Plato's loftiest passages are to be found in *The Symposium*,
which must be ranked as one of the most influential books on love
in Western literature. In it Plato has Aristophanes trace the origins of
love to his belief that, in past times, there were three kinds of humans
– male, female, and a third, androgynous, kind composed of both male
and female. Each type consisted of two individuals who were totally
unified. They had, for example, two faces at the top of a circular neck
but a single head. These individuals, having terrible power, were a threat
to the gods. So Zeus decreed that each individual should be cut in
two. And so began the unending subsequent struggle to find the other
half, with which to be unified. "Now, since the natural form of
human beings had been cut in two, each half longed for the other."
Those who were split from the androgynous unit liked the sex opposite to their own. Women split from a woman were interested in women
only, while men split from men were interested in men only. But the
consequences of this splitting were the same for all three, since each
desired to be united to their missing half. "So, out of their desire to
grow together, they would throw their arms around each other when
they met and become entwined."[2] Similarly, the Alexandrian philosopher, Philo Judaeus, believed the Talmudic fable that Adam was originally androgynous, and that God separated him into his two sexual
components. Judaeus believed that the longing for reunion that love
inspired in the divided halves was the source of the sexual pleasure.
This is not vastly different from what one of the oldest Upanishads
(part of the Hindu scriptures), the *Bṛhadāraṇyaka Upanishad*,
recounts: that in the beginning, the Self was alone and longed for
a second. He therefore split this Self into two, thus giving rise to
husband and wife, from whose union human beings were born.[3]

Love, then, is the desire for unity. It "collects the halves of our
original nature, and tries to make a single thing out of the two parts
so as to restore our natural condition."[4] Note that it "tries" though
nowhere does it say that it succeeds. But this longing is only felt as
an emotion and not articulated or intellectualized. Aristophanes adds,
"Thus, whenever a lover . . . happens to encounter the person who is
their other half, they are overcome with amazement at their friend-
ship, intimacy, and love, and do not want to be severed, so to speak,

from each other even for a moment. These are the people who spend their entire lives with each other, *though they don't know what they want from each other*"[5] (my emphasis). If told of this, lovers "would think they had discovered what they had really desired all along, namely to be made one out of two by being joined and welded together with their beloved."[6] So the definition of love is simple: "the name love is given to the desire for wholeness,"[7] that is, for unity, a unity that may be expressed privately, wished for, sought after, or written about in poetry and literature. It is impossible to achieve, save in thought and through procreation.

The desire for unity-in-love has been celebrated in many works of literature and poetry of all cultures, of which I give only a few examples here. That it should have been so ubiquitously celebrated and written about, in myths and in literature, tells us something significant about the brain's inherited concept of love. That seemingly universal desire is well summarized in the *Conte* of Arthur Rimbaud, reproduced as a preface to this Part. Though only one page long, it is a difficult passage to read and some of its phraseology is ambiguous enough to have been the subject of debate amongst scholars. Yet its overall meaning is straightforward enough. It tells the story of a prince who seeks a glimpse of heaven in that elusive unity that is the hallmark of love. Life provides him with opportunities while he luxuriates in ephemeral sensuous pleasures. But the essential satisfaction, to be derived from unity, escapes him. In the end, he finds that love is an illusion, in the form of a Genie of unavowable beauty who promises an inexpressible and unbearable happiness. He is in fact united to the Genie, because the Prince is the Genie and the Genie is the Prince. Together they die, united. Lover and beloved are annihilated. Jalaluddin Rumi put it even more briefly in the *Mathnawi*. A lover can only be admitted to the house of the beloved if he is annihilated and becomes one with the lover, because "there is no room for two Is in this narrow house."

The unity that the Prince seeks is in fact resolved only in the brain, hence Dante's insistence that he was not writing about Beatrice but about "the glorious lady of my mind."[8] Hence, too, the similar sentiment expressed by Rumi in reference to Shamsuddin Tabrizi, his companion and mentor: "lovers do not find each other; they are in each other all along." But even as an abstraction or an illusion, it can only come to full fruition in death. In his short tale, Rimbaud was expressing, in miniature form, what Plato described and what countless lovers in world literature have experienced. But Rimbaud was doing more than that. He was expressing something that can only be traced to the individuality of the concept in each brain. That individuality can make of love an intensely lonely experience, for the concept does not, often, have its counterpart in reality. The incapacity of biology to deliver what it promotes commonly leads, it seems, to a state of permanent dissatisfaction and therefore inevitably to loneliness. Indeed, the theme of loneliness is implicit in the never-ending search for a state that can never be achieved because it is biologically impossible. Hence passionate love is both individualizing and isolating. It is only when the concept of the loved person and the actual loved person are the same that unity can be achieved. The Prince then is the Genie, but only in the mind.

Since wholeness and unity are not achievable on earth, lovers often look to another world, unknown to us. They hope to achieve what cannot be achieved on earth after death. It is therefore not surprising to find that there is commonly a mystical element in the literature, the desire for the heavens and for God, the desire for annihilation in the loved one and in God, the desire for the expansion of love beyond desire. It is writ large in the world literature of love.

Given the experientially dissatisfied state that results from unsatisfiable brain concepts, many have sought an artistic counterpart to these unsatisfied concepts, trying to satisfy them through art, music or literature. As Thomas Mann wrote: Art is the only way of getting a particular experience.[9] It is a conclusion that Dante would have wholeheartedly agreed with, as would Wagner, both of whom lived in their art the concepts that they could not, according to their own accounts, find in real life. They turned their unrealized experience into art. Yet even art cannot fully satisfy brain concepts, as the struggle of so many artists attests. In the following pages, I shall try to obtain evidence in favor of this brain concept, this universal desire for unity, from the literature of love. Examination of that literature shows only too well how fatal that biologically ingrained concept is. Rimbaud is not the only one to find, in his story, a union in death. Many others before him have sought that union through annihilation, after death, in a heaven that does not belong to this earth.

Chapter 16

The Neural Correlates of Love

It is only relatively recently that neurobiologists have started to probe into the neural bases of romantic love. What we can say today about those neural correlates is therefore, of necessity, limited and sketchy. In particular, the scientific evidence does not allow us to reach definitive conclusions about the all-important question of whether we form a concept of love. The evidence from the literature of love – which is itself a product of the brain – is better and more secure in this regard. Before considering that evidence, it is nevertheless worthwhile to look at what evidence we have today from neurobiology.

More often than not, romantic love is triggered by a visual input, which is not to say that other factors, such as the voice, intellect, charm or social and financial status do not come into play. It is not surprising therefore that the first studies to investigate the neural correlates of romantic love in the human should have used a visual input.[1] They showed[2] that when we look at the face of someone we are deeply, passionately and hopelessly in love with, a limited number of areas in the brain are especially engaged. This is true regardless of gender. Four of these areas are in the cerebral cortex itself and several are located in sub-cortical stations. All constitute parts of what has come to be known as the emotional brain, which is not to say that they act in isolation. Romantic love is of course a complex emotion that includes, and cannot be easily separated from, other impulses such as physical desire and lust, although the latter can be loveless and therefore distinguishable from the sentiment of romantic love. There is a general neurological axiom (which I flatter myself to have been the source of, although it is likely that many others have had similar thoughts) that if you can tell the difference it is because different brain areas, or cells, are involved. It should not surprise us to find

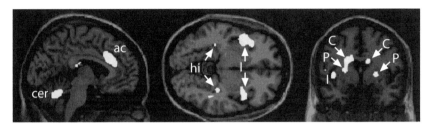

Figure 16.1. Activity (shown in light gray) elicited when subjects view pictures of their loved partner compared to that produced when they view pictures of their friends. The activity, restricted to only a few areas, is shown in sagittal (left), transverse (central), and coronal sections superimposed on slices taken through a template brain. Abbreviations: cer = cerebellum; ac = anterior cingulate; hi = hippocampus; I = insula; C = caudate nucleus; P = putamen. Figure adapted from Bartels A, Zeki S (2000). The neural basis of romantic love. *NeuroReport* **11**(17): 3829–3834, figure 3.

therefore that the neural structures that correlate with romantic love in all its complexity are very distinctive even if they share brain areas with other, closely linked, emotional states.

The areas that are involved are in the cortex (the medial insula, anterior cingulate, and hippocampus) and the sub-cortex (parts of the striatum and probably also the nucleus accumbens), which together constitute core regions of the reward system (Figure 16.1). The passion of love creates feelings of exhilaration and euphoria, of a happiness that is often unbearable and certainly indescribable. And the areas that are activated in response to romantic feelings are largely co-extensive with those brain regions that contain high concentrations of dopamine, a neuro-modulator associated with reward, desire, addiction and euphoric states. Like oxytocin and vasopressin (see below), dopamine is released by the hypothalamus, a structure located deep in the brain and functioning as a link between the nervous and endocrine systems (Figure 16.1). These same cortical regions become active when exogenous opioid drugs such as cocaine, which themselves induce states of euphoria, are ingested. Release of dopamine puts one in a "feel good" state, and dopamine seems to be intimately linked not only to the formation of relationships but also to sex, which consequently comes to be regarded as a rewarding exercise. This increase in dopamine is coupled to a decrease in serotonin (5-HT or 5-hydroxytryptamine), which is linked to appetite and mood. Studies have shown a depletion of serotonin in early stages of romantic love to levels that are common in patients with obsessive-compulsive disorders.[3] Love, after all, is a kind of obsession and in its early stages commonly immobilizes thought and channels it in the direction of a single individual. The early stages of romantic love seem to correlate also with another substance, nerve growth factor, which has been found to be elevated in those who have recently fallen in love compared to those who are not in love or who have stable, long-lasting, relationships.[4] Moreover, the concentration of nerve growth factor appears to correlate significantly with the intensity of romantic feelings.

Oxytocin and another chemically linked neuromodulator, vasopressin, seem to be particularly linked to attachment and bonding. In the human, oxytocin has been shown to induce trust towards other humans, and its involvement in love has been suggested, but not proven so far. Both are produced by the hypothalamus and released and stored in the pituitary gland, to be discharged into the blood, especially during orgasm in both sexes and during childbirth and breast-feeding in females. In males, vasopressin has also been linked to social behavior, in particular to aggression towards other males and to parental behavior. The concentration of both neuromodulators increases during the phase of intense romantic attachment and pairing. The receptors for both neuromodulators are distributed in the many parts of the brainstem that are activated during both romantic and maternal love.

It is noteworthy that sexual arousal activates regions adjacent to – and in the case of the hypothalamus overlapping with – the areas activated by romantic love, in the anterior cingulate and in the subcortical regions mentioned above.[1] Especially interesting in this regard is the activation of the hypothalamus with both romantic feelings and sexual arousal, but not with maternal love. Its activation may thus constitute the erotic component present in romantic but not in maternal attachment. Moreover, sexual arousal (and orgasms), at least in women, de-activates considerable parts of the cortex, some of which overlap the de-activated regions observed in romantic love.[5] This is perhaps not surprising, given that humans often take "leave of their senses" during sexual arousal, perhaps even inducing them to conduct that they might later, in more sober mood, regret. In fact, this intimacy in terms of geographic location between brain areas, engaged during romantic love on the one hand and sexual arousal on the other, is of more than passing interest. If romantic love has at its basis a concept – that of unity – and if sexual union is as close as humans can get to achieving that unity, then the juxtaposition of the areas engaged during these two separate but highly linked states is not surprising. Indeed the desire for unity through sexual union may be a consequence of it.

It may seem surprising that the face that launched a thousand ships did so through this limited set of areas. But the story of Paris and Helen of Troy should in itself be enough to tell us that these neuro-biological results, viewed on their own, can lead to deceptive inter-pretations. For romantic love is all-engaging, transforming people's lives and inducing them to both heroic and evil deeds. It is not sur-prising to find therefore that this core of areas that become engaged during romantic love has rich connections with other sites in the brain, both cortical and sub-cortical. Among these are connections with the frontal, parietal and middle temporal cortex as well as a large nucleus located at the apex of the temporal lobe, known as the amygdala. Increase in activity in the romantic core of areas is mirrored by a decrease in activity, or inactivation, of these cortical zones. The amygdala is known to be engaged during fearful situations and its de-activation, when subjects view pictures of their partners as well as during human male ejaculation, implies a lessening of fear. Also, the all-engaging passion of romantic love is mirrored by a suspension of judgment or a relaxation of judgmental criteria by which we assess other people, which is a function of the frontal cortex (Figure 16.2). This cortical

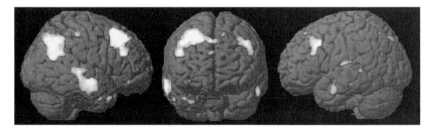

Figure 16.2. Cortical deactivations (shown in white and light gray) produced when subjects view pictures of their loved partners. Figure adapted from Bartels A, Zeki S (2000). The neural basis of romantic love. *NeuroReport* **11**(17): 3829–3834, figure 4.

zone, along with the parietal cortex and parts of the temporal lobe, has also been commonly found to be involved in negative emotions. Its inactivation in romantic as well as maternal states – when faced with the loved one – should not therefore be surprising because when we are deeply in love we suspend those critical judgments that we otherwise use to assess people. The pre-frontal cortex, the parieto-temporal junction and the temporal poles constitute a network of areas invariably active with "mentalizing" or "theory of mind," that is, the ability to determine other people's emotions and intentions.[6] It is noteworthy, from the point of view of the inherited brain concept of "unity-in-love," that one feature of mentalizing in terms of the "theory of mind" is to distinguish between self and others, with the potential of ascribing different sets of beliefs and desires to others and to oneself. To obtain an imagined unity-in-love, so that the self and the other are merged, this process of mentalizing, and thus distinguishing between self and the other, must be rendered inactive or at any rate less potent. But such judgment is also often suspended with the trust that develops between individuals and certainly with the deep bonding that develops between a mother and her child. Here, then, is a neural basis not only for saying that love is blind, but also for the concept of "unity-in-love." We are often surprised by the choice of partner that someone makes, asking futilely whether they have taken leave of their senses. In fact, they have. Love is often irrational because rational judgments are suspended or no longer applied with the same rigour. In Plato's *Phaedrus*, Socrates comments: "the irrational desire that leads us toward the enjoyment of beauty and over-powers the judgment that directs us toward what is right, and that is victorious in leading us toward physical beauty when it is powerfully strengthened by the desires related to it, takes its name from this very strength and is called love."[7] Nor are there moral strictures, for judgment in moral matters is suspended as well. After all, moral considerations play a secondary role, if they play one at all, with Anna Karenina, or Phèdre, or Emma Bovary or Don Giovanni. And morality, too, has been associated with activity of the frontal cortex.[8]

Euphoria and suspension of judgment can lead to states that others might interpret as madness. It is this madness that poets and artists have celebrated, Plato considering it in *Phaedrus* as a productive, desirable state because it comes from God, whereas sober sense is merely human. But of course if it comes from God, it transcends the world of rationality and is beyond the grasp of the intellect or *logos*. Perhaps the neurological explanations, of a de-activation of those parts of the brain that are involved in the making of judgments, makes the frequent apparent irrationality of love more comprehensible. As Nietzsche wrote in *Thus Spoke Zarathustra*, "There is always some madness in love. But there is always some reason in madness," the reason to be sought in the pattern of neurobiological activation and de-activation that romantic love entails, which serves the higher purpose of uniting for biological purposes even unlikely pairs, and thus enhancing variability. If "the heart has its reasons of which reason knows nothing," it is quite literally because reason is suspended. When Blaise Pascal uttered these words in his *Pensées* he could not have known that reason is suspended because the frontal lobes are (temporarily at least) also suspended. In fact, we can draw a neurobiological lesson from this selective suspension of judgment. For, if those in love suspend judgment about their lovers, they do not necessarily also suspend judgment about other things. They could, for example, be perfectly able to judge the quality of a book or of a scientific work. They could also be perfectly able to have a theory of mind regarding persons other than the one they love. The suspension of judgment is selective, and argues for a very specific set of connections and brain operations when it comes to love.

Neural Correlates of Maternal Love

Equally interesting is that this pattern of areas activated by romantic yearnings shares parts of the brain that also become active when mothers view pictures of their own children, as opposed to other children.[1] Maternal and romantic love share a common and crucial evolutionary purpose, that of maintaining and promoting the species. They also share a functional purpose, in that both require that individuals stay together for a period of their lives. Both are thus calculated by nature to ensure the formation of firm bonds between individuals, by making them rewarding experiences. It is not surprising to find that both sentiments share common brain areas. But, given the neurological axiom stated above – that if you can tell the difference it is because different brain areas are involved – it is also not surprising to find that the

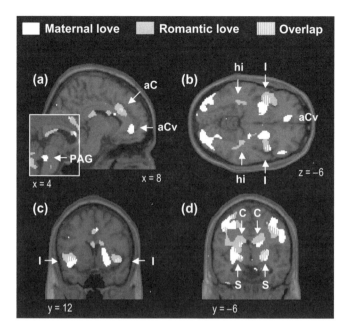

Figure 16.3. Brain activity produced by maternal love and romantic love, in both males and females. Areas specific to maternal love are shown in white, and those specific to romantic love in gray. Note that there are considerable areas of overlap (shown in stripes), although there are also regions that are activated only by maternal or romantic love. Abbreviations: aC = anterior cingulate cortex; aCv = ventral aC; C = caudate nucleus; I = insula; S = striatum (consisting of putamen, caudate nucleus, globus pallidus); PAG = periaqueductal (central) gray; hi = hippocampus. Figure adapted from Bartels A, Zeki S (2004). The neural correlates of maternal and romantic love. *Neuroimage* **21**(3): 1155–1166, figure 3.

pattern of brain activation that correlates with maternal love is not identical to the one that correlates with romantic love (Figure 16.3). An interesting difference lies in the strong activation of parts of the brain that are specific for faces in maternal love. This may be accounted for by the importance of reading children's facial expressions, to ensure their well being and therefore the constant attention that a mother pays to the face of her child. Another interesting difference is that the hypothalamus, which is associated with sexual arousal, is only involved in romantic love. The commonly activated regions between the two types of love are located in the striatum, which is part of the reward system of the human brain. It is also true that in maternal love, just as in romantic love, judgment is somewhat suspended, in that mothers are a good deal more indulgent with their children and perhaps less likely to fault them. Once again, we find that there is a pattern of cortical de-activation produced by maternal love that is remarkably similar to the one produced by romantic love and in particular in the frontal cortex which is involved in the formation of judgments (Figure 16.4). It is a truism to say that most

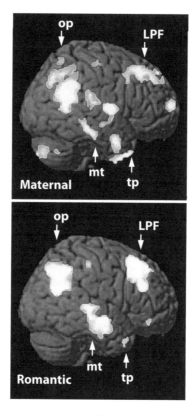

Figure 16.4. Deactivated regions with maternal and romantic love, shown in white and light gray. Abbreviations: mt = middle temporal cortex; op = occipito-parietal junction; tp = temporal pole; LPF = (ventral) lateral prefrontal cortex. Figure adapted from Bartels A, Zeki S (2004). The neural correlates of maternal and romantic love. *Neuroimage* **21**(3): 1155–1166, figure 2.

people develop a preference for the kind of person they want to love, and hence a concept of their potential lover(s); their likelihood of falling in love with that kind of person is that much greater. These preferences come in many different forms and are almost certainly conditioned by, among other things, parental influences, cultural predilections and the kind of person they may have met. A recent study has in fact charted the "average" man with whom women are most likely to fall in love.[9] He is smooth-skinned and remote from the kind of macho type that most believe are attractive to women. The characteristics associated with the most desirable (virtual) man are not only linked to sexual attractiveness but also to factors that suggest a caring attitude. Clearly, this average man, chosen by female subjects in Scotland and in Japan is the result of a concept and may apply only to the environment in which the study was conducted. The importance of the study lies in showing us that we do indeed form a concept of the kind of person we would like to love.

In matters of love and attachment, we can go a little further and sketch in outline the chemistry that underlies the concept of the loved one that the brain forms. Unfortunately we cannot do so for humans yet but we can for much simpler animals – the prairie voles, rats, mice, marmosets and monkeys – but it would be hard to believe that essentially similar, though almost certainly infinitely more complex, mechanisms do not operate in humans.

Perhaps the first step in this inquiry is to look at the chemistry of the human brain areas that are activated during romantic love, especially oxytocin, vasopressin and dopamine. Most brain regions, including sub-cortical regions, that have been determined to contain receptors for oxytocin and vasopressin are activated by both romantic and maternal love. To better understand the role of these chemicals in bonding, we have to rely on recent experiments in prairie voles.

Oxytocin and vasopressin are major neuro-modulator hormones secreted by the posterior pituitary gland and consisting of nine amino acids. They have many effects but most relevant from our point of view is that, not only are they involved in bonding between individuals but they have also been found to be effective in learning and memory, but only in a social context. Both are released when prairie voles have sex. They are intimately linked to dopamine, which is associated with reward. And although prairie voles are a long way from humans, the release of these hormones in other animals, including

humans, under similar conditions makes it likely that their human counterparts are also strongly involved in activities associated with romantic
and maternal love, which is not to say that these are their only functions. The story of voles is actually of great biological interest, especially when one contrasts two species, the prairie and the montane
vole, the former having monogamous relationships (with the occasional
fling thrown in) and the latter indulging in promiscuous sex without
long-term attachment.[10] If the release of these two hormones is
blocked in prairie voles, they too become promiscuous. If, however,
prairie voles are injected with these hormones but prevented from
having sex, they will continue to be faithful to their partners, that is,
to have a monogamous though chaste relationship. One might have
imagined that injection of these hormones into the promiscuous
montane voles would make them virtuous, monogamous, animals too,
but that is not how things work out. This may seem at first paradoxical,
but there is a simple biological way of accounting for it and it is of
substantial interest in the context of concept formation.

Once secreted by the pituitary, neuro-hormones can only act if there
are receptors for them. In the prairie vole there is an abundance of
receptors for vasopressin and oxytocin in the reward centers of the
brain. Receptors for oxytocin and vasopressin are missing or not as
abundant in the reward centers of the montane voles. Hence inject-
ing montane voles with a surplus of these two neuro-hormones does
not make them monogamous, since there are not sufficient receptors
for them in the reward centers. It is as if these two hormones,
strongly implicated from other evidence with bonding, are the ones
that keep voles faithful and monogamous and as if the absence of receptors for them makes their relatives promiscuous animals. There is no
evidence that these two neuro-hormones act in the same way in humans;
it would be surprising if they did, given the infinitely more complic-
ated structure of the human brain. But going again by what I wrote
earlier, namely that evolution uses a good solution over and over again
and adapts it to changing conditions, it would not be surprising if
we find in the vole a vestigial system to account for the sexual and
romantic nature of humans. Mankind is often, but very mistakenly,
considered to be monogamous. The evidence from divorce rates,
adultery and other more or less clandestine and casual encounters, as
well as the flourishing trade in prostitution and pornography, suggests
otherwise, which is not to say that many among the human race do

not maintain monogamous, or serially monogamous, relationships. It would be highly interesting to learn whether (mainly) monogamous humans have a higher concentration of oxytocin and vasopressin, as well as a richer concentration of receptors for them in the reward centers of the human brain compared to their more promiscuous counterparts. One might even find that humans can be divided into three or more categories – ranging from the extremely promiscuous to the strictly monogamous – and that this distribution reflects the distribution of receptors for vasopressin and oxytocin, which is known to vary in species as far apart as voles and humans.

Oxytocin and vasopressin seem to play a crucial role in forming a concept of the kind of partner that an organism wants to be with, at least in the world of vole ideas. They appear to do so by building a strong profile of the mating partner through odor and, once they do so, the odor-derived concept seems to be very stable. The odor comes to be associated with a pleasurable and rewarding encounter with a particular partner. The same works in the visual domain, as has been shown in sheep – once oxytocin is released in the presence of a baby, the sheep will visually recognize the baby and behave in a motherly way toward it until it is grown up. If the gene for either of these two neuro-modulators is disabled before birth by genetic engineering in a mouse, the mouse will no longer be able to form a profile – or a concept – of the mice that it meets.[10] It becomes totally amnesic in this regard and hence promiscuous. It is not outrageous to suggest that this neuro-chemically mediated experience has all the hallmarks of concept formation, but concept formation at a very elementary, chemical, level. The concept formed is that of an individual; it is based on an encounter and sexual experience, is acquired post-natally and is associated with a pleasurable, rewarding, experience with a partner of a particular odor.

Our knowledge of the brain's love system is still far too sketchy, but enough is known to be able to say that there are definitive pathways devoted to love and bonding and that neurochemicals play a crucial role in promoting attachments. In the vole, at least, they seem to play a major role in building a profile or concept of the lover. The concept so formed is extremely simple compared to the concept formed in humans. It does not seem to change with further exposure, as evidently happens in many humans. Moreover, the evidence from voles and other such animals does not and cannot tell us whether they form a concept of love (as opposed to the loved partner), beyond the fact that they have an inherited system for attachment and bonding that results in mating. We have no comparable evidence from neurobiology for humans. We only have hints and guesses – the presence of oxytocin, vasopressin and dopamine, and their release with rewarding experiences and during the formation of attachments. To obtain better evidence that humans also have a concept of love, it is to the literature of love that we have to turn.

Love and Beauty

A beautiful person, as is commonly known, is perhaps the surest way of evoking the sentiment of love. Throughout history, from the days of Plato onwards, the path to love has been described as being through beauty. Dante falls in love with Beatrice because he finds her beautiful, and longs to see that which is hidden in her physique. The Lord Krishna "steals the mind" with his beauty and Majnun, in his love for Leila, is obsessed by her beauty, even if she does not seem beautiful to others. "To see her beauty," he declares, "you must borrow my eyes." Beauty and love are themselves never far from erotic desire, since the most intense love is strongly coupled to sexual desire and the two faculties share common areas in the brain, as described above. It is not surprising to find therefore that an attractive face[11] on the one hand and sexual arousal by visual stimuli[12] on the other both engage the orbito-frontal cortex, as does the experience of beauty.[13] Nor is this the only common brain region engaged by the two aspects of romantic love. The face of a loved person engages the insula and the anterior cingulate, as do sexually arousing visual stimuli. Attractive faces, as well as the faces of a loved person,[1] de-activate not only the frontal cortex but also the amygdala, a nucleus located at the tip of the temporal lobes that is de-activated when viewing the face of a loved person, suggesting that not only is judgment less severe when looking at a loved or desired person but that the studied apprehension with which we often survey faces for discomfiting signs is suspended. Moreover, the orbito-frontal cortex is connected with the amygdala and with other cortical and sub-cortical areas – the anterior cingulate cortex, the putamen and the caudate – that are engaged during the experience of romantic love.[14] Hence the intimate experiential connection between love and beauty probably reflects the intimate anatomical connection between the centers that are involved in these two experiences. So intimate must the anatomical link between them be that the experiences themselves become difficult to disentangle.

The anatomical connections that I refer to above have been derived mainly from the monkey, but it is reasonable to suppose that very similar, if not identical, links will be found to exist in the human brain once anatomical studies in the latter progress far enough. There is another limitation here that is well worth emphasizing. Areas such as the orbito-frontal cortex and the cingulate cortex are large cortical regions and, in the present state of anatomical studies, it is difficult to know which subdivisions of each project elsewhere and which subdivisions are functionally equivalent in the human and in the monkey from which these anatomical studies derive. To go into a discussion of these would be to speculate way beyond what the evidence would permit. Rather, the evidence that there must be a strong neural link comes from studying the literature of love, which is yet another reason why neurobiology should use evidence from products of the brain.

Chapter 17

Brain Concepts of Unity and Annihilation in Love

The concept of "unity-in-love" is such a recurring theme in world literature that it is hard to believe that it does not constitute an essential, inherited brain concept linked to love (Figure 17.1). As we saw, the concept may be strongly linked to mentalizing activity of the brain

(a)   (b)

Figure 17.1. Unity-in-love as represented by (a) a primitive African sculpture from the Lobi tribe in Burkina Faso (author's collection) and (b) A. Burdakov (author's collection, 2005, Courtesy Anton Burdakov).

and the suppression of certain parts of the brain that distinguish between the self and others (see Chapter 16). The concept has three features. First, the inherited brain concept of passionate love – that of unity – does not have an infinite number of facets but only one, which comes therefore to be applied indifferently wherever love prevails – indifferently, that is, to who it is that one loves. As La Rochefoucauld observed in his *Maximes*, "There is only one kind of love but there are a thousand different copies" (*Il n'y a que d'une sorte d'amour, mais il y en a mille différentes copies*). While many works in the literature of love have been addressed to women by men, some of the most romantic and touching poetry addressed to a lover, especially in mystic Persian poetry, has been to same sex lovers, of which the Persian mystics and poets Hafiz, Sa'di and Rumi are good examples. And yet, perhaps reflecting prudishness and certainly unaccomplished scholarship, it has been more acceptable, and easy, for many to present these poems as if addressed to someone of the opposite sex. That they have been able to do so with such ease is almost certainly a reflection of the fact that the underlying concept is the same regardless of the gender of the person to whom love is directed. This re-writing of the intention of lovers has been very common with Western renderings of Persian and Arabic poetry; there was a time when even Shakespeare's sonnets, many addressed to his "lovely boy," were rendered into the feminine. Although these transgressions may be of interest to scholars, they are of little interest to us in the context of the brain concept of love, except for what they imply. And the implication is quite clear, that regardless of gender the concept of love remains the same, although its physical expression may vary. An interesting insight into this is gained from a recent brain imaging study, which showed that viewing attractive faces engages the orbito-frontal cortex, the same region of the brain that is engaged when we look at what we regard as beautiful scenes. The strength of engagement was proportional to the subjective experience of how attractive a face was. Significantly, the activation was not related in any specific way to sexual orientation, in the sense that the strength of activation in men, for example, was proportional to the subjective experience of attractiveness of the viewed face. For men who preferred women, the strength of activation was related to the valence of attraction experienced, and the result was much the same for men who preferred men.[1]

Another feature of the concept of "unity-in-love" is that it has also been applied by humans in very similar, if not identical, terms and with the same wished-for outcome to the love of God. This again is an indication of the limitations of the concept of love, since the same characteristics portray the love of humans for each other and their love of God – at least as judged by human writings. As I shall explore later, there are many works in world literature, as well as in artistic achievements, where the boundary between the sacred and the profane is much eroded. These works can be, and have been, read in both senses. This in itself tells us something about the scope as well as the limitations of brain concepts of love, that it has only one, seemingly inflexible, feature – that of unity – and that feature seems to be equally applicable to both kinds of love. It is not surprising to find, therefore, that a poet can address in a reversible way his passion for union with a lover or with God, as we shall see in Chapter 18, where I also explore its neurobiological implications.

A third feature is inherent in the very concept of unity. Unity implies an obliteration of the self and its merging with the other. It implies, in short, an annihilation: annihilation in the beloved, annihilation in God, who is also the Beloved. But annihilation, in the sense of the merging of two individual entities into one, is not achievable on earth except through death. Hence the ardent and recurring wish for death in the literature of love, for only then, in another world, is this annihilation and subsequent unification possible. The two concepts of unity and annihilation are therefore intimately linked and almost certainly the consequence of our incapacity to achieve the unity that biology has ingrained in our mental constitution as a concept. Is it any wonder that Virgil signals to Dante, in the *Inferno*, the many who have departed this world because of love:

> He showed me Paris and Tristan, and a thousand other shades
> he pointed out and named and said
> that it is love that made them depart this world.

Kant, Schopenhauer and Unity

It is not only in writing about love that the concept of unity takes such a prominent place. Schopenhauer thought much about unity and believed that the closest one could get to it was through the union of sexual love, though even that gave nothing more than a fleeting glimpse. The theme of "oneness" and unity becomes one of the central points in his philosophy, a philosophy that much influenced Wagner, especially when he wrote *Tristan und Isolde*, where the longing for union, the obliteration of the "I" that separates them and the discussion of the "und" that binds them together plays so prominent a role, particularly in its Second Act. The philosophy itself is difficult going and would require many pages to expound, beginning with a review of the work of Kant, which Schopenhauer recommends as a necessity before starting to read his own work. I do so here only briefly and then only to emphasize the theme of unity and its grander implications.

Many philosophers regard Kant as among their greatest. Unfortunately, not enough neurobiologists have recognized the importance of his contribution to our subject. Kant inaugurated a manner of thinking about knowledge and its acquisition that is fundamental to neurobiology. As explained earlier, he supposed that our knowledge of this world depends not only upon the physical reality but also on the contribution that the mind (in our instance, the brain) makes to the acquisition of that knowledge and the limitations that it imposes upon it. All that we know or are capable of knowing, we know through the operations of the mind (the brain). We can therefore never know things as they are (*Das Ding an sich*). But there are, or might be, a whole range of things that our brains are not capable of registering. Consequently, we can therefore never be sure of the existence of such things. It is common knowledge that there are some sensory experiences that we are denied, which other organisms are capable of registering. Those things that lie outside the capacity of our brains to register must forever lie outside our sphere of knowledge, and the existence of God is among these. Kant believed, paradoxically, that he could be religious precisely because the existence of God was, to him, something that lies beyond all possibility of knowledge and thus cannot be questioned.

Those things that we are equipped to experience and thus acquire a knowledge of belong, in Kant's philosophy, to the *phenomenal* world, while those that we are incapable of experiencing belong to the *noumenal* world. Using philosophical arguments, Schopenhauer argued in *The World as Will and Representation* (*Die Welt als Wille und Ausstellung*) that the phenomenal world is merely the perceivable part of the noumenal world, which must remain forever occult. This led him to suppose that human beings are merely the outward manifestations, in the phenomenal world, of the unified and timeless noumenal world, where there are no distinctions because there is nothing but an undifferentiated oneness. And to him the closest that humans could come to experiencing that undifferentiated oneness was in a loving sexual relationship. But such a relationship is brief, and the participants return to individuality without achieving the ultimate union, that of oneness. The latter can only be achieved in death. And this is the ultimate wish not only of Tristan and Isolde but of countless other lovers.

This desire for unity and oneness, with love and sexuality being the closest but still illusory way of achieving it, is characteristic not only of humans but sometimes even of gods, or in the projection of human feelings into those of gods, as in the Hindu legend of the God Krishna and his lover Radha. For them, too, the ultimate way of achieving that union lies in extinction, in the supreme unity of Brahman, the single supreme, transcendent and timeless, omnipotent and omnipresent Being. But this is only achievable in death. Only then is the incessant longing for the other half extinguished and love itself ceases to exist. Is it not surprising that in his great operatic exposition of love Wagner should have described his opera as one dealing "with a single emotion, that of longing without end and without satisfaction" and that he should have portrayed the lovers as ecstatically yearning for death, where they see the promise of the "utmost rapture." Schopenhauer himself was surprised to find that his outlook had precedents in Hinduism and Buddhism, which regard humans as illusory manifestations of an undifferentiated and timeless oneness, to which one should aspire to return. It is in fact not surprising that different cultures should have emphasized this desire for oneness and used love as a vehicle for achieving it. As I shall try to show, the similarity does not rest with Hinduism or Buddhism. It is characteristic of all great love literature. What we are witnessing here is the reflection, in the artistic world, of the inherited brain concept that uses this desire for unity as a means of promoting the success of the species. The real surprise would have been if different cultures of different times had reached different conclusions, given the essential similarity in brain concepts, at least at this level of analysis.

In the mystical and occult writings that belong to the Hindi and Buddhist scriptures, the *Tantras*, the union and the desire for its attainment are given cosmic dimensions, with man and woman being merely the earthly aspects of the cosmic Śiva and Śakti. "In the ritualized sexual union of the man and the woman all the polar opposites are to be united – there is to be a re-conquest of the primordial unity, the ultimate unified reality behind appearance."[2] Elsewhere, as in the *Gitagovinda* of Sri Jayadeva, the twelfth century Bengali poet, the Lord Krishna, 8th avatar (reincarnation) of Vishnu, indulges in trysts with cowherdesses until he falls desperately in love with a married woman, Radha, with whom he aims to be united in love. By thus giving the god Krishna a human aspect and setting, and human desires too, the ultimate search and desire for sacred and cosmic unity is transferred not only to humans in general, but by humans to the gods themselves.

So intense is this desire for unity that, in its service, even genders are sometimes transgressed and the lover (the god, Lord Krishna) tries to experience the erotic feelings of Radha by taking on a feminine role during sexual encounters. Conversely, with love for the Lord Krishna being at least in part erotic in nature, all male saints and those who aspire to union with Him must adopt a feminine stance. The fourteenth to fifteenth century Indian poet Surdas, celebrating the love of Krishna and Rhada in a Hindustani dialect, writes:

> You become Radha and I will become Madhava, truly
> Madhava; this is the reversal which I shall produce. I shall
> braid your hair and will put (your) crown on my head.

And, Surdas says, "Thus the Lord becomes Radha and Radha the son of Nanda."[3] Radha, too, is urged to make love to Krishna in the "inverse" mode and so she mounts him. Similarly, in Act 2 of *Tristan und Isolde*, Tristan declares "I am Isolde, you Tristan" while Isolde says "I am Tristan, you Isolde."

Nor is the supreme god always male. In the Hindi Tantric tradition, gods were subordinate to goddesses and men to women. But the ultimate aim was always the same: "the worship of a Goddess (Devi) in all her beauty and voluptuousness was a way for her devotee to dissolve the union of soul and bond and savour(s) the sweetness called supreme Brahman,"[2] Brahman being the Single Unitary Deity and the sum total of the Universe and all that is in it.

In Hindu culture, the principle and creator of all things and the totality of the Universe – Brahman – cannot be loved: Brahman is the Self, the two united where there is no distinction between lover and beloved. Love itself becomes irrelevant, for its aims have been achieved, or do not even arise in the one Self. Since unity is achieved and love is therefore extinguished, so is the unquenchable longing for it, a longing so prominent in love literature. In the Sufi[4] tradition, the Iberian-Arabic Islamic scholar Muhyiddin Ali Ibn al-Arabi used the term *wuhdat al wujud*, which also signifies a yearning for the same state, an annihilation in God. This term is usually translated into "unity of being." In fact, *wujud* also means "found" or "finding" and both it and *mawjud* also mean "present" or "presence." It is thus a complex term and is perhaps better rendered into "unity of existence." There is an ambiguity here, in that existence does not necessarily imply annihilation. Moreover, since God, in the Sufi tradition, is the perfect and the eternal, He is one to whom no human, and therefore created, person can have total access, thus mirroring in the human love of God the endless and unquenchable longing that is a hallmark of human love. In fact, in Arabic literature, the difficulty of complete union (*wuhda*) with the divine, even in annihilation (*fana'*), is implicitly acknowledged through use of the metaphor of ocean to describe the unity, since its waves, which take on different forms, are individual but ephemeral; they rise and fall back into the vast depths of the ocean, "which, psychologically, symbolizes so perfectly the *longing* of the individual for union and annihilation in the whole"[5] (my emphasis).

A picture of that desire for annihilation in order to achieve unity is often found in the world literature of love. In the Tristan and Isolde legend, as interpreted in Richard Wagner's opera, the central preoccupation of the lovers, especially in Act 2, is the "and" that will unite them and give them the "single breath of a single bond." It is their realization that this unity can only be achieved after death, in a mystical transfiguration (*Verklärung*), that makes them wish ecstatically for death (see Chapter 20). In one version of the Arabic-Azeri myth of Majnun-Leila (see Chapter 19), it is Majnun's realization that his unified concept of love with Leila is not true, even in the mind, that hastens his death. Rumi never ceases in his poetry to dream of that union. The ninth century Persian poet, mystic and theologian, Mansur Al-Hallaj, who longed for death so that it removes the distracting "I" that stands between lover and beloved, expresses the same sentiment when addressing himself to God, with whom he desires union, one that can only be achieved after death:

> I am He whom I love,
>   and He whom I love is I:
> We are two spirits
>   dwelling in one body.
> If thou seest me,
>   thou seest Him,
> And if thou seest Him,
>   thou seest us both.[6]

The list is endless and testifies to the central position of unity, and its corollary – annihilation – in concepts of love. Since the concept transcends cultures and time, it is hard to believe that it is not an ingrained brain concept.

Chapter 18

Sacred and Profane

There is an ambiguity, which has been used to advantage, in some affective states and especially in that pertaining to romantic and sacred love. The apparent ease with which the two have become interchangeable in the literature of love suggests that the brain systems dealing with these emotions are themselves inextricably linked and probably share common brain areas and pathways. This conclusion is of course tentative because there is no experimental evidence in its favor. The only evidence comes from the literature of love. A link between simple perceptual ambiguity and the ambiguity inherent in so exalted a sentiment as love may seem absurd. But, as described earlier, the brain repeats a solution that has been found to be expedient over and over again, to ensure its success.

We have seen how abstraction lies at the base of categorization and concept formation, and that concepts themselves therefore have an abstract side. We have seen how the brain has a system for categorizing some things as having a different magnitude to other things. Magnitude itself becomes a concept, mediated through a unique brain area in the parietal lobe and applied indifferently to what it is that differs in magnitude, provided only that there is a difference in magnitude. Much the same applies to patterns that occur irregularly in time, the brain seemingly being capable through a unique area, located in the frontal cortex, to determine such an irregularity whatever its source. This is not to say that the brain does not have other systems for differentiating between different irregular patterns. Obviously, a temporal irregularity in the visual domain is mediated through the visual cortex and recognized instantly as being visual while an auditory one is mediated through the auditory cortex, and so on.

Much the same applies to love. Love, with the desire for unity at its core, is applied in equal measure to romantic and to sacred love. They are both encompassed within a single concept, that of love; sacred and profane are merely two facets of it and share many characteristics that are defining of love: possessiveness, jealousy, exclusivity, and of course the desire to be united. Indeed, so conflated are the two concepts neurally that some cultures do not even make a distinction between the two; on the contrary, they regard sexual love as the closest one gets to union with God, and celebrate love-making as a religious undertaking and a path to God. This ambiguity can be found especially in texts where the writer seeks a path to union with God through love and union with an earthly person. Scholars and critics have argued endlessly about whether some of these texts are to be interpreted in a sacred or profane sense. To the neurobiologist who is trying to understand something about the brain by studying this literature, the different interpretations are equally valid. Indeed, the issue becomes, critically, not so much whether one interpretation or the other is the more plausible, but why two interpretations can be given and argued over for so many centuries. The answer must surely lie in a simple neurobiological fact, that the brain areas and systems dealing with the emotions of love themselves are not equipped to disentangle the two elements, since the two are entangled in the brain itself. The brain concept of love, with unity at its core, is apparently equally applicable to divine and profane love.

The merging of the two aspects of the same sentiment, love, can be discerned in the earliest cultures. Hence the prediction that when the brain mechanisms underlying religious experience come to be studied and compared to those engaged during romantic love – that is, whether the experience is an intense desire for unity with God or a romantic experience yearning for unity with the lover – contiguous brain areas that may even overlap substantially will be found to be engaged. The distinction between the two kinds of love depends upon other recognition systems in the brain, and sometimes even that is ineffective. It is for this reason that, in the examples given below, I do not take sides or value one interpretation more than the other. Both interpretations are valid because they represent a brain reality, or brain realities. To that extent, the reversibility of the sacred and the profane is an example of ambiguity generated by the brain. But there are differences with the kind of ambiguity that I discussed earlier. Like perceptual ambiguity, sacred and profane love may ride

serenely with one another, as with Dante. Unlike perceptual ambiguity, they may come into conflict, as in the example of Petrarch, or one
may be the vehicle for the other, as with Rumi, Hallaj and other Sufi
poets or in the Indian (Sanskrit) Bhakti tradition of intense devotion
and total servitude to the divine.

The Greeks, as well as other ancient cultures, projected their
human sentiments and deified them in gods of human construction.
There are many gods in Greek and ancient traditions, mostly concerned
with factors that are beyond human control – the seasons, the wind,
the sun, and, of course, love. That love is beyond one's control is
evident to most, and hence the allocation of a god (or more usually
goddess) of love is in keeping with the general tendency to give
the uncontrollable a divine status, and invoke its help when help is
needed. There is however an element of both sacred and profane in
the gods of love. They are not only gods and goddesses of love,
and by this very fact inject a divine element into love; they are often
associated with fertility as well, clearly implying a sexual component.
To the Phoenicians, Astarte is the goddess of love and fertility.
Xochiquetzal in Aztec culture serves much the same purpose, as do
Turan in Etruscan culture, Rath in Balinese, Qadesh in Egyptian, Nambi
in Masai, Morongo in Zimbabwean, Inernes in Micronesian, Inanna
in Sumerian, Freya in German, Eros in Greek and many others in
different cultures. Sometimes, the goddess or god is that of sacred
love and ecstasy mingled with sexual pleasure, as with the Egyptian
goddess Qadesh and with the Roman god Liber. There is even a
goddess (Lofn) for illicit love. Aphrodite, the Greek goddess of love,
beauty and sexual pleasure, had many priestesses who represented
her and sexual intercourse with them was regarded as a form of god
worship. The list is endless. And however the Greeks may have dis-
tinguished different kinds of love – erotic, fraternal, affectionate – it
is neurobiologically significant that they commonly embodied love and
desire in a single god. This is not to say that all gods and goddesses
of love always represented fertility as well. But the long list of those
who did is sufficient to suggest a strong association in the minds (and
hence the brains) of those who created the gods in the first place,
namely ordinary humans.

The association of the profane with the divine is also very much
evident in literature. *The Song of Songs* [also known as *The Song of
Solomon* or *The Canticle of Canticles*] is replete with erotic imagery

and speaks of the love of a woman and a man. No person who is not religiously minded or is not a religious exegete could possibly interpret lines such as

> Let me kiss him with the kisses of his mouth: for thy love is better than wine [Chapter 1, line 2]

or

> Thou hast ravished my heart, my sister, my spouse; thou hast ravished my heart with one of thine eyes, with one chain of thy neck.
> How fair is thy love, my sister, my spouse! how much better is thy love than wine! and the smell of thine ointments than all spices! [Chapter 4, lines 9–10]

in any sense other than an erotic one. Indeed the worldly imagery used is such that *The Song of Songs* was only admitted into the Canon in the second century, its canonization having been long opposed by religious scholars. But it has often been interpreted in an allegorical sense. This would be surprising, given the text, had it not been that, for the brain, the sacred and the divine concepts of love are subdivisions of the same concept, that of love, thus making it easy to mutate one interpretation into another. Many scholars, both Jewish and Christian, have asserted that the *Songs* could not be a depiction of worldly love. In the Jewish tradition, it has been interpreted to reflect the love of God for his people, and Christian scholars have taken up this tradition by interpreting the *Songs* to be a depiction of God's love for his Church or the love of God for the Virgin Mary. Christian exegetes saw in the *Songs* a prefiguring of the marriage of Christ (male) to his Church (female), a comparison that is rich in sexual connotation. Others justified a religious or mystical interpretation by what they believed to be improbabilities in the text. Bernard of Clairvaux argued against all reason that, in the lines quoted above, "kisses of his mouth" could only be interpreted in a spiritual sense since a man does not kiss a woman with the kisses of his mouth but with his mouth! Today, such an argument seems to us nothing more than a shallow excuse to infuse a sacred meaning into a profane text. What is interesting is that both interpretations can and have been given to the same texts. In a sense, therefore, there is no correct interpretation. Had there been one, the argument would not have lasted for so many millennia. What is reflected in this literature is a brain reality – that the brain's concept of love is one that is all-encompassing and cannot easily distinguish between the sacred and the profane.

Nor is the entanglement of the sacred and the profane only spiritual; it even expresses itself at the carnal level, the erotic element being an essential component of romantic love. Consider this passage from St. Teresa of Avila. She had had amorous flirtations in her youth and later, when she took the religious route, had been often castigated for having rapturous relations with Christ in her dreams, and accused of having been possessed by the devil. This is how she described one of her visionary dreams, using language that would not sit uneasily in a pornographic book:

> Beside me on the left appeared an angel in bodily form . . . He was not tall but short, and very beautiful; and his face was so aflame that he appeared to be one of the highest ranks of angels, who seem to be all on fire . . . In his hands I saw a great golden spear, and at the iron tip there appeared to be a point of fire. This he plunged into my heart several times so that it penetrated my entrails. When he pulled it out I felt that he took them with it, and left me utterly consumed by the great love of God. The pain was so severe that it made me utter several moans. The sweetness caused by this intense pain is so extreme that one can not possibly wish it to cease, nor is one's soul content with anything but God. This is not a physical but a spiritual pain, though the body has some share in it – even a considerable share.[1]

No less interesting is Bernini's famous depiction of her ecstasy at the Cornaro Chapel in Rome (*The Ecstasy of St. Teresa*, Figure 18.1). To some, this sculpture, with the rapturous face of St. Teresa, is a depiction of the moment of orgasm. Others have argued that Bernini, himself religiously devout, would not have done so consciously, that he was depicting instead the rapture during the experience of God, the so-called "sleep of God," and have compared it stylistically to his *Beata Ludovica Albertoni* at the Cappella Altieri in Rome.[2] A more realistic neurobiological interpretation would be that the religious Bernini certainly did not *consciously* intend to depict anything profane in his sculpture; rather, that the sculpture is a manifestation of the neurological entanglement of spiritual and profane love in his brain. That entanglement even extends to language. It is not at all bizarre,

Figure 18.1.   Gian Lorenzo Bernini, *The Ecstasy of St. Teresa*. Cornaro Chapel, Rome.

in the neurological sense, that we use the same word – love – to describe heavenly, spiritual or romantic associations. Very much the same is true of the visions of St. Teresa herself. I doubt very much that so religious a person would have *consciously* intended to express profane longings in her writings and then cloak them in religious sentiment as a protection. Rather her description, like the sculpture of Bernini, reflects the neurobiological reality. Hence, from a neurobiological viewpoint, which interpretation – the sacred or the profane – is the correct one is an irrelevancy. They both are and, once again, this impossibility of reaching a definitive conclusion itself tells us something about the neural mechanisms underlying the sentiment of love.

If the *Song of Songs* is somewhat too explicit to have a spiritual content for those who are not religious scholars, the dividing line between sacred and profane is a great deal more difficult to draw in other works of literature, whether one is religiously inclined or not.

Perhaps nowhere is this more evident than in Arabic and Sufi literature, where the "beloved" can be easily interpreted to refer to God
or to an actual person, to whom the poet may have strong emotional
attachments. Arabic and Persian mystical poetry often express lofty
spiritual sentiments, a longing for and a desire to be united with God.
But God, who is beautiful, is often addressed as the "Beloved," a term
that is also applied in the same poetry to a person. Hafiz often said
that he could see the image of God in the face of a beautiful youth
or of his beloved. There is nothing surprising in this. In common
language today, we often describe a very beautiful woman as a
goddess or a very handsome man as having "god-like" features. Like
Plato before them, the Sufis in general imagined that the path to divine
love commenced with earthly love, which was merely a preparation
for the former.[3] Indeed, many Sufis believed that human beauty
was an earthly manifestation of divine beauty. As with Plato, they
explained their tendency to contemplate and worship the limited and
ephemeral earthly beauty as a means of attaining Absolute and
boundless Beauty. In fact, there was a period when Sufis organized
evenings known as the *samā* (listening), whose purpose was to flirt
with female singers and gaze at beautiful youths. In general, these were
given a somewhat religious character and too much sensuality or
wine-drinking were frowned upon. The purpose was to contemplate
beauty and, above all, to see God through the beauty that He has
created. They argued that appreciating earthly beauty paved the way
to the contemplation of divine beauty and served as a bridge to the
love of the divine. For them, contemplation of a beautiful person was
the contemplation of God, since only God could produce a beautiful
person. The term commonly used for a beautiful youth is *shāhid*, which
in Arabic means witness but could also be interpreted to mean one
who is present. Thus God is present in the face of a beautiful youth.
The tenth century Arabic mystic poet, Sarraj, declares: "For Him, there
is a *shāhid* in every thing, which demonstrates that He is one."[3]

Death in Venice, the novella of Thomas Mann, has many precedents
in the poetry of Hafiz, Attar, Rumi, Sa'adi and other Sufis.

It would, I think, be a mistake to think of these gatherings (which
were actually common until relatively recently) as being solely exercises
in sensuality, an excuse to arouse erotic desires under the cloak of
respectable religious experience. It would equally be a mistake to think
of them as solely religious experiences or contemplative exercises

devoid of sensual, romantic and erotic connotations. They are in fact both, and that they are and can be both at the same time is a fact for which we must seek a neurobiological basis, even though we are today far from being able to do so with any great precision. Some translators, projecting their own assumptions into these works, suppose that "beloved" only refers to God, by capitalizing the B and rendering it as "Beloved." The truth is that it belongs to both heavenly and earthly love. As Annemarie Schimmel explains in her book *Mystical Dimensions of Islam*,[4] ". . . the nostalgia of the lover and the longing for union was expressed by symbols taken from human love; often a strange and fascinating combination of human and divine love permeates the verses of the mystics" in which an author "may describe God in terminology taken from a pure love relation and a few lines later use language that lends itself to an exclusively pantheistic interpretation." Thus, "The ambiguity of the experience of love, as it emerges from these mystical theories and practices, resulted in the use of erotic symbolism by the mystics and of mystical terms by the profane poets. The true, pure mystics have sometimes tried to explain the symbolism of earthly love and wine as completely allegorical."[4] It can indeed be said that we use the term mystical as an acknowledgment of the fact that there is a single concept of love in the brain, and that earthly and heavenly love are merely subdivisions of it.

Consider this passage from Jalluludin Rumi, addressed to Shamsuddin Tabrizi, to whom Rumi had a powerful attachment that, reflecting the neurobiological reality, is as ambiguous as St. Teresa's love for Christ. It may be a spiritual seeking for a union with God, but it is no less a celebration of a relationship with another human:

> What is to be done, O Moslems? for I do not recognize myself.
> I am neither Christian, nor Jew, nor Gabr, nor Moslem.
> I am not of the East, nor of the West, nor of the land, nor of the
>   sea;
> I am not of Nature's mint, nor of the circling' heavens.
> I am not of earth, nor of water, nor of air, nor of fire;
> I am not of the empyrean, nor of the dust, nor of existence, nor of
>   entity.
> I am not of India, nor of China, nor of Bulghar, nor of Saqsin
> I am not of the kingdom of 'Iraqian, nor of the country of Khorasan
> I am not of the this world, nor of the next, nor of Paradise, nor of
>   Hell

I am not of Adam, nor of Eve, nor of Eden and Rizwan.
My place is the Placeless, my trace is the Traceless;
'Tis neither body nor soul, for I belong to the soul of the Beloved.
I have put duality away, I have seen that the two worlds are one;
One I seek, One I know One I see, One I call.
He is the first, He is the last, He is the outward, He is the inward;
I know none other except 'Ya Hu' and 'Ya man Hu.'
I am intoxicated with Love's cup, the two worlds have passed out of
    my ken ;
I have no business save carouse and revelry.
If once in my life I spent a moment without you,
From that time and from that hour I repent of my life.
If once in this world I win a moment with you,
I will trample on both worlds, I will dance in triumph for ever.
O Shamsi Tabriz, I am so drunken in this world,
That except of drunkenness and revelry I have no tale to tell.
                                              From *Divan-i-Shams*[5]

Note that the capitalization of He and of Beloved imposes a spiritual
or divine interpretation, one that some scholars will dispute. If these
words had not been capitalized, the more plausible interpretation would
be a profane one, given Rumi's strong emotional and indeed romantic
attachment to *Shamsuddin*. It merely reflects the reality of the brain,
which forms a concept of love that encompasses both the divine and
profane, which, united within a single concept, become inseparable.

In an earlier chapter, I wrote of "unity" as constituting a fundamental, and unrealizable, concept since two individuals must forever
remain separate. The only possible solution to this problem is that of
extinction and annihilation, when even the concept itself no longer
exists. Annihilation is what Tristan and Isolde desire, as do Majnun
and Leila. We find much the same desire in literature dedicated to
the love of God and quite often the desire to be extinguished in the
lover is interchangeable with the desire to be extinguished in God.
The similarities here are striking. In his book *Das Meer der Seele* [*The
Ocean of the Soul*], Helmutt Ritter writes that, in many Sufi poems,
"Love of God as love of an unattainable object . . . expresses itself
on earth in forever unquenched longing . . . both for closeness to
God . . . , as well as disclosure of His essence and His person"[3] (my
ellipsis), a sentiment that both Thomas Mann, with his "permanent
dissatisfaction" (see Chapter 21) and Richard Wagner with his "longing

without end and without satisfaction" (see Chapter 20) would have understood well. And just as Majnun dismisses Leila, proclaiming "Be gone from me! Love for you so engages me that I have no time for you," so Ritter reports that when a Sufi was asked why he did not want to see God, he replied, "To me that beauty is too sublime that someone like me should see it." But if he knows that it is sublime, he must already have a concept of it, even a vague one, in his brain. Another Sufi asks to be resurrected blind, "for You're too lofty and sublime that any eye should see You."[3] – sublime and lofty as brain concepts of course, never to be lived in reality but only as synthetic brain concepts.

A supreme example of the conflation of heavenly and earthly love is to be found in Dante where, right from the start, in *La Vita Nuova* he invests Beatrice with heavenly qualities, describing her even in the second Canzone as a "tender angel" and quoting Homer to the effect that she was not the daughter of a mortal man but of a god. And all this while he reminds his reader, even as he progresses to the *Paradiso* in *The Divine Comedy*, that it is of an earthly person, Beatrice, that he is still writing. Charles Singleton has written in his book *Journey to Beatrice*[6] how, in *La Vita Nuova*, Beatrice had shown, "in her role in the poet's life, a miraculous resemblance to Christ; how, in fact, she had been seen, in a vision recounted at the center of the work, to die amidst signs which can call to mind no other death than Christ's, and then to rise to Heaven attended by angels and the cry of Hosanna in an ascension which is most like His." Singleton argues convincingly for a theological basis in Dante's description of the appearance of Beatrice in the *Divine Comedy*, basing himself largely on St. Bernard's *Sermons for the Season of Advent*. The argument runs that the Advent of Christ is triplex: His first coming – which has been – and His last – which shall be; in addition there is a third Advent, which is "spiritual and occult," for He comes to the receptive soul daily, "in spirit and invisibly." This third Advent is neither in the past nor in the future but is now and it occurs not once, as the first and third Advents, but repetitively. In this third Advent, St. Bernard declares in his fifth sermon, "He is hidden, visible only to the elect who see Him in themselves." The third Advent is thus the Sanctifying Grace that comes *in mentem*. It has a name or names, given by both St. Bernard and St. Thomas Aquinas. The names are: Wisdom and Grace and Sanctifying Grace, the very names that

Dante gives Beatrice. Though Beatrice is not of course Christ, the unconscious implication is obvious. Singleton declares, "those words must call to our mind Beatrice as she comes attended by her seven handmaids who are the seven infused Virtues. . . . And this being so, who would Beatrice be, if not Wisdom and Grace?"[6] She is in fact a substitute for Christ.

The conflation lasts to the very end. It is notable that, in the very last cantos of *The Divine Comedy*, Beatrice is replaced as the poet's guide by St. Bernard. Truly, this earthly love is unattainable, and the mind substitutes for it another love that is also unattainable on earth, namely heavenly love (it is worth repeating that Dante's journey is that of a man on earth, not one who is dead). St. Bernard tells Dante of the blessedness of the Virgin mother and begs her to give Dante the grace to contemplate the light of Divine Majesty. At the very end, he is admitted to a glimpse, no more (for he is still alive), of the mysterious Trinity and the Union of Man with God. The Light of Beatrice has been replaced by the Light of another woman, the Virgin Mary, *figlia del tuo figlio*, daughter of your son.

As Dante imparts a divine element to Beatrice, so does Petrarch in his *Canzoniere*, where he declares that as he hopes to gaze on the image of Him (Christ) who he longs to see in heaven, so he searches in others for the real Laura[7] (poem 16). But with Petrarch, we see another element of this two-faceted concept of love: the divine and the profane come into conflict. Petrarch sees his love for Laura as diminishing his love for God. He laments the squandered days: "Father of the Heavens, after the squandered days" (*Padre del ciel, doppo I perdutti giorni*) (poem 62), begs for forgiveness for his wandering and lustful thoughts and pleads with Him who suffered on the Cross to return him to a better place (*miglior luogo*) (poem 62). His love for Laura may have led him to a greater, spiritual love of God but the two were always in conflict, even after her death. Love had him burning for twenty-one years, and then for another ten after her death. But now:

> God on high, I render myself to you
> Penitent and saddened by my such ill-spent years

While sacred and profane are often conflated, thus permitting the reader to arrive at both a sacred and a profane interpretation, or to see one through the other, there are other cultures in which the two are made explicitly similar, or where the profane is regarded as the desirable and indeed only route to the sacred and to the union with the Lover. Perhaps the most extreme and explicit form of that desire for unity with the lover and, through the lover, with God, is to be found in the Bhakti tradition and in the legend of the Hindu god, Krishna, described earlier (Chapter 17). The Bhakti movement of devotion prescribes the virtues of possessing and being possessed by God and, for this, sexual union is regarded as the occasion where individuals come to closest possession. Hence, sexual relationship is regarded, and celebrated, as a means of getting closer to God. The adulterous love affair of Krishna-Radha is thus portrayed as reflecting the ultimate union, with God and the Universe. It is not therefore to be shunned, as in the Christian tradition, but to be embraced and practiced. As I described in Chapter 17, the intense desire for union even leads the devotees in some Hindi traditions to transgress gender boundaries, for only by doing so can they achieve union (see Chapter 17). Such crossing of lines is also there in Western literature, including even sacred literature, although perhaps not quite so explicitly. Examples are Dante's comparison of Beatrice to Jesus, and Petrarch's calls upon Jesus to deliver him from his lustful ways. But the thirteenth to fourteenth century Italian Franciscan friar Jacopone da Todi (Jacopo Benedicti) is a good deal more explicit, indeed not much less so than St. Teresa:

> Love, love, longed for Jesus; love, love, I yearn to die embracing thee; love, love, Jesus, my sweet bridegroom; love, love, I implore thee for death; love, love, Jesus so beloved, thou givest thyself to me by transforming me into thee.

Seemingly, so potent is the inherited brain concept of unity that almost any path for achieving it is acceptable.

I have chosen only a few examples here, from different cultures. The thought imposes itself: did these disparate authors, from different cultures, know of each others' writings? Once again, the answer is immaterial. The link one sees between the profane and the divine is a link in the concept of love, in the brain. That concept involves unity with the beloved or the Beloved, a unity that can only be achieved in death and extinction, whether the beloved is a person or is God.

Chapter 19

The Metamorphosis of the Brain Concept of Love in Dante

The work of Dante Alighieri is an interesting projection into art of the unsatisfied and seemingly commonly unsatisfiable sentiment of romantic love, in terms of both the inherited concept of unity-in-love and the acquired concept of the kind of person that one wants to love. It therefore provides interesting literary evidence for both kinds of brain concepts, and their consequences in the field of love. The originality of Dante's journey to Beatrice is that it is a journey of the mind and in the mind, the love having been kindled by his first sight of Beatrice but never subsequently satisfied. Through his work, one can trace some important consequences of this unquenched desire – its origins, the concept of the loved-one formed, the mental development of the concept and the near-impossibility of not only not finding a counterpart to that brain concept in real life but also of the difficulty of representing it, even in art. It also illustrates an important point, the metamorphosis of the synthetic concept in the brain. In Dante, this change is brought about not only by external experience but by the internal development of the concept itself, through what is perhaps inappropriately called the imagination, and I have already emphasized that the acquired concept can develop internally in the brain even when the object that is its basis is absent. Though Dante's work towers above much else written during his period, it is nevertheless worth recalling that idealization of a woman, usually someone other than a wife, was common in the culture to which Dante belonged.[1] This emphasizes the importance not only of the cultural context within which Dante worked, but of cultural contexts in general in the formulation of concepts. It also raises the question of why this kind of idealization should have occurred so commonly in literature. Dante's "love at a distance" is representative of courtly love in general and of the writings of many

troubadour poets and princes. But even before Dante, the general ascend-
ance to the heavens through earthly and commonly chaste love is a
recurring theme among the Persian mystics and, before them, in the
writings of Plato.

The love affair between Dante and Beatrice Portinari is one of the
most famous in Western literature, and also one of the most bizarre.
It is bizarre in at least three ways: it was a childhood love affair that
triggered the concept of the perfect, idealized, woman in his brain
and led to a life-long passion, although the two met in the first decade
of life, when they were not even in their teens. It is indeed doubtful
whether they ever exchanged any words. What seems more certain is
that they exchanged glances. He saw her on two or three occasions;
she smiled at him on one and did not on the other. The uncertainty
in her intentions that this reflected sent him into deep depression. She
married a rich banker at the age of fourteen and died soon thereafter
but remained in his mind throughout his life, a potent symbol of love
and beauty. It is bizarre, next, because there is no indication that his
profound love for her was ever reciprocated, except in his imagination. It is bizarre, too, because in spite of these very brief encounters
and lack of reciprocity Beatrice became the main preoccupation of
Dante's life – even in spite of his marriage and his political involve-
ments – and the inspiration for the creation of one of the most prized
literary achievements in Western culture. This is important to bear
in mind because, together with their rare and fleeting encounters, it
suggests that the entire love affair is a creation of Dante's and his alone,
with little or no input from Beatrice save two or three fleeting views.
Dante tells us as much in his first book, *La Vita Nuova* (*The New Life*),
when he declares that he will write about "*la gloriosa donna de la mia
mente*" (the glorious lady of my mind). He was to marry Gemma Donati
but she does not figure in any of his writings, and we can only
presume that this was a marriage of convenience and convention, not
of passion. In fact, there is only one other female figure who takes a
prominent place in Dante's work – Donna Gentile. She appears in
the second half of *La Vita Nuova* as a real person, creating a tension
in him between his love of Beatrice and her. But she remains an
ambiguous figure. In the *Convivio*, written some ten years after *La
Vita Nuova*, Dante equates her with Lady Philosophy, who instills
in him the philosophical virtues of Wisdom, and consoles him for
Beatrice's death. Her existence as a real person has been doubted.[2]

Dante seems to have preferred to stick to the glorious lady of his mind. It is perhaps as well for posterity that he did so and did not actually marry Beatrice and that she could, therefore, remain entirely a brain concept, the concept of love and of a woman that he could glorify in a work of art. When Dante declared in *La Vita Nuova* that he intends to write of her (Beatrice) as no man had ever written about a woman (*"io spero di dicer di lei quello qua ma non fue detto d'alcuna"*), he was in fact going to write not of Beatrice but of the glorious lady of his mind, his concept of her.

Dante's allegorical journey is the journey of a *living* man on this earth, and he emphasizes more than once that he will take this same route again, but as a dead soul. This is important to bear in mind, for the metamorphosis of his concept of Beatrice and his love for her is taking place in his brain as a living person. It begins with desire and expands love beyond desire, into a vision of beauty and hope and ultimately union with God. Nor is Dante alone in thus writing of the metamorphosis of the concept of love in the brain of a lover. Nur-Eddin Abdulrahman Jami, the thirteenth century Persian (Sufi) mystic and poet whose book *Salaman and Absal* is an allegory of sacred and profane love, has this to say: "Beholding in many souls the traits of Divine beauty, and separating in each soul that which it has contracted in the world, the lover ascends to the highest beauty, to the love and knowledge of Divinity, by steps of this ladder of created souls," a theme not dissimilar to the one expounded by Dante and, before him, by Plato in *The Symposium*. Both Dante and Jami are antedated also by the story of Majnun and Leila, which has several versions. The origin of that love story, popular even today throughout the middle and far east, lies in a poem by a sixth century Arab poet, Umru'l Qays, of the period known as the *Jahiliyeh* (age of ignorance), a century before the advent of Islam. Its more celebrated version is by the twelfth to thirteenth century Azeri poet and writer Ilyas Ibn Yusuf Nizami. It tells, as is common, of the passionate but hopeless and doomed love of Majnun (which in Arabic means mad) and Leila (which means night), an interesting and neurobiologically very appropriate choice of names. In summary, Majnun is consumed by his passion for Leila but, belonging to a different tribe and being poor, is prevented from marrying her. She is instead given in marriage to another, conventionally more suitable man, although the marriage remains unconsummated and the unquenched and unsatisfied longing of Leila for Majnun continues. Majnun begins to glorify Leila in his poetry and shuns society, preferring to live in caves in the company of beasts. Gradually his concept of Leila metamorphoses and he builds an idealized portrait of her in his poetry, by which I mean of course that he builds up his own unique concept of Leila. The idealized brain concept that he has of her is so different from her that the real Leila becomes secondary in importance to, a shadow of, the "glorious" Leila of Majnun's creation. In fact, Majnun, invoking the eternal brain concept of unity-in-love, feels that he and Leila have become one – which in a sense they have since he has created her in his mind and this mental portrait of her is unique and belongs to him alone. "They said to Majnun: 'Leila has come!' He said: 'I am myself Leila!' and then stuck his head under his garment again." [3] When told that he can, after a prolonged period of longing, see Leila, he replies that he does not want to see any woman, and that remembering Leila (through the record and concept in his brain) "is more dear to me than Leila herself." [3] When she comes to see him, he says to her, "Be gone from me! Love for you so engages me that I have no time for you!" [3] In one version, Leila dies before Majnun, and he exclaims, "Thanks be to God," just as Dante "kills off" Beatrice in his mind, in the central canzone of *La Vita Nuova* (see below). The unity that Majnun seeks is in fact already in him, in the brain concept that he has of Leila and of love, just as the unity that Rimbaud's prince sought was in his brain concept of love. Their passionate love remains unconsummated, as in Wagner's *Tristan und Isolde*, and also as in the latter they die symbolically buried together, to achieve that unity in the nether world.

Closer in time to Dante, Francesco Petrarch wrote in his *Canzoniere* passionate poems of love and eroticism to a woman, Laura, whom he first saw at a church in Avignon. It is said that this was the pursuit of a hopeless love from the start, for she was already married and, here again, we witness a conceptual change as Petrarch's love for Laura becomes conflated with his love of God, to whom he ultimately surrenders his love. There are strong similarities in this conceptual development of a woman in Dante and Petrarch, for neither of them seems to have known the women they were exalting in any real sense and certainly not in the biblical sense. Indeed, the existence of Laura herself has been doubted, the implication being that she was entirely the creation of his brain. The allegation was actually made even during Petrarch's lifetime by his friend, Cardinal Giacomo Colonna, drawing an outraged rebuttal from him: "You say that I invented the beautiful name of Laura . . . so that others would speak of my (poetic) merit . . . that indeed there was no Laura except the one in my poetic imagination . . . I wish indeed that she had been a fiction and not a madness"[4] (my ellipsis). Scholars may search, perhaps as vainly as in the past, for the real Laura, for whether she existed or not. Whatever their findings, Colonna's accusation will remain true and Petrarch's rebuttal false. For Laura *was* an invention of Petrarch's brain. How else could it be when she herself (assuming her to have existed at all) rejected him and apparently had only very limited exchanges with him?

Love at a distance, love that remains perpetually unsatisfied and therefore remains in the mind alone, as a concept, are also dominant themes in troubadour poetry. Denis de Rougement writes that, "there is, in the whole of occitan lyrics, and in petrarquesque and dantesque lyrics, a single theme: love, and not love that is satisfied . . . but on the contrary love that is perpetually unsatisfied."[5] Perhaps we should be precise here and say that when we speak of love that remains unsatisfied we are speaking of unsatisfied in terms of the inherited concept of love and the acquired concept of the lover formed in the brain, for by what other yardstick can we proclaim that it is unsatisfied? This concept of love that remains perpetually unsatisfied is not unique to the troubadours and the Cathares either. Some have traced it to earlier times, to Arab mystics, to the Latin poetry of the eleventh and twelfth centuries or to Christian religious influences. Denis de Rougemont traces it to religious Manicheans' beliefs that lie at the basis of heretical Christian sects of the Albigensis. The latter had created a "Church of Love" in which chastity was a fundamental virtue. Earlier still, the intense, nostalgic and poignant yet sweet joy that love in separation (known in Hindi as *viraha*) entails is celebrated in the legend of Krishna-Radha. Views about the derivation of the doctrine of the "perpetually unsatisfied love" have thus been disputed, but these disputes do not much concern us here. We can leave it to scholars to try and trace the origins of the doctrine of unsatisfied love, of whether it originated in Arabia or among the Sufi mystics or the Cathares. For the neurobiologist the link is evident, and it is in the brain, in the common incapacity to find in real life the counterpart to the brain concept of love, leaving literary and artistic creation the only means of trying to satisfy that concept. But that may not be the only reason for celebrating the love that remains perpetually unsatisfied. In Chapter 16 I wrote of a neuro-modulator, dopamine, the release of which has been linked to reward and hence a "feel-good" state. In fact, more recent studies have suggested that dopamine is linked not only to reward itself but to the *expectation* of reward, and that its release correlates more with desire than with pleasure.[6] The reward itself, when obtained, may not satisfy the synthetic concept in the brain, and biology has seen to it that as soon as a climax is reached, it turns immediately into an anti-climax.

The Divine Comedy itself may, in the words of Charles Singleton,[7] be thought of as a journey "of the soul from sin to grace" and follows a common theological pattern that was well known in the days of Dante. While acknowledging the conflation of the sacred and the profane in Dante's work (see Chapter 18), what I am interested in here is to look at the concept of love formulated by Dante and the difficulty of experiencing that love in real life, even in a work of art that is the creation of the brain in response to the unsatisfied concept. It is as well to remember again that Dante's allegorical journey to grace and to the heavens is the thought journey of a man on this earth, and must be read as such.

There is a distinctly Platonic flavor to Dante's love affair with Beatrice. In both *Phaedo* and *The Symposium*, arguments are made in favor of love beginning as attraction and desire and metamorphosing gradually into the philosophical virtues of Wisdom, Truth and Universal Beauty. The prevalence of this transmutation in all cultures, from physical to spiritual love, suggests that to a large extent the brain concept is only capable of developing in certain ways. For Dante, this metamorphosis was probably much aided when the vernaculars, starting with Provençal, came to use the word *amor* and *amore* in both sexual and sacred senses, its previous use in the sacred sense having been frowned upon as being compromised by its use in the other sense.[8] This dual use of the word "can be said to have facilitated Dante's extraordinary enhancement of his angel-like lady, Beatrice, and his exaltation of her and his love for her."[9] Indeed he tells us at the beginning of *La Vita Nuova* that soon after seeing Beatrice, Love (Amor) governed his soul and that, through the force and power that his (Dante's) *imagination* (which is his concept) gave to Love, he was able to execute the wishes of the latter. Dante is clearly dealing with the internal (brain) reality and comes close to saying so.

Dante was acquainted with the ingenious view of Greek philo-sophers, that objects take their form by virtue of what the observer vests in them. In the *Convivio*, (Tractate III, ix), he writes, "In truth, Plato and other philosophers affirmed that our vision was brought about, not because the object of sight came to the eye, but because the visual power went out to the object," though he adds that "this opinion is censured as false by the Philosopher [Aristotle] in his book *On Sense and the Object of Sense*."[10] Evidently the Aristotelian view prevailed with Dante because when he first sees Beatrice, "the animal spirit, the one abiding in the high chamber [*la secretissima camera*] to which all the senses bring their perceptions, was stricken with amazement, and speaking directly to the spirits of sight said these words, 'Now your bliss has appeared'." But though metamorphosed in *The Divine Comedy*, and especially in the *Paradiso*, into an object of Wisdom and Truth, the relationship has an early erotic component, the physical desire acknowledged through its denial. In his commentary to Canzone XVIII of the *Vita Nuova* he writes, "I speak of certain beauties pertaining to her whole body [and then] I speak of certain beauties pertaining to particular parts of her body." But "so that here and now every perverse thought may be extinguished, let him who reads this remember what has been mentioned previously concerning this lady's greeting, which is an act performed by her mouth; namely that it was the goal of all my desire so long as I was able to receive it," thus deceiving himself and the reader that the thought of kissing her never crossed his mind! There are erotic allusions in the *Convivio* too. There he says, "the sight of this lady was so generously ordained for us – not just to see her face, which she shows us, but to long to win what she keeps hidden" (Tractate xiv, 13). Writing long before Freud had started to profane the secrets of fantasy, he was able to convey unashamedly the idea of Beatrice as the "mother" and himself as a "child" who falls asleep "like a little boy crying from a spanking," since he was protected from having to acknowledge the source of his phant-asms. Dante's writing thus leaves little doubt that, though she was to be metamorphosed into Truth and Wisdom by him in his work, cul-minating in the *Paradiso*, his love of her was the love of a woman and started as such. There is acknowledgement, too, that the complete joy one desires in a relationship with a woman may never happen. In the *Convivio* (Tractate III, xii) he writes that "In other intelligences she exists in a lesser fashion, as it were like a mistress in whom no lover can take complete joy, but *contents his longing by looking at her*" (my emphasis). Death was a solution to this predicament earlier in his life, as it has been to so many artists. In Canzone XXIII of *Vita Nuova* comes the surprising dream, possibly even the wish, of *her* death, which in fact anticipates her real death. In the introduction to his translation of the work, Mark Musa[11] has emphasized that this Canzone occupies the important, central, part of the *Vita Nuova*, whereas her actual death is mentioned in passing later, without comment, as if it is the death in the mind that is the more important event. With her death, the brain is, after all, free to develop its concepts, unhindered by what is imposed from the outside, by the ever-changing external reality. Death is of course a solution to what is not achievable. Perhaps also anticipating the death wish of Wagner's Tristan and Isolde, to whom romantic love was also an illusion, or just a brain concept, he also wishes his own death (before her real death), writing:

> I said, "Death, I hold you very dear;
> by now you ought to be a gracious thing
> and changed your scorn for sympathy
> since in my lady you have been at home
> I yearn so to become one of your own
> that I resemble you in every way
> My heart begs you to come"

But even as the *Comedy* develops, the vision of Beatrice as a flesh and blood woman does not transmute completely into the spiritual dimension until the very last cantos of the *Paradiso*. In Canto XXVII of the *Purgatorio*, Dante is much reassured when Virgil explains to him that the flame into which the angel has commanded him to enter is the last obstacle remaining between him and Beatrice. He has the status of a child at whom Virgil smiles "like to a child won over by an apple" ["*come al fanciul si fa ch'è vinto al pome*"]. This same Freudian theme, of himself a child but this time with Beatrice as a mother, recurs late in the *Paradiso* where, in Canto XXII, he appears oppressed and turns to Beatrice "like an infant turns to the one in whom he confides most." Beatrice in turn comforts him "like a mother, who succours her pale son with that reassuring voice," by telling him, "Don't you know that you are in heaven," [*mi disse: Non sai che tu se' in cielo?*] (Botticelli's illustration of this Canto shows Dante cuddled tenderly in the arms of Beatrice, much as an infant would). This common enough oedipal dimension may have its origins in the common brain areas that are engaged during romantic and maternal love.[12] I say *may* because the scientific experiments as yet give us only hints and first approximations, and the detailed neural mechanisms in terms of cell responses remain unknown. Moreover, whereas brain imaging experiments show the significant areas of overlap between regions engaged in romantic and maternal love, no such experiments have been conducted on son–mother relationships. But given the common oedipal instincts, it would not be at all surprising if we find significant overlap between brain areas engaged in romantic and filial love.

It would be easy, in the transformation of Beatrice to divine status, to lose sight of the origins of the sentiment and the transformation. But, in Platonic style, the origin and source – the romantic passion of a man for a woman – though becoming of lesser importance, are never indifferent. Dante assures the reader that the same Beatrice with whom he was smitten at first sight and who had engulfed him in passion and desire years before is still alive in his brain even towards the end of his allegorical journey, as he explains in Canto XXVI of the *Paradiso*:

> I said, at her pleasure, sooner or later,
> let remedy come to my eyes, which were the gates
> through which she entered with that fire that ever burns me

And the theme is taken up again in Canto XXVII of the *Paradiso*:

> The mind amorous, preoccupied with my lady alone,
> my wish to return my eyes to her was ever more ardent;
> and if art or nature has made a trap to catch the eyes and
>   so possess the mind
> in human flesh or in its portrait,
> all this would be as nothing
> compared to the divine delight which shone upon me,
> when I turned to her radiant face;

In Canto XXX of the *Paradiso*, he recalls that

> From the first day that I saw her face
> in this life, to this very moment
> the sequence of my song has never ceased

The reader is thus reminded that, even though she is transformed into an almost angelic and divine status, she also remains a woman, indeed the same woman who triggered the passion in the first place.

But of course Beatrice is a concept in Dante's brain, a synthetic concept that develops with time. Just as it is difficult to find a real-life equivalent to the synthetic brain concept, so the translation of that concept into a work of art or even works of art (which will constitute particular examples only of the overall synthetic concept) is an almost hopeless task. Unlike Michelangelo, who often did not undertake a task for fear that he could not match his brain concept in a work of art, or left many of his sculptures unfinished, Dante completed his work. But, like Michelangelo, he nevertheless laments the impossibility of representing perfection, the perfection that resides in brain concepts, for every artist:

> But now this sequence must desist
> from following her beauty, in verse,
> as every artist must.

The impossibility of representing his concept [of Beatrice and of love] is acknowledged again in Canto XXXI of the *Paradiso*:

> And if I had in language as much wealth
> as in imagination, I should still not try
> to describe the smallest of her delights

a canto that also, interestingly, it is not illustrated by Botticelli.

But the sentiment of love, its search for that elusive unity and its overwhelming power to dictate and shape life, is too grand for most to fathom, and lovers – as in the words of Plato's Aristophanes – do not even know what they want from each other. As with so many others, Dante concedes in the last canto (Canto XXXIII) of the *Paradiso*, that his powers of description fail him, for his concept is much too grand for words:

> Oh how feeble is speech and how inadequate
> to the concept! And speech, compared to what I saw, is such
> that it is not enough to call it little

Finally his highest fantasy (the concept itself, derived from the senses) fails him

> Here, the highest fantasy failed me.

but his desire and will are caught up, somewhat vaguely, in the turning of the wheel of

the love that moves the sun and the other stars

The Divine Comedy is of course a monumental work that treats many subjects besides that of love and Beatrice. Dante's work revolves around the changing concept of love, its expansion to grander and even mystical dimensions, but one that, as in Plato's prescription, is triggered by the sight of, and desire for, a beautiful though unattainable woman. In this conceptual transformation, he looks not for her but for his concept of her, forever protected from the vicissitudes of *external* change and subject to internal change only, through the metamorphosis of the brain concept of love and of Beatrice. In the end, Beatrice, the earthly woman whom he could never love as a woman, herself changes from being an earthly and desirable but unattainable woman to the embodiment of beauty, wisdom and virtue. Thus transformed, she leads him in successive stages through Hell, Purgatory and Paradise to the Empyrean. But love is grander than that, and it is St. Bernard, not Beatrice, who finally ushers him into the highest level of the Empyrean. In a sense, the 100 cantos constituting *The Divine Comedy* can be interpreted to end in a failure imposed by the very nature of brain concepts, the impossibility of achieving them and even of understanding them. In the end, Dante merely merges his desire and will into an inseparable concept of love, and ultimately of union not only with the beloved but, through the beloved, with God as well – hence *l'amor che move il sole e l'altre stelle*.

Dante and Petrarch idealize a real, individual, woman – a woman of supreme importance in their life. Umr'ul Qays and Nizami idealize a woman (Leila) in someone else's life and in the process also idealize the ardent lover (Majnun) who is oblivious to all else save his concept of the beloved. The Arabic and Persian mystics rarely speak of an individual. Instead they sing the glories of the idealized beloved. Whatever the course and mode adopted, there is a strong thread that connects these different approaches not only to each other but also to the much older Platonic doctrine expressed in *The Symposium*. Were Dante and Petrarch aware of Plato's writings? Yes. Were they aware of what the Arabic and Persian mystic poets had written centuries before their time? Perhaps and perhaps not. Were the Islamic mystic poets aware of Plato? Possibly. The links between these different authors may or may not be traced historically through actual documents. Neurobiologically, the matter is quite different. The links are there in the inherited and acquired concepts of love that the brain has and formulates. These concepts do not seem to differ very much, even when applied in different cultures. At this level, humanity is everywhere the same, as indeed are their brains.

Chapter 20

Wagner and *Tristan und Isolde*

The *Conte* by Arthur Rimbaud that prefaces this Part summarizes, in miniature and perhaps extreme form, an inevitable and seemingly universal wish of lovers, itself an inherited brain concept linked to love. At the height of passion, their desire is not only for their lover but above all to be united to their lover, to dissolve all distance and substance between them, to feel as one indissoluble entity. In practice, this is unachievable because the lovers must remain two separate individuals. Built into this passion is therefore the inevitability of separation. Such inevitability can render the passion of love an isolating and intensely lonely experience. The lover seeks to find the true reflection of the concept in his or her brain, a search that – if statistics are anything to go by – is vain and fruitless for a very significant number of individuals. One solution is to annihilate the inherited brain concept of unity and the ideal that goes with it, and this can only be achieved through death. There are many instances of this in world literature but perhaps the supreme example is to be found in Richard Wagner's great masterpiece, *Tristan und Isolde*. It is of much neurobiological interest. In a curious way, it is the projection into art of the unrealistic demands of biology, mediated through the agency of inherited brain concepts.

The myth of Tristan and Isolde is an ancient Celtic one, and there have been many versions of it, although all speak of the tragic and fatal inevitability of romantic love. That it should be a myth, which by definition has no specific author but reflects rather the collective thought, is significant. As Denis de Rougemont has emphasized: "We need the myth to express the obscure and inexpressible [*inavouable*] fact that passion is linked to death," adding that "The myth reigns wherever passion is dreamed of as an ideal, not feared as a malignant fever; wherever its fatality is called for, invoked and imagined as a beautiful and desirable catastrophe, and not merely a catastrophe."[1] Is it any wonder that Wagner set the fatal myth to music so beautiful that, on first hearing it, Giuseppe Verdi could hardly believe it came from a human source?

Wagner's three-act romantic opera dispenses with all the details and, from the start, portrays the lovers as ultimately lonely and isolated, a feeling that, in his Salzburg production of the opera in the early 1970s, Herbert von Karajan managed to convey and heighten through a stage setting that was almost totally bare. When I asked him about his intentions, Karajan told me that he had wanted to heighten the sense of loneliness where one least expected it, namely in romantic love. The lovers, in their desire for that elusive unity, are not only imprisoned in solitary fantasy but also in knowledge about the ineluctable destiny of passionate love. Wagner, the great womanizer, wrote it relatively late in life, after a passionate and probably unconsummated love affair with Mathilde von Wesendonk, the wife of a rich banker at whose home in Zurich he stayed, and who had inspired the *Wesendonk Lieder*, which presaged *Tristan und Isolde*. Whether consummated or not, Wagner understood instinctively, like Thomas Mann after him, that the concept of love in his brain could not be achieved in life, but only through art. In a letter to Liszt, his father in law, he wrote: "Since never in my whole life have I tasted the real happiness of romantic love, I mean to raise the greatest of monuments to that most beautiful of dreams." This expresses the identical sentiment that Thomas Mann was to express much later, when he wrote that literature was "the sole and painful way we have of getting a particular experience,"[2] that of satisfying the concept in the brain. In his work Wagner conveyed the idea that the brain concept, as it relates to romantic love, has no counterpart in real experience and, perhaps paradoxically, can only be achieved through its annihilation, in death. If his letter to Liszt is to be believed, his most intense experience of romantic love came in his work of art, *Tristan und Isolde*. It was, for him, the sole and painful way of getting the particular experience.

In Wagner's version, the relationship of Tristan and Isolde becomes entirely ascetic, indeed perhaps one of the most ascetic relationships in romantic love ever described. The nearest thing to physical consummation that I have seen in a production of *Tristan* was in the 2005 Bayreuth staging by Christoff Marthaler where, in the Second Act,

Isolde makes a brief suggestive movement to undress Tristan and proceeds to unbutton her corsage before King Marke hastily buttons it up again. This asceticism and indifference to physical consummation merely serves to heighten the impossibility of achieving the concept of love, as experienced by the great lovers in literature, in life. Indeed, even the beloved is a concept in the lover's brain; what the lover loves above all is the concept in his or her brain. This is what de Rougemont refers to as the "double narcissism" of love in Wagner's *Tristan*, that is, the narcissism of both Isolde and Tristan. "They love each other, but each one loves the other from him or herself, not from the beloved;"[3] hence Isolde sings of Tristan in Act 1 as being "Chosen by *me*, lost to *me*" (my emphasis). Critics have often objected that these are male depictions of love and that the selfishness of Isolde, as well as other heroines, is one depicted by a male. In fact, a reading of love literature written by women suggests that selfishness is not gender bound. If one surveys at random the poems of the sixteenth century Italian poetess Gaspara Stampa, considered to be among the greatest of Italian Renaissance women poets, one will be hard put to find a poem that is not in reference to the suffering that *she* is going through. The repetition of this theme throughout suggests that she is almost indifferent to the fate of her lover. Much the same impression of utter selfishness and narcissism is gained from reading the passionate love letters of Julie de Lespinasse, the eighteenth century French authoress. Where it comes to selfishness and narcissism in love, men have little to teach women and even less to learn from them.

The ascetic relationship of Tristan and Isolde is not unique to Wagner's thinking; it was characteristic, as we saw, of courtly love, when the chaste love of a woman at a distance was exalted. But the feverish, and often tragically resigned and despairing, musical accompaniment depicting unfulfilled desire that Wagner provided as a counterbalance to the coolly cerebral libretto of Acts 2 and 3 sets it apart as one of the most powerful affirmations of the inevitable fate of romantic love. The theme is taken up right from the start, in the *Prelude*. In his own program notes for the first performance, Wagner wrote that "it represents the incessant projection and recoil upon itself of a single emotion – *that of longing without satisfaction and without end*"[4] (my emphasis). The *Prelude* was originally referred to as the *Liebestod* (love-death) and Wagner described it as a progression "from the first timidest lament of unappeasable longing, the tenderest shudder, to the most terrible outpouring of an avowal of hopeless love," the music "traversing all phases of the vain struggle against the inner ardor until this, sinking back powerless upon itself, seems to be extinguished in death."[4] I have already alluded to the philosophy of Schopenhauer, which Wagner had been much impressed with, and which emphasized that we are merely the outward manifestations of the timeless and unified noumenal world, to which we aspire. The theme of unity-in-love, but after death, is strongly emphasized in *Tristan*.

Neurobiologically, and from a neuroesthetics viewpoint, there are three aspects of Wagner's opera that are important. They emphasize in turn the theme of unity or union-in-love, the impossibility of achieving this and that the loved one is in fact a concept in the lover's brain. Also, the musical accompaniment heightens the sense of the unfinished and the ambiguous, thus creating a grand tapestry that encompasses many of the themes of passionate love.

The first occurs in Act 1 when Brengäne, Isolde's maid, substitutes the love potion for the death potion that Isolde is determined to take. This love potion is perhaps best understood metaphorically, as a concept unleashed in the protagonists' brains and over which they have no control. That is the interpretation I give it here, as a concept developed in the brain and against which any fight is futile. The concept that the love potion unleashes is that of union with the lover. Tristan curses the potion (and thus the brain concept) in Act 3; once the love potion, that brain concept, had begun to work its effects, "No healing /no sweet death / can ever release me / from yearning's distress." The potion in fact imprisons the protagonists in a passionate desire from which there seems to be no escape.[5] In their imaginative production of the opera in Paris in 2005, Peter Sellars and Bill Viola projected two movies side by side during the course of Act 1, of a man and a woman walking slowly to their cells in prison. There they gradually strip and hand over all to the prison warders. They are left totally naked, vulnerable and powerless, imprisoned in desire and seemingly aware of its outcome, even before taking the potion: "Head destined for death / Heart destined for death" Isolde laments as she gazes at Tristan in Act 1. Later in the Act, Tristan – just before taking what he mistakenly supposes is the potion of reconciliation – bemoans the looming threat of permanent dissatisfaction: "Heart's deceit / wishful dreaming / the only consolation / in eternal mourning / Beneficent draught of forgetfulness / I drain you unwaveringly." And having substituted the love potion for that of death, Brengäne too realizes the terrible consequences of what she has done in Act 1: "Inescapable / eternal misery / instead of an early death." She curses "Love's spiteful draught" because it "extinguishe[s] the light of reason" in Act 2, which love indeed does by inactivating the evaluating and judgmental frontal cortex.

The desire for unity with the lover, that ubiquitous brain concept, is writ large throughout the opera. Tristan sings in Act 2 of "the single bond / of a single breath" and together they dream of being "Ever, ever one" while Isolde sings of that "sweet little word – and." To Isolde, the love they share is the love of Tristan *and* Isolde, not the love of Tristan *or* Isolde. These separate entities break the bond and unity of love. If one of them were to die alone, she asks, would not that bond be broken? To which Tristan replies that the only thing that could die is what troubles them, and prevents Tristan from ever loving Isolde and her alone, namely the unattainable unity. And Tristan receives this response from Isolde, opening the way for their joint death in love:

> Yet this little word: *and,*
> were it destroyed,
> how else but together
> with Isolde's own life
> would death be given to Tristan?[6]

In the ensuing duet they yearn for self-obliteration, to be replaced by the dreamed-of unity, which can, given the biological realities, only be achieved in death. They sing "Thus would we die/ that together / ever one / without ending/" and look forward to the time when there will be no longer a Tristan *and* an Isolde, since they will be unified in one indissoluble bond.

Much of the opera can be described briefly, but accurately, as the gradual realization of the impossibility of realizing the concept of a total union of two individuals in love in this world, its annihilation through death remaining the only solution. The contrast of Day with Night in Act 2 heightens the contradiction between the unachievable reality and the concept in the brain. The brain concept reigns supreme in imagination only (Night) when it does not clash with the harsh reality that obtrudes (Day). The imagination is of course to be understood in terms of untrammeled brain concepts. The supreme power of the Night in giving freedom to the imagination had been celebrated before. Of particular interest is the poem of the eighteenth century German author and philosopher Georg Phillip von Hardenburg, who is better known through his pen name of Novalis and with whose work Wagner was almost certainly acquainted. Entitled *Hymnen an die Nacht* (Hymns to the Night), it was a lament for his dead fiancée, Sophie. As with Tristan and Isolde in Act 2, Novalis bemoans the fact that the harsh realities of Day keep him from being united with his lover. But he then experiences such a vivid dream of her that he almost touches her. It is then that he starts believing in the sovereignty of the Night ("*und erst seitdem fühl ich ewigen, unwandelbaren Glauben an den Himmel der Nacht und sein Licht, die Geliebte*") and begins to yearn for the moment when light will no longer frighten away Night. It is then that Love and death will supervene, since the sleep will be forever: "*wenn das Licht nicht mehr die Nacht und die Liebe scheucht – wenn der Schlummer ewig und nur Ein unerschöplicher Traum sein wird.*"

Just as Novalis did, both Tristan and Isolde lament the ugliness of the Day and exalt the sovereignty of the imagination at Night in Act 2. Tristan laments the light and wishes for it to be extinguished, bemoaning that he cannot get rid of the Day's insolence even at Night. He would like to extinguish Day which is "spiteful, the most bitter foe" for there is "no distress, no anguish, which it does not revive with its beams." To which Isolde responds by asking what lies evil Day had told to make him betray her, who was destined for him. This in turn elicits this response from Tristan:

> From the light of Day
> which made you appear to me
> a traitor
> I wished to flee
> into Night,
> to take you with me,
> where my heart would bid me
> end all deception,
> where the vain premonition
> of treachery might be dispelled,
> there to pledge to you
> eternal love,
> to consecrate you to Death
> in company with myself.

The brain concept of a total union in love is unrealizable on earth, and can only be dreamed of elsewhere, in a heaven that succeeds life. And so, in the midst of the celebration of love, the death-wish appears, when Tristan declares:

> When I recognized
> sweet death
> offered to me
> at your hand;
> when a bold and
> clear presentiment
> showed me what
> expiation demanded;
> there dawned gently
> in my heart
> the lofty power of Night;
> my Day was then accomplished.

And together they sing:

> Descend,
> O Night of love,
> grant oblivion
> that I may live;
> take me up
> into your bosom,
> release me from
> the world!

Release from the world! Death! Wagner makes this into a duet, and it prefaces the central theme, that they must die together for only then can they achieve the dreamed of unity. Tristan yearns for the "single bond/ of a single breath." In exclaiming, "Let Day / give way before death" (and not give way, as one might have imagined, to Night), he articulates the thought that even the Night of the imagination cannot promise the brain concept of unity. It is, as Dante finds at the end of *Paradiso*, too grand a concept to even imagine. Isolde replies, saddened, "Should Day / and Death / both reach / our love?"

The endless yearning for that unity through death continues even in spite of brief moments of doubt and attachment to the brief but disorienting delights of earthly love. Isolde implores him to stay alive for "just one hour" and not deprive her of the "eternally brief, final worldly joy." And if Tristan must die, it must be for love, not from the physical wounds inflicted on him:

> do not die from the wound.
> Unite us both,
> Extinguish the light of life!

At the end of the opera, in the *Liebestod*, Isolde ends by singing:

> in the universal stream
> All – of the world-breath –
> to drown,
> – to founder –
> – unconscious –
> utmost rapture!

before following Tristan in death, just as von Aschenbach, in *Death in Venice*, gets up to follow Tadzio when promised the "richest expectations" in another world. How similar "richest expectation" is to "utmost rapture."

There is no clearer, more poignant, statement of the desire for that unity that is elusive on earth, even at Night when the imagination reigns supreme. For imagination too and the brain concepts that underlie it have limits. In Wagner's opera, the concept of love was born in Tristan in Act 1, when he was given the love draught by Brangäne, Isolde's faithful maid. Although he had hailed that love potion in Act 2 for opening up "The wonderous realms of Night / where I had only been in dreams," he curses it in Act 3, just as von Aschenbach cursed the smile of Tadzio as "a fatal gift." For when Tristan took the love draught in Act 1 and the concept of love for Isolde was born,

> then was the most searing
> magic unleashed:
> that I might never die
> But inherit eternal torment!

Some producers have tried to resurrect Tristan and Isolde at the end of a performance. In his Covent Garden production of the opera in

1971, Peter Hall had Tristan and Isolde rise at the end of the opera and leave the stage holding hands. A Wagner purist in the audience shouted, "Disgusting!," presumably believing that it was a negation of what Wagner had intended. In fact, Wagner had originally referred to the present *Liebestod* as the "*Verklärung*" (Transfiguration), and the Tristan legends speak of Tristan and Isolde being buried side by side, with a vine growing from one grave and an ivy from the other, the branches of the two intertwining and thus representing eternal unity in death. There is a supreme, and probably unintended, irony in Peter Hall's production, for only the living can see this unity in another world; only they can fathom the death and hypothetical rebirth of the unattainable concept. This irony was well projected in the 2007 Munich production by Peter Konwitschny, who has Tristan and Isolde holding hands to leave the stage. As they leave, a curtain is drawn to reveal two white coffins reverentially contemplated by King Marke and Brangäne.

Wagner made full use of the imaginative powers of the brain in composing the opera, though he himself knew nothing formally about the brain or its rules. Indeed, his music, if studied systematically in relation to neural activity, could teach us something about the brain and its rules. The work is marked by two striking features. There is first the ambiguity in the famous dissonant Tristan chord, about which so much has been written. The ambiguity resides in the progression of the four-note chords, not in the chords themselves. The first chord is unambiguous and diatonic in only one minor key, the "hidden" D#/Eb minor and in its parallel F major. On entering, the second chord abruptly contradicts the seeming A minor of the beginning, thus enhancing the expectation and curiosity of the listener. The chord is left unresolved and therefore ambiguous throughout the opera. Not until the coda in the last Act is it finally resolved, thus engaging the expectation of the listener maximally and imaginatively. This ambiguity is often thought of as a musical metaphor for the deep *Sehnsucht* (yearning) of the two protagonists, the irresolution coming to represent, musically, the notion that their union can never be complete in this world. It represents, in a sense, the unfinished, unachievable desire of the two lovers to be united.

The imagination of the listener is heightened and engaged further by the long silences and the prolonged dwelling on a single note, often without orchestral accompaniment. Prolonged moments of silence are a feature of the *Prelude*, which is in fact a summary of the theme of the entire opera. The orchestra resumes after a first long silence by a *sforzando*, and then a *più forte*, followed by a slow descent into *piano*, as if to express failure and resignation in the admission of the inevitable consequence of romantic love. The long silences, coupled with the ambiguity in the progression of the chord, led one music expert to ask whether anyone "has ever composed silence as eloquently as Wagner."[7] The two together constitute the musical counterpart of the *non finito* in art. But whereas in visual art the unspoken message is conveyed through the visual medium, and the unfinished interpreted by the brain, in *Tristan* the meaning is conveyed essentially through music but the ambiguous is also resolved by the brain. Wagner once said, "Do not worry if you do not understand the libretto; the music makes everything perfectly clear," just as a description in a work of art is unnecessary because, in the words of Naum Gabo, a work of art has failed if "it needs to be supplemented and explained in words."[8] In writing it, Wagner said that he had lost control of it, since it all flowed from his "sub-conscious." He came close to expressing the wish that there would never be a perfect performance of *Tristan*, for if there were, the audience would be driven mad! In a sense, he wanted his masterpiece to remain forever unfinished, in denying it also the perfection that it deserved. Or was it perhaps an acknowledgment that the perfect concept of the opera that he had could never be realized.

That the love affair remains unconsummated means essentially that it is also unfinished. In its unfinished status it bears a relationship to the unfinished in a work of art, which is also left in that state because the concept in the painter's brain cannot be realized. The unfinished is, as discussed above, related to ambiguity, since both not only engage the brain but also allow the viewer or the listener to complete the work of art according to their own brain concepts. Wagner uses ambiguity and the unfinished to maximum effect in *Tristan*. As with Michelangelo's *Rondanini Pietà* or Vermeer's *Music Lesson*, the listener becomes maximally and imaginatively engaged in completing the work. I am in fact deliberately comparing Wagner's musical work with examples derived from visual art to emphasize that, in spite of differences in medium, the underlying organization of the brain in terms of its concept formation is fundamentally uniform at this level of analysis. Indeed, it is characteristic of the genius of Wagner that he combined the ambiguous (characteristic of many works of art) and the unfinished (characteristic of others in a single work) to convey the notion that the concept in the brain is unachievable. But in essence it is the same message – that of inachievability – that is conveyed by Dante, or by Thomas Mann, or by Michelangelo or Cézanne. Is there not, after all, some similarity between Cézanne uniting a whole canvas but only in the brain of the viewer, in spite of unfinished patches, and Wagner uniting a whole opera in the brain of the listener, despite the repetitive irresolution and ambiguity? Is there no similarity between Frenhofer, in Balzac's story, failing to achieve the concept in his brain and destroying his canvas before dying, and Tristan and Isolde wishing death because they cannot reach their concept of love? Is there no similarity between von Aschenbach's quest for perfection in nothingness and Tristan and Isolde's quest for nothingness to achieve their perfection of happiness? That such disparate products of the human brain and its creativity should deal with what are, in essence, the same concepts and resolve them in similar ways tells us something about the nature of concepts formed in the brain. Collectively, they give support to the view expressed in this book, of a clash between synthetic brain concepts and the experience of particulars in daily life. The literature of love and the works of art also tell neurobiology that, by studying these manifestations of the brain directly, it can find evidence for the belief that there are brain concepts in art and in love that can be of inestimable value in learning about the brain and how it functions.[9]

Chapter 21

Thomas Mann and *Death in Venice*

In Thomas Mann's letters, lectures, and above all in his literary output there are many transparently veiled references to the impossibility of achieving in real life the concepts in his brain. Much of this has been perceptively dissected out in Anthony Heilbut's magisterial biography, entitled *Thomas Mann: Eros and Literature*.[1] Heilbut gives an admirable summary of Mann's psychological outlook, and it is not dissimilar to that expressed by Wagner as the motive force for the composition of *Tristan und Isolde*: "We can read him now as someone almost overwhelmed by longing. His idea of love involves a psychological imbalance between a lover, consumed by passion, and the elusive object of his desires. There are no happy endings; the pursuit is all. Worship of beauty is its only reward; in his old age he seconded Michelangelo's lyric, 'love has ravished me, beauty has me spellbound'."[1]

Mann much admired Wagner who, along with Schopenhauer and Nietzsche, was one of the predominant influences in his intellectual life. *Tristan und Isolde* was the work that he preferred, considering that the "ever-yearning chromaticism of the *Liebestod* is a literary idea," which of course in a sense it is. This admiration no doubt reflects a fundamental belief in Mann that was almost identical to the one portrayed by Wagner and earlier still by Dante, namely the difficulty of realizing in life the concept formed in the brain, in this instance the concept of love, art remaining the best and possibly the last and only refuge for doing so. Mann admits as much in his story about Schiller, *A Weary Hour*: Art "At bottom is a compulsion, a critical knowledge of the ideal, *a permanent dissatisfaction*" (my emphasis), a statement that is almost identical in sentiment to that expressed by Wagner in *Tristan und Isolde* and especially in its *Prelude*, of "longing without end and without satisfaction." Permanent dissatisfaction in relation to the ideal invades Mann's stories even before he produced *Death in Venice*. It is there in a novella entitled *Tristan* (1902), in *The Blood of the Walsungs* (1905) and in *Tonio Kröger* (1903). A critical knowledge of the ideal is of course a critical knowledge of the ideal formed in the brain and by the brain. Indeed, it can be argued that having a critical knowledge of the ideal formed in one's brain is the certain way to permanent dissatisfaction, a serious affliction where the ideal formed in the brain relates to love. For it is more than likely that the ideal cannot be met in reality or, if met, can only be short-lived. But an artist can try to re-create it in his art, a therapeutic measure that compensates for the disappointment, though even that remains uncertain. And so it was for Mann. Literature, to him, was the only way of achieving the experience and living the ideal.

The fleeting glimpse of the ideal constituted in the brain, and the imperative of not blemishing it through reality, are central preoccupations of Mann and explored by him in stories antedating *Death in Venice*. *Tristan* is the story of a powerful infatuation that, as in Wagner's *Tristan und Isolde*, remains unconsummated. It is a chance encounter in a sanatorium between a writer, Herr Spinell, and the wife of a somewhat coarse businessman, Frau Kloterjahn. It is not for nothing that the novella bears the title *Tristan*, and that the *Sehnuchtsmotiv* (longing motif), and especially Act 2, of *Tristan und Isolde* should constitute such a prominent part of it. In his descriptions, Mann shows that he was much impressed by the irresolution and the long silences in the *Prelude* and the *Liebestod* of Wagner's work. He writes (in his novella *Tristan*): "The *Sehnuchtsmotiv*, roving lost and forlorn like a voice in the night, lifted its trembling question. Then silence, a waiting. And lo, an answer: the same timorous, lonely note, only clearer, only tenderer. Silence again. And then, with that marvelous muted *sforzando*, like mounting passion, the love-motif came in." In describing it, Mann emphasizes the importance of the imagination, the concept, and the power of reality and the blemishes that intrude into the concept, as Wagner does in contrasting day and night in the Second Act of *Tristan*.

Early in the novella, Frau Kloterjahn asks Spinell to describe a woman to her. He replies:

"That I cannot do. Or, rather, it would not be a fair picture. I only saw the lady as I glanced at her in passing, I did not actually see her at all. But that fleeting glimpse was enough to rouse my fancy and make me carry away a picture so beautiful that – good Lord! How beautiful it is!" She laughed. "Is that the way you always look at beautiful women, Herr Spinell? Just a fleeting glance?"

"Yes, madame; *it is a better way than if I were avid of actuality, stared them plump in the face, and carried away with me only a consciousness of the blemishes they in fact possess.*" (my emphasis).

Elsewhere, the same sentiment rebounds in the letter that Herr Kloterjahn writes to Spinell, in response to what is perceived by the former to be an offensive letter addressed to him: "My wife wrote me once that when you meet a woman you don't look her square in the face, but just give her a side squint, so as to carry away a good impression, *because you are afraid of the reality*" (my emphasis). Indeed, it can be said that the idea of longing, in the knowledge that what is being longed for does not exist in this world – for it is a concept of the brain that can never be realized when one is faced with the cold facts and details – seems to have been central to Mann's thought, although Mann of course never acknowledged this directly and never wrote about the brain, even in spite of his profound medical knowledge.

In trying to appreciate Mann's work in the present context, two factors about his psychological make-up and thinking are worth emphasizing. He was, to begin, an arch bourgeois, living an upper middle-class and outwardly respectable life, with a wife and a large family. But this existence, which he was in fact much attached to, was counterbalanced by inner yearnings of a different kind, of a "forbidden love", in a world that was not always accepting of them. This tension between the two recurs throughout his work and in many confessional statements. The arch bourgeois continually contrasts the reputable with what he deems to be disreputable. The two are anti-podean, almost enemies. In pursuing Tadzio through the streets of Venice, Von Aschenbachs's "Mind and heart were drunk with passion, his foot-steps guided by the dæmonic power whose pastime is to trample on human reason and dignity,"[2] which of course the brain does by inactivating the frontal cortex, the brain's seat of judgment, as described earlier. In spite of this, Mann never fails to see the disreputable as the inspirational source for the reputable; he is continually absorbed by the humble and even the seemingly sordid and depraved origins of great ideas, as indeed Konstantinos Kavafis was in his poetry, with the difference that Kavafis never saw these humble experiences as anything but enriching and beautiful. It is a theme Mann returns to again and again. In *Tonio Kröger*, he writes: "And because in their innocence they assume that beautiful and uplifting results must have beautiful and uplifting causes, they never dream that the 'gift' in question is a very dubious affair and rests upon extremely sinister foundations" (*Tonio*). In *Death in Venice*, he writes, "Verily it is well for the world that it sees only the beauty of the completed work and not its origins nor the conditions whence it sprang; since knowledge of the artist's inspiration might often but confuse and alarm and so prevent the full effect of its excellence." For Kavafis instead, the "gift" was neither sinister nor dubious. It was beautiful, a sensuous moment frozen in time because it has no sequel, and can only develop internally, in the brain of the artist, as a concept, just as Beatrice developed in Dante's brain and his alone. In one of his poems entitled *Their Beginning*, Kavafis writes:

> Their illicit pleasure has been fulfilled.
> They get up and dress quickly, without a word.
> They come out of the house separately, furtively;
> and as they move off down the street a bit unsettled,
> it seems they sense that something about them betrays
> what kind of bed they've just been lying on.
> But what profit for the life of the artist:
> tomorrow, the day after, or years later, he'll give voice
> to the strong lines that had their beginning here.

Notice, they had their beginning here, but developed internally in the brain of the artist.

Time and again, Mann wishes that he was an ordinary person, not one possessed by "dæmonic" powers. It is, he says, "the normal, respectable, and admirable that is the kingdom of our longing" (*Tonio*). How he longed "To sleep . . . To long to be allowed to live the life of simple feeling, to rest sweetly and passively in feeling alone, without compulsion to act and achieve" (*Tonio* original ellipsis). The impulse to live in art, and through art, the ideal that is formed in the brain is, to him, a curse and not a blessing: ". . . you ought to realize that there is a way of being an artist that goes so deep and is so much a matter of origins and destinies that no longing seems to it sweeter and more worth knowing than longing after the bliss of the commonplace" (*Tonio*). Notice that he writes of "origins and destinies," implying that many experiences are involved in the formation of the brain concepts. In writing that the world should not know of the "origins nor the conditions whence [a work of art] sprang" he is acknowledging this even more explicitly.

The sinister and sordid origins of the inspiration that produces great art imply a sublimation of the impulses. And sublimation, which is a critical theme in *Death in Venice*, is worth considering briefly here. Its earliest, and greatest, exponent was Plato and the most remarkable exposition of it is in *The Symposium*. Love begins as infatuation by a beautiful person, and in ever higher steps ends with the love of universal truth and beauty. The particular becomes unimportant though not indifferent. The source of the love for the ideal, universal, truth and beauty becomes ever farther removed from the destination. It is merely the trigger, sublimated into a grand vision of beauty, as the sight of Beatrice was for Dante. We know that Mann consulted both *Phaedrus* and *The Symposium* extensively while writing *Death in Venice*. And he rejects the Platonic notion that the source of the vision of beauty, which lies in erotic impulses, can ever be eradicated.

Death in Venice (*Der Tod in Venedig*) was first published in 1913, having been serialized the previous year in two issues of *Die Neue Rundschau*. It is almost certain that all the details in the book are factual. Many of the central facts were indeed confirmed by Count Wladyslaw Moes, who in real life was the actual beautiful Polish boy who had been vacationing at the Hotel des Bains in the Lido of Venice with his mother and sisters. The novella was an immediate success, reprinted many times and translated into at least twenty languages. Almost one century after its first publication, its popularity has not diminished. Indeed, it has increased, perhaps aided by the film version produced by Luchino Visconti.

Gustav von Aschenbach, a successful and recently ennobled author, takes a trip to Venice after a chance encounter with a disturbing man in Munich instils in him the need for travel, a change of air. Settled at the Hotel des Bains, he is transfixed by the sight of a sickly but beautiful Polish boy, Tadzio. But of course what he sees is a real-life image of the concept in his brain or mind, and Mann comes as close

as one might expect, for someone writing at his time, to saying so –
"with an outburst of rapture he told himself that what he saw
was beauty's very essence; *form as divine thought, the single and pure
perfection which resides in the mind,* of which an image and likeness,
rare and holy, was here raised up for adoration" (my emphasis). The
two flirt visually, in that the attention of von Aschenbach is acknowledged by Tadzio, making the boy up to a point actively complicit in
the unfolding drama. There is something disturbingly seductive in this
silent visual complicity, and Mann's description again recalls the Day
and Night motif of the Second Act of *Tristan und Isolde*: "Uneasiness
rules between them, unslaked curiosity, a hysterical desire to give rein
to their suppressed impulse to recognize and address each other; even,
actually, a sort of strained but mutual regard. For one human being
instinctively feels respect and love for another human being *so long as
he does not know him well enough to judge him; and that he does not,
the craving he feels is evidence*" (my emphasis). But, welcome though
this exchange is, it is also fatal, as fatal perhaps as the potion that Tristan
drinks in Act 1 of *Tristan und Isolde*: "Aschenbach received
[Tadzio's] smile and turned away with it as though entrusted with a
fatal gift," just as Tristan, given the "fearful [love] draught" in Act 1,
laments in Act 3. "Then was the most searing magic unleashed/
that I might never die/but inherit eternal torment."

Almost from first sight of Tadzio, Aschenbach's inner struggle
begins. The boy represents beauty, indeed reflects a beautiful concept
in Aschenbach's own brain. The reflection in real life of so beautiful
a brain concept is not easy to find, and if found is likely to be ephemeral.
But one can try to create it in a work of art, which may come to reflect
the concept in the brain. As with Michelangelo, for whom the best
of artists sought nothing more than to break the marble spell to reveal
the beauty in the mind of the artist,[3] so for Aschenbach, too, "Was
not the same force at work in himself when he strove in cold fury to
liberate from the marble mass of language the slender forms of his
art which he saw with the eye of his mind and would body forth to
men as the mirror and image of spiritual beauty." Every sight of Tadzio,
on the beach, embracing another boy, merely heightens Aschenbachs's
infatuation and along with it the tension within him. He composes
his work within sight of Tadzio, in whom he finds inspiration. But
this is all at a distance, and one senses that, throughout, Aschenbach
is inwardly resolved not to advance too far, a dilemma especially well

portrayed by Dirk Bogarde in Visconti's film version. Echoing again the Second Act of *Tristan und Isolde*, von Aschenbach comes to the conclusion "that what seemed to him fresh and happy thoughts were like the flattering inventions of a dream, which the waking sense proves worthless and insubstantial." This compares nicely to Tristan's lament in Act 2 of Wagner's opera: "for spiteful Day/the most bitter foe/ hatred and grievance/ . . . is there any distress/is there any anguish/ which it does not revive." Or to the lines in one of Shakespeare's sonnets:

> Thus have I had thee as a dream doth flatter,
> In sleep a king, but waking no such matter

for in sleep, during the night, the brain and its imagination reign supreme and do not have to contend with the reality that does not conform to the brain's concepts.

The apprehension of such beauty in reality is of course dangerous; the beauty is bound to be ephemeral and hence frustrating. The brain must arm itself against it. Seeing the boy in the lift, Aschenbach notes with satisfaction that the boy's teeth "were imperfect, rather jagged and bluish, without a healthy glaze, and of that peculiar brittle transparency which the teeth of chlorotic people often show." "He is delicate, he is sickly" Aschenbach thought. "He will most likely not live to grow old. *He did not try to account for the pleasure the idea gave him*" (my emphasis). Elsewhere he thinks, "He is sickly, he will never live to grow up." It is a pity that this important detail is omitted in Visconti's reasonably faithful film version, for it is a crucial point in the present context and serves two contrasting purposes. It is on the one hand a protective thought, acting to shield von Aschenbach, even if momentarily, from the abyss to which he is destined, by suggesting that the ideal beauty he perceives in the boy is transient. Hence Aschenbach's secret pleasure at the thought. The ideal in the Platonic system, and as traditionally understood, implies the immutable. But the object that is perceived as beautiful changes and decays, *if it continues to be experienced*. At the same time, the brain's concept of beauty, which is a synthetic concept, is modified by the acquisition of new experience, and hence the ideal itself, in terms of brain concepts, is never immutable. The thought that the perceived beauty is ephemeral in turn implies that it cannot be the ideal or at least will not remain so for long. It is a consoling thought, especially for one so intoxicated – as both Mann and his confessional self, Aschenbach, were – by the fatal prediction in the opening lines of August von Platen's poem, also entitled *Tristan*: "Wer die Schönheit angeschaut mit Augen/ ist dem Tode schon anheim gegeben" ["He who has set eyes on beauty is already a prey to death"]. It is therefore, on the other hand, also a manner of wishing fervently that the beautiful will not transmute into the ugly through gradual decay. Best if it were to die, or if the perceiver were to die, while still beautiful. In contrast, Konstantinos Kavafis managed to "freeze" the ideal moment in his memory, to re-create it later in his art, as in the following poem, entitled *One Night*:

> The room was cheap and sordid,
> Hidden above the suspect taverna.
> From the window you could see the alley,
> Dirty and narrow. From below
> Came the voices of workmen
> Playing cards, enjoying themselves.
>
> And there on that ordinary, plain bed
> I had love's body, knew those intoxicating lips,
> red and sensual,
> red lips so intoxicating
> that now as I write, after so many years,
> in my lonely house, I'm drunk with passion again.

In spite of differences in setting, in the story itself and in the gender of the protagonists, the similarity in theme of *Death in Venice* to *Tristan und Isolde*, whose Second Act was interestingly also composed in Venice, is striking. Both end in death after the crushing realization by the protagonists that their ideal of love cannot be achieved, indeed that the only means of doing so is its annihilation in death. Seemingly, the hero of *Death in Venice* had already reached this conclusion long before arriving in Venice. For there was in von Aschenbach "another yearning, opposed to his art and perhaps for that very reason a lure, for the unorganised, the immeasurable, the eternal – in short for nothingness. He whose preoccupation is with excellence longs fervently to find rest in perfection, *and is not nothingness a form of perfection?*" (my emphasis). Nothingness, after all, is immutable. Aschenbach's unmaking is the realization that, as with Tristan and Isolde, his yearning is un-satisfiable. Being as bourgeois as Mann himself was, Aschenbach has sublimated his true infatuation with beauty into his work, into the creation of art. He knows that "a man can still be capable of moral resolution even after he has plumbed the depths of knowledge" (*Venice*), but, it seems, only up to a point. Working while watching Tadzio on the beach, being inspired by him, he begins to realize that moral resolution, when faced with the overpowering concept and demand of the brain, is also a sham. "When Aschenbach put aside his work and left the beach he felt exhausted, he felt broken – conscience reproached him, as it were after a debauch."

There is little doubt that the novel is a confessional one, with Mann himself, though married, having been attracted to many young men both before and after publication of his novella. Most of these attractions, perhaps all, seemingly never resulted in lasting relationships, their transient nature being implied in this entry in his diary, dated 11 July 1950 and reminiscent of the poetry of Konstantinos Kavafis: "As it is, in three days I won't see the boy anymore, will forget his face. But not the experience of my heart. He will join that gallery about which no literary history will speak." Even late in life, as a renowned and much admired author, he was much infatuated by a waiter in a Zurich restaurant, confiding in his diary that "World renown is wonderful but it cannot compare with the smile in his eyes."

In essence, the sublimation of Aschenbach's art is fraudulent, as all sublimation is. It amounts to an admission of failure in achieving the desire, as Freud also recognized (see Chapter 22). The man "who had written *The Abject*, in a style of classic purity renounced bohemianism and all its works, all sympathy with the abyss and the troubled depths of the outcast human soul" now understands, in a passage appropriately addressed to Phaedrus (the very Phaedrus after whom one of Plato's most lofty discourses on love is named) that such sublimation is a mockery. "For mark you, Phaedrus, beauty alone is both divine and visible; and so it is the sense way, the artist's way, little Phaedrus, to the spirit. But now tell me, my dear boy, do you believe that such a man can ever attain wisdom and true manly worth, for whom the path to the spirit must lead through the senses? Or do you rather think . . . that it is a path of perilous sweetness, a way of transgression, and must surely lead him who walks in it astray? For you know that we poets cannot walk the way of beauty without Eros as our companion and guide. . . . love is still our desire – our craving and our shame" (my ellipsis).

In the end, watching from his deckchair, Aschenbach sees Tadzio in the sea and imagines him to be returning his gaze. "The watcher sat just as he had that time in the lobby of the hotel when first the twilit grey eyes had met his own . . . It seemed to him the pale and lovely Summoner out there smiled at him and beckoned; as though, with the hand lifted from his hip, he pointed outward . . . into an immensity of richest expectation. And, as so often before, he rose to follow" (my ellipsis). Anthony Heilbut writes that "This final stroke is Mann's cruellest, for the sexual prowl is revealed as a death trek."[1] But romantic love is also revealed as a death trek in *Tristan und Isolde*, and in Dante's love of Beatrice and in the legend of Majnun and Leila. Even love of God is a death trek. St. John of the Cross declared that only in dying from love, being united with God and thus losing himself and perishing will he be able to say "Now I live." They all have their "richest expectations" in another world, after death. Is not the "höchste Lust" (utmost rapture) that ends Wagner's great opera an expectation of riches in another world? And does not Dante, looking at the heavens from the earth as a living man, and faltering like a geometer who does not understand the concept of the circle, have the same "richest expectations" when, gazing upon the heavens, he turns his will and desire to "the love that moves the sun and the other stars" (*"l'amor che move il sole e l'altre stelle"*)?

Chapter 22

A Neurobiological Analysis of Freud's *Civilization and Its Discontents*

My emphasis in this book has been on the synthetic concepts formed by the brain in its quest for knowledge, and the frequent impossibility of satisfying those concepts, thus leading to a dissatisfaction that may be temporary or permanent. I have tried to argue that creativity, in its most general sense, has often been the route of choice, and commonly the only one available, to alleviate the suffering and discontent that results from this state. This makes it interesting to consider Freud's views on human discontent published some 75 years ago in his *Civilization and Its Discontents*, commonly regarded as among the most influential of his more general books, and to consider how the two sets of views are related.

In *Civilization and Its Discontents*[1] Freud's starting point is that, in spite of all the magnificent achievements of civilization, mankind remains discontented with its state; it is especially so with regard to relationships, either between individuals or between an individual and the family, the community or society at large. What is it that brings about this discontent? To answer this, Freud asks a fundamental question, to which he gives complex answers. The question is breathtakingly simple: "what do people seek in life?". The answer, of course, is "happiness." This, in Freud's view, is equivalent to satisfying the pleasure principle: "As we see, what decides the purpose of life is simply the programme of the pleasure principle. This principle dominates the operation of the mental apparatus from the start. There can be no doubt about its efficacy, and yet its programme is at loggerheads with the whole world, with the macrocosm as much as with the microcosm." Freud did not, indeed could not, specify the neurological basis of that principle because, at the time he was writing, the brain had not been charted in the detail that we have today. His neurobiological insight was nevertheless profound, as was his question. For the seeking of happiness must be ultimately related to the satisfaction of something in the brain, some neurobiological principle. Since Freud's time, neurobiologists have discovered that there are reward and pleasure centers in the brain. However imperfectly they may be described today, it is significant that there are such brain centers, and that they constitute part of the machinery that requires to be satisfied. Reward center is probably the wrong way to describe what is essentially a large conglomeration of cortical and sub-cortical centers, whose cells are intricately connected and whose physiological profile depends upon the sustained and controlled release of neuro-modulators such as dopamine, oxytocin, vasopressin and serotonin. How these neuro-modulators work is not known with any great precision but there seems little reason to doubt that the pattern of cell firing mediated by them is strongly related to satisfaction and satiety. Let us, then, accept the general principle that, in their behaviour, humans do try to satisfy the reward centers and that this satisfaction constitutes the neurological basis of the pleasure principle that Freud spoke of. For Freud, the satisfaction of the "pleasure principle" (which we shall call the pleasure center) comes into conflict with the aims of civilization in general, which tries to curb individual satisfactions in favor of the common good. "A good part of the struggles of mankind," he writes, "centre round the single task of finding an expedient accommodation – one, that is, that will bring happiness – between this claim of the individual and the cultural claims of the group; and one of the problems that touches the fate of humanity is whether such an accommodation can be reached by means of some particular form of civilization or whether the conflict is irreconcilable."

What are the factors that impede the satisfaction of the pleasure principle(s) or, in more modern language, the pleasure and reward centers of the brain? One of them is undoubtedly human variability, to which Freud makes only brief reference by acknowledging "how variegated the human world and its mental life are." Yet variability is one of the most fundamental factors that prevent the satisfaction of the reward centers. The pleasure principle is largely based upon the gratification of instinctual demands, be they of love, sexuality, aggression, greed or the experience of beauty. But these are broad categories, within which there are many refinements. Not all people find the same means of gratifying their love, or sexual impulses, nor are the demands of greed in one individual identical to that of another. Indeed, the hallmark of the human race is its variability. Charles Darwin emphasized that the organs that are most variable are those that are developing fastest. In humans, the greatest variability is to be found in the brain. We can infer this with fair certainty, by observing the variability in men's behavior. If we were to study the kidneys or the livers from two individuals who are wide apart in location and ethnicity, we would find precious little difference. But if we were to study the external and observable manifestations of the brain – in terms of aptitudes, capacities and behavior of two individuals from the same village, with the same background – we are more than likely to find huge variations. In spite of these differences in aspirations, conduct, and abilities, society imposes a more or less uniform code of conduct on us all. And of course society isolates transgressors and avenges itself ruthlessly against them; it can afford to do so because its revenge is institutionalized and anonymous. Its concern is with social groupings; as with the evolutionary process, of which it is a product, it is indifferent to individual fate. Worst of all, for Freud, is the uniform conduct and uniform aspiration imposed by religion, because "Religion restricts this play of choice and adaptation, since it imposes equally on everyone its own path to the acquisition of happiness and protection from suffering," that is, without taking into account human variability and the variety of human needs. The demands of religion and civilization where instincts are concerned are especially pernicious where sexuality (an important and, at times, a dominant force in human conduct) is concerned. Societies commonly impose strong prohibitions in this area, not taking into account human variability in this, as in other domains. For Freud, "The requirement, demonstrated in these prohibitions, that there shall be a single kind of sexual life for everyone, disregards the dissimilarities, whether innate or acquired, in the sexual constitution of human beings; it cuts off a fair number of them from sexual enjoyment, and so becomes the source of serious injustice."

In Freud's view, it was not just the difficulty of satisfying instinctual demands in relation to one other person that was the root cause of human happiness. It went beyond and involved almost all important human affairs. For, "when one considers the inadequacy of regulating human relations in the family, the community and the state and when we consider how unsuccessful our efforts to safeguard against suffering in this particular area have proved, the suspicion dawns upon us that a bit of unconquerable nature lurks concealed behind this difficulty as well, in the form of our mental constitution." What could that mental constitution be? In the Freudian system, it is a struggle between conscious and unconscious processes, and between the ego and its censoring system, the superego. Yet it seems to me that we should go beyond these and look at perhaps an even more basic element of our mental or neurobiological constitution. That basic factor, which seriously prevents the satisfaction of the pleasure principle, or the optimal excitation of the reward centers in the brain, is the synthetic concept, and sometimes also inherited concepts, as in that of unity-in-love. As I have emphasized throughout, the synthetic concept is built up from many experiences and is capable of constant modification with the acquisition of new experience. The momentary or individual experience is, by contrast, of one particular example or situation only and may not – and commonly does not – satisfy the synthetic concept in the brain. Here then is another interpretation of what Freud called our "mental constitution" – an interpretation based not so much on the contradictory claims of the id, ego and superego but on the brain's role as a knowledge-seeking organ. The conflict between the requirements of the brain and the satisfaction of the pleasure principle (through the pleasure centers) is indeed "irreconcilable" as Freud maintained, although the reasons as I see them are different from those given by Freud. Thus the over-arching problem of variability is not the only irreconcilable contradiction. The one rooted in the biology of the brain in its role as a knowledge-seeking and knowledge-acquiring organ, with a capacity to form synthetic concepts that are commonly left unsatisfied, is another. I believe, therefore, that Freud did not frame the question broadly enough when he wondered "whether . . . accommodation can be reached by means of some particular form of civilization or whether the conflict is irreconcilable." It is of course trite to point out the obvious, that in a system as variable as human behavior it would be surprising if some very lucky individuals did not find the capacity of satisfying the pleasure centers of the brain through means that are beyond the reach of others. Yes, there are happy marriages, happy relationships, and happy social interactions, but there is also a significant number of people, almost certainly in the majority, who remain discontented with one important aspect of their life or another.

There is, it seems, a significant contradiction between the demands of biology for human variability and the demands for conformity of another biological system – that of society. The contradiction is all the more surprising because the aims of both systems are in fact the same – the promotion and protection of the species, or, to be more precise, the promotion through natural selection of genetic elements that lead to a greater reproductive rate than others. Such biological contradictions must not, I believe, be considered in a negative light only, even in spite of the difficulties they create for the individual. Even though of supreme importance in Western civilization (well, sometimes, at any rate), the individual is, in a sense, of little importance to biology once it has reproduced and passed the genes along. In protecting the species and maximizing its chances of survival and development, evolution seems to employ two principles that have the same aim but contradictory prescriptions, something that Freud did not really appreciate. In general, biology with evolution as its agent tends towards those conditions that maximize the frequencies of reproductively successful genetic elements in a population. Aggression, aggrandisement, love, sexuality, and the display of behavior that is likely to attract are all means of maximizing the chances of reproductive success. The mechanisms acting as engines for these – the love system no less than the aggression systems of the brain, as well as the complex neurological machinery that induces the protective parental care until the offspring are themselves ready to reproduce – are extremely stable and well protected. But the morality and social rules that society – that is, collective brains – have developed are also themselves tailored to achieve the very same aims. For example, the family unit and the moral prohibition on adultery both act as protective shields that promote the nurturing of the offspring in a stable environment and hence try to ensure its future success in distributing genes with a greater reproductive rate. Yet both are diametrically opposed to the reproductive urge that also promotes promiscuous activity, which is likely to lead to the same biological success. The aggressive and acquisitive instincts promote the well-being of the species as well as its reproductive capacity, yet the moral prohibition that controls excesses in these behaviors has the very same aim – that of protecting and promoting the well-being of the species, and hence its chances of reproduction. We thus find that the moral system, though developed by collective brains and though having the same ultimate aims as the instinctual biological system, is nevertheless often in opposition to it. But being in opposition to it does not mean that the moral system does not sometimes use the identical method to promote its aim as the biological system from which it is derived. The prohibition in some religions on the use of condoms or indeed any form of contraception, or of spilling one's seed onanistically and therefore unnecessarily [from a biological point of view, which happens to be the same as the religious point of view], has one aim – that of increasing the number born. Biology (if it could actually speak audibly) would also prescribe fornication without the use of condoms, for its aims are identical to the moral one. Unwittingly, the morality of some religious institutions here gives a forceful helping hand to biology, which it otherwise tries to stigmatize, but in pursuit of the same aim. The power in this contest is very much on the side of biology. Indeed, morality, though ultimately biological in origin, may be said to be a constant fight against biology and, in that fight, biology has always – in the long term – been the winner. The horrors of war have not prevented men from repeating them, even with the massive destructive power that we now possess. Hence, too, the dismal failure of the message that we should love one another, and the very limited success of the call to monogamy. The call to us to love one another, Freud says, is "a commandment which is really justified by the fact that nothing else runs so strongly counter to the original nature of man." And civilization recognizes, if only silently, that the contest between the biological and the moral systems is unequal. As Freud states in his book, "Everybody knows that it has proved impossible to put [moral restrictions] into execution, even for quite short periods . . . Civilized society has found itself obliged to pass over in silence many transgressions which, according to its own prescripts, it ought to have punished." Where strong moral prohibitions have prevailed, as in incest, biology has played a critical role, since this is a system that reduces variability.

It is when one reads Freud's summary of what have been thought of as prescriptions to overcome the unhappiness that is, in his view, the human lot that one begins to sense the inadequacy, from a neurobiological point of view, of his analysis. Freud writes as if there are two wholly distinct entities, the external reality and the internal reality, without acknowledging that there is one reality, brain reality, which is shaped by both external and internal influences. Humans,

Freud says, try to overcome the impositions that prevent them from satisfying the pleasure principle by disengaging themselves from reality. He writes, "Life, as we find it, is too hard for us; it brings us too many pains, disappointments and impossible tasks. In order to bear it . . . [w]e cannot do without auxiliary constructions . . . there are perhaps three such measures: powerful deflections, which cause us to make light of our misery; substitutive satisfactions, which diminish it; and intoxicating substances, which make us insensitive to it . . . the substitutive satisfactions, as offered by art, are illusions in contrast with reality, but they are none the less psychically effective, thanks to the role which phantasy has assumed in mental life." To the extent that each one of these approaches constituted a renunciation of reality, each was considered unsatisfactory by him. It is here that I find Freud's analysis in turn inadequate because it fails to take into account that the only reality is the brain's reality – deeply shaped by the external environment but also independent of it. The reality that the brain creates is the product of its knowledge-acquiring system. It results in the formation of synthetic concepts. These concepts are, in my view, the ideals created by the brain. Though such a formulation is remote from the Platonic formulation, which sees the ideal as existing in the outside world, it is also at one with the latter, because in both systems that Ideal is almost impossible to achieve. It is this inaccessibility in the real world of the counterpart of the synthetic concept (ideal) formed in the brain that constitutes, for me, one of the root causes of human discontent.

It is perhaps best to begin with Freud's final way in which happiness is sought, namely the enjoyment of beauty. For Freud, "Beauty has no obvious use; nor is there any clear cultural necessity for it. Yet civilization cannot do without it." There is an obvious contradiction here, for if society cannot do without it, it must satisfy some deep-seated psychological, and therefore neurobiological, need. In fact, as we have seen, the sight of something beautiful does engage the reward system of the brain and is therefore, at this neurobiological level of analysis, no different from other factors, such as the gratification of instinctual impulses that also engage the reward center. If civilization cannot do without it, it is because it is an essential part of our neurobiological make-up. Far from being useless, it is neurobiologically essential.

The other points he raises are in accord with this general view, of a sharp distinction between the internal and external realities. One way of alleviating suffering is to renounce instinct, or to shift "the instinc-tual aims in such a way that they cannot come up against frustration from the external world. In this, sublimation of the instincts lends its assistance." But sublimation, as Thomas Mann observed astutely at the end of *Death in Venice*, is a fraud and a sham. It is an open acknow-ledgment that the synthetic concept in the brain cannot be achieved: "For you know that we poets cannot walk the way of beauty without Eros as our companion and guide . . . love is still our desire – our craving and our shame" (my ellipsis), Mann declares at the end of his novella. Freud admits as much when he writes that the intensity of enjoyment derived from sublimation "is mild as compared with that derived from the sating of crude and primary instinctual impulses." Moreover, it is only applicable to a select few because most do not possess artistic, scientific or literary gifts which they can use to sublimate and transform their instincts." Even so, to Freud "it is impos-sible to overlook the extent to which civilization is built up upon a renunciation of instinct, how much it presupposes precisely the non-satisfaction (by suppression, repression or some other means) of powerful instincts." This is of course also true in my formulation. The renunciation of instinct (which I would expand to mean the renun-ciation of trying to find in daily life the counterpart of the inherited and acquired concepts, working together, of the brain) contributes significantly to civilization because the search for the counterpart is now transferred into the realm of art and literature, and creativity in general.

Yet another method is a condition in which "the connection with reality is still further loosened; satisfaction is obtained from illusions, which are recognized as such without the discrepancy between them and reality being allowed to interfere with enjoyment. The region from which these illusions arise is the life of the imagination." But imagination is derived from many realities – it is in fact a re-working of the realities that the brain has experienced, which end up becoming brain reality. Freud adds, "at the time when the development of the sense of reality took place, this region [of the imagination] was expressly exempted from the demands of reality-testing and was set apart for the purpose of fulfilling wishes which were difficult to carry out." The description is obtuse and off the mark. Imagination is not exempt from the rigours of reality; quite the contrary, it is brain reality coming into play, because the external reality (from which the brain reality itself was largely created) no longer satisfies the brain, its synthetic concepts and, ultimately, its reward centers. Imagination develops from interaction of the brain's concept-forming system with the external reality.

Freud believes that "At the head of these satisfactions through phantasy stands the enjoyment of works of art – an enjoyment which, by the agency of the artist, is made accessible even to those who are not themselves creative." But the brain of the spectator is also creative when viewing works of art, and great works of art are great because they correspond to many different concepts in many different ways. Works of art also make the world of fantasy safe and largely beyond the reach of criticism, disapproval or the law. Like imagination, fantasy is not, I think, a loosening of the connection with reality. Rather it is using the reality that the brain has created from its interaction with the external world to disengage itself from particular experiences and approximate as much as possible to the synthetic concept formulated by the brain and in the brain, unhindered by restrictions, prohibitions or the failure to find a counterpart to what is desired in the external world.

Another route considered by Freud, and found unsatisfactory, is that prescribed in Eastern cultures and practised by Yogas – the aim being to stifle and kill off those instincts that, because of the difficulty of satisfying them, bring suffering. "If it succeeds, then the subject has, it is true, given up all other activities as well – he has sacrificed his life; and, by another path, he has once more only achieved the happiness of quietness." The problem here is that this renunciation is a controlled effort to renounce brain realities, with the open acknowledgment that they are unachievable.

It is only when he writes of love that Freud comes close to acknowledging, though without saying so, the supremacy of the brain concept in regulating affairs (in this instance of an inherited brain concept, that of unity), and the dissolution of that unstable boundary between the internal and external realities. For, "At the height of being in love the boundary between ego and object threatens to melt away. Against all the evidence of his senses, a man who is in love declares that 'I' and 'you' are one, and is prepared to behave as if it were a fact," but, it seems, only momentarily in more intense moments. With the moment lived, the boundary re-emerges, instilling in lovers like Tristan and Isolde and Majnun and Leila the ardent wish to be annihilated so that the boundary between them can be dissolved in another world, after death.

I have devoted this chapter to an analysis of Freud's work, not only because I admire and have regularly advised my students to read it, but also because I essentially agree with the problem that he outlines, namely of the discontent of humans and the near-impossibility of finding a solution to that discontent. I also agree with his statement that this discontent is the result of something unconquerable in our "mental constitution." It is only that I see the root causes of that discontent in a somewhat different system compared to Freud, or rather have a different view of what our mental constitution means in this context.

In suggesting that the brain, through its very efficiency, also brings untold misery, much of what I have said in this book is gloomy. That humanity, or large segments of it, should forever be doomed not to find adequate happiness because of a failure to satisfy the synthetic concepts that the brain develops in its quest for knowledge seems to project a message of disillusion, of a fatality from which there is no escape and against which there is no appeal. But biology is full of apparent paradoxes and contradictions and, just as we pay a substantial price in misery for the splendors of our brain, so the misery itself generates splendors in its turn. I have mentioned above the contradictory ways in which biology tries to ensure the well-being of the species and its capacity to procreate. In human discontent, too, we find a powerful paradox in that the brain also has the capacity to turn that discontent into creative achievements, in works of art, literature or music, either by realizing the concept itself in a work of art or by drawing attention to its inevitability. Hence the disadvantage imposed by the huge advantages of the knowledge-acquiring system that the brain is, is itself turned into an advantage of creating new works that enrich mankind and in turn introduce new concepts. Nor should we think only of art, music and literature as being the sole faculties within the creative world. Creativity applies as well to a child who builds a sand castle, to those who perfect the art of conversation, to management skills and to many other human activities and actions. Indeed, the difficulty lies in identifying actions and activities from which the creative element is exempt. Thus creativity and imagination are attributes with which all brains are blessed to varying degrees and that all brains impart to what they are doing to varying degrees. Creativity therefore is, in a way, the brain's way of making up for its shortcomings.

Notes

Introduction

1 The literal English translation is "Splendours and miseries of courtesans". However, its common English title is *A Harlot High and Low*.

Chapter 1

1 Hubel DH, Wiesel TN (1977). The Ferrier lecture. Functional architecture of macaque monkey visual cortex. *Proc R Soc Lond B* **198**: 1–59.
2 Zeki S (1978). Uniformity and diversity of structure and function in rhesus monkey prestriate visual cortex. *J Physiol* **277**: 273–290.
3 Zeki S (1974). Functional organization of a visual area in the posterior bank of the superior temporal sulcus of the rhesus monkey. *J Physiol* **236**: 549–573.
4 Piazza M, Pinel P, Le Bihan D, Dehaene S (2007). A magnitude code common to numerosities and number symbols in human intraparietal cortex. *Neuron* **53**(2): 293–305.
5 Unpublished results from my laboratory.
6 Sergent J, Ohta S, MacDonald B (1992). Functional neuroanatomy of face and object processing: A positron emission tomography study. *Brain* **115**: 15–36; Tong F, Nakayama K, Vaughan JT, Kanwisher N (1998). Binocular rivalry and visual awareness in human extrastriate cortex. *Neuron* **21**: 753–759.
7 Epstein R, Kanwisher N (1998). A cortical representation of the local visual environment. *Nature* **392**: 598–601.

8 Kawabata H & Zeki S (2004). Neural correlates of beauty. *J Neurophysiol* **91**: 1699–1705.

9 Bartels A, Zeki S (2004). The neural correlates of maternal and romantic love. *NeuroImage* **21**: 1155–1166; Aron A, Fisher H, Mashek DJ, Strong G, Li H, Brown LL (2005). Reward, motivation, and emotion systems associated with early-stage intense romantic love. *J Neurophysiol* **94**(1): 327–337.

Chapter 2

1 Schopenhauer A (1819). *Die Welt als Wille und Vorstellung.* Translated by EFJ Payne (1966) as *The World as Will and Representation*, Volume 2. Dover, New York.

2 Kant I (1783). *Prolegomena.* Translated by PG Lucas (1953). Manchester University Press, Manchester.

3 Zeki S (1999). *Inner Vision: An Exploration of Art and the Brain.* Oxford University Press, Oxford.

Chapter 3

1 Schopenhauer A (1854). *Über das Sehen und die Farben: Ein Abhandlung.* Translated by EFJ Payne (1994) as *On Vision and Colors: an Essay.* Berg, Oxford.

2 Kant I (1781). *Kritik der reinen Vernunft*, first edition. Translated by WS Pluhar (1996) as *Critique of Pure Reason.* Hackett, Indianapolis.

3 Helmholtz H von (1911). *Handbuch der Physiologischen Optik*, Volume 2. Leopold Voss, Hamburg.

4 Hering E (1877). *Outlines of a Theory of the Light Sense.* Translated by LM Hurvich and D Jameson (1964), Harvard University Press, Cambridge.

5 Land E (1974). The retinex theory of colour vision. *Proc R Inst Gt Br* **47**: 23–58.

6 Newton I (1704). *Opticks.* Dover, New York.

7 A detailed description of color-generating mechanisms is given in: Zeki S (1993). *A Vision of the Brain*, Blackwell, Oxford.

8 Lewandowsky M (1908). Über Abspaltung des Farbensinnes. *Monatsschrift für Psychiatrie und Neurologie* **23**: 488–510. Translated and annotated by J Davidoff and G Fodor (1989) as "Disconnection of the

colour sense by focal disease of the brain". *Cognit Neuropsychol* **6**: 165–178.

9 Malraux A (1951). *Les Voix du silence*. NRF, Pleiade, Paris.

10 Zeki S, Watson JDG, Lueck CJ, Friston KJ, Kennard C, Frackowiak RSJ (1991). A direct demonstration of functional specialization in human visual cortex. *J Neurosci* **11**: 641–649; Bartels A, Zeki S (2000). The architecture of the colour centre in the human visual brain. *Eur J Neurosci* **12**: 172–193; Wade AR, Brewer AA, Rieger JW, Wandell BA (2002). Functional measurements of human ventral occipital cortex: retinotopy and colour. *Philos Trans R Soc Lond B* **357**: 963–973.

11 A more detailed description of visual imperfections resulting from specific cerebral lesions is given in: Zeki S (1993). *A Vision of the Brain*. Blackwell, Oxford.

12 Kawabata H, Zeki S (2004). The neural correlates of beauty. *J Neurophysiol* **91**: 1699–1705.

13 Hubel DH, Wiesel TN (1977). The Ferrier lecture. Functional architecture of macaque monkey visual cortex. *Proc R Soc Lond B* **198**: 1–59.

14 Senden M von (1932). *Raum- und Gestaltauffassung bei Operierten Blindgebornen*. Translated by P Heath (1960) as *Space and Sight*. Methuen & Co, London.

Chapter 4

1 Zeki S (1978). Functional specialization in the visual cortex of the rhesus monkey. *Nature* **274**: 423–428; Zeki S, Watson JDG, Lueck CJ, Friston KJ, Kennard C, Frackowiak RSJ (1991). A direct demonstration of functional specialization in human visual cortex. *J Neurosci* **11**: 641–649.

2 Zeki S (1990). A century of cerebral achromatopsia. *Brain* **113**: 1721–1777.

3 Zeki S (2005). The Ferrier Lecture 1995. Behind the seen: the functional specialization of the brain in space and time. *Philos Trans R Soc Lond B* **360**: 1145–1183; Zeki S (1991). Cerebral akinetopsia (visual motion blindness). *Brain* **114**: 811–824.

4 Moutoussis K, Zeki S (1997). A direct demonstration of perceptual asynchrony in vision. *Proc R Soc Lond B* **265**: 393–399.

5 Arnold DH & Clifford CW (2002). Determinants of asynchronous processing in vision. *Proc R Soc Lond B* **269**: 579–583.

6 Kant I (1781). *Kritik der reinen Vernunft*, first edition. Translated by WS Pluhar (1996) as *Critique of Pure Reason*. Hackett, Indianapolis.

7   Zeki S, Bartels A (1999). Toward a theory of visual consciousness. *Conscious Cogn* **8**: 225–259.

Chapter 5

1   Zeki S, Marini L (1998). Three cortical stages of colour processing in the human brain. *Brain* **121**: 1669–1685.
2   Logothetis NK, Pauls J, Poggio T (1995). Shape representation in the inferior temporal cortex of monkeys. *Curr Biol* **5**: 552–563.

Chapter 6

1   Frazer JG (1930). *The Growth of Plato's Ideal Theory*. Macmillan & Co, London.
2   Plato, *Parmenides* 130b,c. In Hamilton E, Cairns H (eds) (1961). *The Collected Dialogues of Plato*. Bollingen series LXXI. Princeton University Press, Princeton.

Chapter 7

1   Plato, *Phaedo* 96b,c. In Hamilton E, Cairns H (eds) (1961). *The Collected Dialogues of Plato*. Bollingen series LXXI, Princeton University Press, Princeton.
2   This refers to an anecdote recounted by Madame du Deffand (1697–1780) in a letter to Horace Walpole and mentioned by Voltaire in a note to *La Pucelle d'Orleans*. It is a comment made on the transportation by the Cardinal de Polignac of the decapitated head of Saint Denis from Montmartre to Saint Denis. "Ah, monseigneur, I said to him, I think that in such a situation, it is only the first step that counts."
3   Quoted in Heilbut A (1997). *Thomas Mann: Eros and Literature*. Papermac, London.
4   Newman E (1949). *Wagner Nights*. Putnam & Co, London.
5   On the BBC programme *The Ticket*, broadcast September 11, 2005.
6   Freud L (1954). *Encounter III: I* (July). Martin Secker and Warburg, London.

Chapter 8

1 This Part is largely based on: Zeki S (2004). The neurology of ambiguity. *Conscious Cogn* **13**: 173–196, in which there is a detailed bibliography for the more interested reader.
2 Zeki S (1984). The construction of colours by the cerebral cortex. *Proc R Inst Gt Br* **56**: 231–257.

Chapter 9

1 Sergent J, Ohta S, MacDonald B (1992). Functional neuroanatomy of face and object processing: A positron emission tomography study. *Brain* **115**: 15–36; Kanwisher N, McDermott J, Chun MM (1997). The fusiform face area: a module in human extrastriate cortex specialized for face perception. *J Neurosci* **17**: 4302–4311; Tong F, Nakayama K, Vaughan JT, Kanwisher N (1998). Binocular rivalry and visual awareness in human extrastriate cortex. *Neuron* **21**: 753–759.
2 Moutoussis K, Zeki S (2002). The relationship between cortical activation and perception investigated with invisible stimuli. *Proc Natl Acad Sci USA* **99**(14): 9527–9532.
3 This of course raises the unresolved question of how signals belonging to two different classes – faces and houses – are routed to the respective specialized areas of the brain.
4 Crick F, Koch C (1995). Are we aware of neural activity in primary visual cortex? *Nature* **375**: 121–123.
5 Zeki S, Bartels A (1999). Toward a theory of visual consciousness. *Conscious Cogn* **8**: 225–259; Zeki S (2003). The disunity of consciousness. *Trends Cogn Sci* **7**: 214–218.
6 Zeki S (1983). Colour coding in the cerebral cortex: The reaction of cells in monkey visual cortex to wavelengths and colours. *Neuroscience* **9**: 741–765.
7 Moutoussis K, Zeki S (2002). The responses of wavelength selective cells in macaque area V2 to wavelengths and colors. *J Neurophysiol* **87**(4): 2104–2112.
8 Zeki S, Aglioti S, McKeefry D, Berlucchi G (1999). The neurological basis of conscious color perception in a blind patient. *Proc Nat Acad Sci USA* **96**: 14124–14129.
9 Kennard C, Lawden M, Morland AB, Ruddock KH (1995). Colour identification and colour constancy are impaired in a patient with

incomplete achromatopsia associated with prestriate cortical lesions. *Proc R Soc Lond B* **260**: 169–175.

Chapter 10

1 Bartels A, Zeki S (2000). The architecture of the colour centre in the human visual brain: New results and a review. *Eur J Neurosci* **12**: 172–193.

2 Wade AR, Brewer AA, Rieger JW, Wandell BA (2002). Functional measurements of human ventral occipital cortex: Retinotopy and colour. *Philos Trans R Soc Lond B* **357**: 963–973.

3 Peterhans E, von der Heydt R (1989). Mechanisms of contour perception in monkey visual cortex. II. Contours bridging gaps. *J Neurosci* **9**: 1749–1763.

4 Sergent J, Ohta S, MacDonald B (1992). Functional neuroanatomy of face and object processing: A positron emission tomography study. *Brain* **115**: 15–36; Malach R, Reppas JB, Benson RR, Kwong KK, Jiang H, Kennedy WA, Ledden PJ, Brady TJ, Rosen BR, Tootell RB (1995). Object-related activity revealed by functional magnetic resonance imaging in human occipital cortex. *Proc Natl Acad Sci USA* **92**(18): 8135–8139.

5 Gregory R (1972). Cognitive contours. *Nature* **238**: 51–52.

6 ffytche D, Zeki S (1996). Brain activity related to the perception of illusory contours. *NeuroImage* **3**: 104–108; Hirsch J, DeLaPaz RL, Relkin NR, Victor J, Kim K, Li T, Borden P, Rubin N, Shapley R (1995). Illusory contours activate specific regions in human visual cortex: evidence from functional magnetic resonance imaging. *Proc Natl Acad Sci USA* **92**(14): 6469–6473.

7 Adams DL, Zeki S (2001). Functional organization of macaque V3 for stereoscopic depth. *J Neurophysiol* **86**: 2195–2203; Poggio GF, Fischer B (1977). Binocular interaction and depth sensitivity in striate and prestriate cortex of behaving rhesus monkey. *J Neurophysiol* **40**: 1392–1405.

8 Cragg BG (1969). The topography of the afferent projections in circumstriate visual cortex studied by the Nauta method. *Vision Res* **9**: 733–747; Zeki SM (1969). Representation of central visual fields in prestriate cortex of monkey. *Brain Res.* **14**: 271–291; Lyon DC, Kaas JH (2002). Evidence for a modified V3 with dorsal and ventral halves in macaque monkeys. *Neuron* **33**: 453–461.

9   Leopold DA, Wilke M, Maier A, Logothetis NK (2002). Stable perception of visually ambiguous figures. *Nat Neurosci* **5**: 605–609.

10 Kleinschmidt A, Büchel C, Zeki S, Frackowiak RS (1998). Human brain activity during spontaneously reversing perception of ambiguous figures. *Proc R Soc Lond B* **265**: 2427–2432; Lumer ED, Friston KJ, Rees G (1998). Neural correlates of perceptual rivalry in the human brain. *Science* **280**: 1930–1934.

11 Sterzer P, Russ MO, Preibisch C, Kleinschmidt A (2002). Neural correlates of spontaneous direction reversals in ambiguous apparent visual motion. *NeuroImage* **15**: 908–916.

12 Zeki S, Perry RJ, Bartels A (2003). The processing of kinetic contours in the brain. *Cereb Cortex* **13**: 189–202.

Chapter 11

1   Schopenhauer A, quoted in Hofstader A, Kuhns R (eds) (1964). *Philosophies of Art and Beauty.* University of Chicago Press, Chicago.

2   This painting is at the Royal Collection in London: http: //www. royalcollection.org.uk/egallery/object.asp?object=405346&row=0&detail= about.

3   Zeki S (2004). The neurology of ambiguity. *Conscious Cogn* **13**: 173–196.

4   Schopenhauer A (1819). *Die Welt als Wille und Vorstellung.* Translated by EFJ Payne (1966) as *The World as Will and Representation*, Volume 2. Dover, New York.

5   Zeki S (1999). *Inner Vision: an Exploration of Art and the Brain.* Oxford University Press, Oxford.

6   Tolnay C (1934). Michelangelo's Rondanini Pietà. *Burlington Magazine* **65**: 146–157.

7   Winckelmann J (1764). *Gesichte der Kunst des Alterthums* (*History of the Art of Antiquity*). Dresden.

8   Goethe JW von (1805). *Winckelmann und sein Jahrhundert.* Cotta, Tübingen.

9   Potts A (1994). *Flesh and the Ideal: Winckelmann and the Origins of Art History.* Yale University Press, New Haven.

10 Reynolds, Sir J, in Wark RR (ed.) (1997). *Discourses on Art.* Yale University Press, New Haven and London.

11 Winckelmann (1764); quoted in Potts (1994).

Chapter 12

1 Linscott RN (ed.) (1980). *Complete Poems and Selected Letters of Michelangelo*, third edition. Translated by C Gilbert. Princeton University Press, Princeton.

2 Symonds JA (1904). *The Sonnets of Michael Angelo Buonarroti*. Smith, Elder & Co, London.

3 Clements RJ (1961). *Michelangelo's Theory of Art*. New York University Press, New York.

4 Blunt A (1940). *Artistic Theory in Italy*. The Clarendon Press, Oxford.

5 Quoted in Clements (1961).

6 Vasari G, *Le vite de' piu eccellenti pittori, scultori ed architettori*. G Milanesi (ed.), Florence 1878–85, Volume I. Quoted by Schultz J (1975). Michelangelo's unfinished works. *Art Bulletin* **58**: 366–373.

7 Clark K (1972). *The Nude: A Study in Ideal Form*. Princeton University Press, Princeton.

Chapter 13

1 Quoted by R Shiff (2000) in Mark, motif, materiality: The Cézanne effect in the twentieth century, in *Cézanne Finished, Unfinished*, catalogue of the exhibition at the Kunstforum, Vienna, Hatje Cantz, Ostfildern-Ruit.

2 Belting H (1998). *Das unsichtbare Meisterwerk: Die Modernen Mythen der Kunst*. Beck, Munich.

3 Boehm G (2000). Precarious balance: Cézanne and the unfinished, in *Cézanne Finished, Uunfinished*, catalogue of the exhibition at the Kunstforum, Vienna, Hatje Cantz, Ostfildern-Ruit.

4 Quoted by T Maloon (2000). Tableau/Peinture: Critical responses to Cézanne's unfinished work, in *Cézanne Finished, Unfinished*, catalogue of the exhibition at the Kunstforum, Vienna, Hatje Cantz, Ostfildern-Ruit.

5 Letter to Émile Bernard dated 23 October 1905, in Rewald J (ed.) (1978). *Paul Cézanne: Correspondances*. Grasset, Paris.

6 Bernard E (1910). *L'Ésthetique fondamentale et traditionelle – d'apres les maitres de tous les temps*. Paris.

7 Zola quoted in Coquiot G (1919). *Paul Cézanne*. Ollendorf, Paris.

8 Baudelaire C, in *Charles Baudelaire: Ecrits sur l'art*, Moulinat F (ed.) (1992). Livre de Poche, Paris.

9 Letter of 21 Nov 1895 to his son Lucien, in Bailly-Herzberg J (ed.) (1980–91). Volume 4, *Correspondance de Camille Pissaro*, 5 Volumes,

Paris 1980–91. Quoted by T Maloon, in *Cézanne Finished, Unfinished*, catalogue of the exhibition at the Kunstforum, Vienna.
10 Rewald J (ed.) (1978). *Paul Cézanne: Correspondances*. Grasset, Paris.
11 Joachim Gasquet, "Ce qu'il m'a dit . . ." (1921). In Doran PM (1978). *Conversations avec Cézanne*. Macula, Paris.
12 From Bernard E (1908), Julien Tanguy, dit le 'Pére Tanguy', *Mercure de France*, 76: 600–616.

Chapter 14

1 Balzac H de (1979). *Le Chef-d'Oeuvre inconnue*. Gallimard, Paris (Editions de la Pleiade).
2 Balzac wrote: "*Massimilla Doni* et *Gambera sont*, dans les *Études philosophiques*, l'apparition de la musique, sous le double forme d'*execution* et de *composition*, soumise a la même épreuve que la pensée dans L[ouis] Lambert, c'est a dire l'oeuvre et l'exécution tuées par la grande abondance du principe créateur, ce qui m'a dicté *Le Chef-d'oeuvre inconnu* pour la peinture [. . .]" (original emphasis). Balzac is here referring to two other of his stories that address the same theme. See René Guise (1979). Introduction to *Le Chef-d'oeuvre inconnu* in *La Comédie humaine* X, La Pleiade, Gallimard, Paris.
3 Mitterand H (1966). *Emile-Zola, Les Rougon-Macquart*, Volume 4. Gallimard, Paris (Editions de la Pleiade).
4 Letter to Cézanne dated 25 June 1860, reproduced in *Les Rougon-Macquart*, Volume 4. Gallimard, Paris (Editions de la Pleiade).
5 Pierre-Louis Rey, preface to the Pocket Classiques edition of *l'Oeuvre*, Pocket 1992.

Chapter 15

1 Not all languages, e.g. Italians speak of *inamorarsi*. But the term is used in French, Japanese and Chinese (Mandarin) – languages spoken by a significant proportion of mankind.
2 Plato, *Symposium* 191b. In Hamilton E, Cairns H (eds) (1961). *The Collected Dialogues of Plato*. Bollingen series LXXI. Princeton University Press, Princeton.

3   Siegel L (1978). *Sacred and Profane Dimensions of Love in Indian Traditions as Exemplified in the Gitagovinda of Jayadeva.* Oxford University Press, Delhi.
4   Plato, *Symposium* 191d. In Hamilton E, Cairns H (eds) (1961). *The Collected Dialogues of Plato.* Bollingen series LXXI. Princeton University Press, Princeton.
5   Plato, *Symposium* 192c. In Hamilton E, Cairns H (eds) (1961). *The Collected Dialogues of Plato.* Bollingen series LXXI. Princeton University Press, Princeton.
6   Plato, *Symposium* 192e. In Hamilton E, Cairns H (eds) (1961). *The Collected Dialogues of Plato.* Bollingen series LXXI. Princeton University Press, Princeton.
7   Plato, *Symposium* 193a. In Hamilton E, Cairns H (eds) (1961). *The Collected Dialogues of Plato.* Bollingen series LXXI. Princeton University Press, Princeton.
8   Dante Alighieri, *La Vita Nuova.* Translated by M Musa (1992). Oxford University Press, Oxford.
9   Quoted in Heilbut A (1997). *Thomas Mann: Eros and Literature.* Papermac, London.

Chapter 16

1   Bartels A, Zeki S (2000). The neural basis of romantic love. *NeuroReport* **11**(17): 3829–3834; Bartels A, Zeki S (2004). The neural correlates of maternal and romantic love. *Neuroimage* **21**(3): 1155–1166.
2   Aron A, Fisher H, Mashek DJ, Strong G, Li H, Brown LL (2005). Reward, motivation, and emotion systems associated with early-stage intense romantic love. *J Neurophysiol* **94**(1): 327–337.
3   Marazziti D, Akiskal HS, Rossi A, Cassano GB (1999). Alteration of the platelet serotonin transporter in romantic love. *Psychol Med* **29**: 741–745.
4   Emanuele E, Politi P, Bianchi M, Minoretti P, Bertona M, Geroldi D (2006). Raised plasma nerve growth factor levels associated with early-stage romantic love. *Psychoneuroendocrinology* **31**: 288–294.
5   Georgiadis JR, Kortekaas R, Kuipers R, Nieuwenburg A, Pruim J, Reinders AA, Holstege G (2006). Regional cerebral blood flow changes associated with clitorally induced orgasm in healthy women. *Eur J Neurosci* **24**(11): 3305–3316.
6   Gallagher HL, Frith CD (2003). Functional imaging of "theory of mind". *Trends Cogn Sci* **7**(2): 77–83.

7 I am aware of the contradictions in the views of love and judgment expressed by Plato in *Phaedrus* and in *The Symposium*, which scholars have debated. I prefer to read each of these dialogues as self-contained ones which raise points that are of interest in a neurobiological context.

8 Moll J, Zahn R, de Oliveira-Souza R, Krueger F, Grafman J (2005). Opinion: the neural basis of human moral cognition. *Nat Rev Neurosci* **6**: 799–809.

9 Perrett DI, Lee KJ, Penton-Voak I, Rowland D, Yoshikawa S, Burt DM, Henzi SP, Castles DL, Akamatsu S (1998). Effects of sexual dimorphism on facial attractiveness. *Nature* **394**(6696): 884–887.

10 Insel TR, Young LJ (2001). The neurobiology of attachment. *Nat Rev Neurosci* **2**: 129–136.

11 O'Doherty J, Winston J, Critchley H, Perrett D, Burt DM, Dolan RJ (2003). Beauty in a smile: The role of medial orbitofrontal cortex in facial attractiveness. *Neuropsychologia* **41**(2): 147–155.

12 Redouté J, Stoléru S, Grégoire MC, Costes N, Cinotti L, Lavenne F, Le Bars D, Forest MG, Pujol JF (2000). Brain processing of visual sexual stimuli in human males. *Hum Brain Mapp* **11**(3): 162–177.

13 Kawabata H, Zeki S (2004). Neural correlates of beauty. *J Neurophysiol* **91**: 1699–1705.

14 Cavada C, Compañy T, Tejedor J, Cruz-Rizzolo RJ, Reinoso-Suárez F (2000). The anatomical connections of the macaque monkey orbito-frontal cortex. *Cereb Cortex* **10**(3): 220–242.

Chapter 17

1 Kranz F, Ishai A (2006). Face perception is modulated by sexual preference. *Curr Biol* **16**(1): 63–68.

2 Siegel L (1978). *Sacred and Profane Dimensions of Love in Indian Traditions as Exemplified in the Gitagovinda of Jayadeva*. Oxford University Press, Delhi.

3 Madhava is one of the many titles of Krishna, and Nanda was the foster father of Krishna.

4 A term derived from the Arabic *suf*, which means wool and was used to designate the generally humble personality and dress of the practitioners of a mystical doctrine that emphasizes the path to God through love.

5 Schimmel A (1975). *Mystical Dimensions of Islam*. University of North Carolina Press, Chapel Hill.

6 From *Kitab al-Tawasin*, in *The Mystics of Islam*, by Reynold A Nicholson. The capitalization of He introduces an ambiguity here, which

is discussed later. In fact, Al-Hallaj can be read in both sacred and profane senses.

Chapter 18

1 Teresa of Avila, in *The Life of Teresa of Jesus, The Autobiography of Teresa of Avila*, translated and edited by EA Peers (1960), from the Critical Edition of P Silverio de Santa Teresa, CD. Chapter XXIX. Image Books, New York.
2 See http: //www.franciscanos.org/santoral/ludovicaalbertoni.htm for a photograph of the statue.
3 Ritter H (1955). *Das Meer der Seele*. Translated by J O'Kane with editorial assistance of B Radtke (2003) as *The Ocean of the Soul: Man, the World and God in the Stories of Farid Al-Din Attar* (Handbook of Oriental Studies). Brill Academic Publishers, Leiden and Boston.
4 Schimmel A (1975). *Mystical Dimensions of Islam*. University of North Carolina Press, Chapel Hill.
5 From Divan-i-Shams by Rumi. In Nicholson RA (ed.) (1898). *Selected Poems from the Divani Shamsi Tabriz*. Cambridge University Press, Cambridge.
6 Singleton, C (1978). *The Journey to Beatrice*. John Hopkins University Press, Baltimore and London.
7 Francesco Petrarca, *The Canzoniere*. Translated by FJ Jones, 2 Volumes (2001). Troubadour, Leicester.

Chapter 19

1 Petrie J, Salmons J (eds) (1994). *La Vita Nuova*, by Dante Alighieri (Belefield Italian Library).
2 Donke P (1997). *Dante's Second Love* (Society for Italian Studies).
3 Ritter H (1955). *Das Meer der Seele*. Translated by J O'Kane with editorial assistance of B Radtke (2003) as *The Ocean of the Soul: Man, the World and God in the Stories of Farid Al-Din Attar* (Handbook of Oriental Studies). Brill Academic Publishers, Leiden and Boston.
4 My non-literal translation, to render the meaning.
5 De Rougemont D (1972). *L'Amour et l'Occident*. Librairie Plon, Paris.
6 Berridge KC (2007). The debate over dopamine's role in reward: the case for incentive salience. *Psychopharmacology* **191**: 391–431.

7 Singleton, C (1978). *The Journey to Beatrice*. John Hopkins University Press, Baltimore and London.

8 A parallel can be found in the use of the Arabic word "'ishq" [passionate love] in the description of relations between man and God, a usage that many, including Sufis, objected to.

9 Nelson L (1986). *The Poetry of Guido Cavalcanti*. Garland, New York.

10 Dante Alighieri, *Convivio*. Translated by WW Jackson (1909). The Clarendon Press, Oxford.

11 Musa M, trans (1992). *La Vita Nuova*, by Dante Alighieri. Oxford University Press, Oxford.

12 Bartels A, Zeki S (2004). The neural correlates of maternal and romantic love. *Neuroimage* **21**(3): 1155–1166.

Chapter 20

1 "Le mythe agit partout où la passion est rêvée comme un idéal, non point redoutée comme une fièvre maligne; partout où sa fatalité est appelée, invoquée, imaginée, comme une belle et désirable catastrophe, et non point comme catastrophe" in De Rougemont D (1972). *L'amour et l'Occident*. Librairie Plon, Paris.

2 Quoted in Heilbut A (1997). *Thomas Mann: Eros and Literature*. Papermac, London.

3 De Rougemont D (1972). *L'amour et l'Occident*. Librairie Plon, Paris.

4 Newman E (1949). *Wagner Nights*. Putnam & Co, London.

5 It is interesting to note that Béroul, in his version of the myth (never completed), somewhat more realistically, had the effects of the love potion wearing off after three years. Isolde therefore ceases to be infatuated by Tristan and returns to King Mark. This version fits the realities, as reflected in divorce statistics, much better. I have suggested, in keeping with biological realities, that a marriage contract should be for five years, renewable by common consent every three years thereafter.

6 Translations taken from the libretto accompanying the recording by Herbert von Karajan and Berliner Philharmoniker, 1972 (EMI Classics).

7 Crosby DH (1999). Beyond analysis: Richard Wagner's Tristan und Isolde. http://www.wagner-dc.org/crosby99_lec.html.

8 Gabo N (1959). *Of Divers Arts*. The AW Mellon Lectures in the Fine Arts, National Gallery of Art, Washington. Pantheon Books, Bollingen Foundation, New York.

9 Text consulted apart from those given in the notes above: McGee B (2000). *The Tristan Chord*. Henry Holt & Co, New York.

Chapter 21

1 Heilbut A (1997). *Thomas Mann: Eros and Literature*. Papermac, London.
2 I have used throughout this chapter the authorized translation of Thomas Mann's short stories by Lowe-Porter: *Mann, Thomas, Death in Venice and Other Stories*. Everyman's Library (1940).
3 "The best of artists have no thought to show that which the marble in its superfluous shell does not include To break the marble spell is all that the brain that guides the hand can do." Michelangelo, Sonnet dedicated to Vittoria Colonna

Chapter 22

1 Freud S (1930). *Das Unbehagen in der Kultur. Civilization and Its Discontents*, translated and edited by J Strachey (1961). WW Norton & Co, New York.

Name Index

Page numbers given in **bold** indicate an illustration

Subject Index

Page numbers given in **bold** indicate an illustration